ONLY A
DAMN FOOL

Dagny Taggart *taking on fuel and water in Colonia Harbor, Yap.*

ONLY A
DAMN FOOL

*Taylor Hancock
and Carol Brooks Hancock*

David McKay Company, Inc.
NEW YORK

Library of Congress Cataloging in Publication Data

Hancock, Taylor.
Only a damn fool.

1. Dagny Taggart (Yacht) 2. Voyages and travels—
1951- I. Hancock, Carol Brooks, joint author.
II. Title.
G477.H34   910'.45   79-15442
ISBN 0-679-51251-9

1 2 3 4 5 6 7 8 9 10

MANUFACTURED IN THE UNITED STATES OF AMERICA

To
Dagny Taggart

達妮泰姣娣

. . . a helluva gal!

Contents

I. THE IDEA   1

Coronado / One-Upmanship / This Is the Place? / Jane

II. THE BOAT   9

*This Is the Boat? / The John Morley / As Long As We're
Here . . . / This Is the Boat / The Islander / The Long Wait*

III. THE PREPARATION   29

*Generation Gap / First Progress Payment! / A Name Is a
Name Is a Name / Diesel Power / The Red Duster / Hot
Stuff / Take Three Aspirin; Push
Liquids / Chuck / Farewell Columbus / The Anchor
Winch / In All Her Glory / Gathering in the
Sheaves / Carol Joins Our Crack Team / Will It Ever Get
Launched! / Gentlemen, Start Your
Launching! / April / Out of the Yard / Bob / The
Beginning in Sight! / Luxury Tour / Grand
Reunion / Firearms / The Royal Hong Kong Yacht*

Club / Waiting for Our Ship to Come In / Jane's Fighting Ship / The Lost Box / First Slipping / This Ain't No Chris Craft! / Surveying / Hong Kong Transport / Pep Talk / Life in a Hong Kong Ship Yard / The Dreaded Typhoon / Hong Kong Morning Breakfast Watch / Anthony Wong and Fei Pohl / Carol's Sacred Bulkhead / The Last Lap / SSB, VHF, ADF, RDF / My Kingdom for a Skipper / Sail Power / Next to Last Day / Last Full Day / Freddy the Rat

IV. THE VOYAGE

123

The South China Sea / Person Overboard / Cruising the Coast of Luzon / Letters of Credit and All That / First Landfall / I'll Take Manila / Trouble Right Here in River City / The Autopilot / Getting the Hell out of Manila / Philippine Roulette / To Gimbal or Not to Gimbal / First Shark / Entrance to the Mighty Pacific / Mystique of the Mizzen Staysail / The Second Battle of the Philippine Sea / The Body Beautiful / Where the Hell Are We? / Continuous Assault by the Sea / Where's the Wind Coming From? / Joanne / Where the Hell Is Yap? / Dick Justice of the Gull / What, No Drinking Permit? / Those Wonderful Seabees! / Wally Kluver, Barefoot Banker / Dismissal, Desertion, Mutiny / Farewell to Yap / Fire at Sea / No Choice: Sail or Else / The Japanese Retake Guam! / In Deep Water Again / Oh, What a Beautiful Morning! / On the Way to Ponape / Keeping It Clean at Sea / Channel? What Channel? / Paradise Enow! / Kolonia, Not Colonia / The Seven Korean Virgins / The Ginger House / The Great Seabee Mutiny / Good Old Jack Adams / So Long Old Taylor / Good Old Air Micronesia

ONLY A
DAMN FOOL

I

The Idea

Only a damn fool would venture across the mighty Pacific Ocean in a new sailboat, against the prevailing winds, at a time dangerously close to the typhoon season, with an amateur crew, none of whom had ever made the trip before—in fact, none of whom had ever made *any* long sailing voyage before. Perhaps that's not entirely true. Perhaps one shouldn't be considered a damn fool for making such a trip if he or she were a master mariner, master mechanic, master carpenter, master navigator, master plumber, master fisherman, radio technician, diesel engineer, sailmaker, rigger, medical doctor, nurse, priest, psychologist, gourmet chef, quartermaster, expert scrounger, national rifle champion, accomplished forger, inspirational leader, and hard-driving rugged, son-of-a-bitch.

Where in the world does one get the idea of making such a ridiculous trip? You don't just wake up one morning, nudge your sleeping companion, and say, "Hey, get up! I just got a great idea. We'll buy a sailboat in Taiwan and sail it to California!"

No, even to a wild-hare mind like mine, even to one who has always struck out boldly and foolishly with arms flapping down the path of adventure, for an idea like that to get in and take hold of the gray matter and the red corpuscles, it takes some pretty sneaky and roundabout turns of events to get the show on the road.

CORONADO

It began in one of those role-reversal situations made possible by the feminist movement of the 1960s and 1970s. I was an accompanying spouse at a conference of the international Council of Shopping Centers of which Carol was a member. The program that day for accompanying spouses consisted of fashion displays and dress shopping tours—all of which were pretty low on my priority list.

We were at one of my favorite spots, at what has to be rated among the greatest hotels in the world: the Hotel del Coronado in San Diego. It was October, which is probably the best month for good weather in Southern California. I had spent the morning in our room working on a business report, had joined Carol for a lunch meeting that was part of the conference, and had decided to goof off for the afternoon. I walked down to the beach to try my luck at body surfing. Since I found myself in the unusual but happy situation of not being pressed for time, I thought I would wander along the shore for a spell, particularly since waves from a mild storm and a recent high tide had tossed all sorts of interesting goodies up on the sand—an old stove, a jaunty straw hat which I promptly made a part of my permanent wardrobe, an unexplained miniature pylon, and a comb! Combing the beach, what *else* would one find but a comb?! It was a little eerie, almost as if each pleasant item had been purposely placed there for me to find and enjoy.

By this time I had walked along the strand a couple of miles or so to the fence around the U.S. Naval Air Base on North Island. Navy fighter jets in groups of three were making close-wing practice landings and runs over the airstrip. A military jet, particularly a sleek, fast fighter, always gives me a lump; and this was no exception. What a glorious day! The jets jetting and the surf surfing . . . Hey! That surf really has gotten big out there! Let's give it a try.

But wait a minute—you know the rules about not diving or surfing alone. This beach is desolate, and those jet pilots aren't about to look after you.

Yeah, I know, but look at that great surf! It's breaking just right. And besides, I've got my fins—why the hell have I been carrying them all this time?

Well, natch, I went in. And, natch, it was great. I'm not the best body surfer in the world, but no one enjoys it more. And the waves *were* big, but ridable. The tough part, as always with body surfing, was swimming out through the big breakers after riding into the shore. Only three or four times—as the waves crashed above me and beat my face in the sand—did I think I had run out of air and surely would die; just enough to make it interesting.

Jogging back along the hard wet sand I felt more right with the world than I had in years. As I neared the beach in front of the hotel, I wanted to grab or hug each person there and say, "Oh friend, don't you wish *this* could be the real world, here with the sand and the water and the surf and the sea birds and the clouds and the sky and the life by the side of the ocean!"

I carried this euphoria with me to the hotel room; I was amazed to note that my short walk and body surfing had taken several hours. In fact, before I could get dressed and long before the anesthetic wore off, Carol was back from the wars, telling me of her meetings, her contacts, her conquests. Sharp as a tack, she soon noticed that I was not listening to her business stories quite as avidly as usual. When she asked why, I of course laid the above vignette on her.

She came back with: "Well, what are you going to do about it, just sit there?"

Carol's question caught me short. What was I going to *do* about it? I hadn't given the matter a lot of thought, other than dreamily to wish that I could just go on beachcombing and body surfing the rest of my life—with perhaps a little sailing, snorkeling, and skin diving tossed in. Here I was, your typical fifty-two-year-old corporate lawyer, married to your typical active feminist, twenty-one years my junior, who managed a shopping center. We had the typical family of four—hers, mine and ours—ranging from age two to twenty-six. Could I seriously consider becoming a corporate dropout and spending the rest of my life doing what I wanted to do, when I wanted to do it, with whom I wanted, and all that?

When I answered Carol's question I was a lot more cavalier on the outside than on the inside: What am I going to do about it? Well, just maybe one of these fine days we can manage to break away from the lousy traffic, smog, crime, drugs, and welfare state that we're suffering under and find a spot that has all those things I'm raving and ranting about, where we can get back to nature, appreciate our family, slow down the pace of life, live off the land or off the sea, with whatever modest help we can furnish as a result of our labors to date on this terrestrial sphere—even though inflation eats up accumulated capital or fixed dollar annuities so fast this may be an even bigger dream.

Carol's reaction, which I suspected then and suspect now was deliberately contrived to prod me into some kind of commitment, was something like: "You talk pretty big, but don't think you can con me into believing that you would leave that precious company of yours, walk away from your responsibilities, and do something for yourself for a change! No way!"

I rose to the bait: "Just don't be so sure about that, young lady. Hell, I've taken bigger steps before."

You just wait, 'enry 'iggins, you just wait.

ONE-UPMANSHIP

If you usually don't read prefaces, you have just been had. That was it.

THIS IS THE PLACE?

Well, now that we had *that* all settled, there were left only the little details of where to go, when to leave, how to get there, and how to exist after we get there.

For many years my work had taken me all over the world, which gave me a tremendous disadvantage in trying to select a place to hide away. No matter where I was, or where I considered settling down, I could always think of someplace else that might have a little better climate, or be safer, or offer more economical living, or be closer to medical or cultural facilities, or closer to friends and relatives back home, or something.

My own three favorite general areas, in all of which I had spent time, were the Caribbean, the Mediterranean, and the island groups off of Northwest Africa. It was difficult to give up consideration of some of the South Pacific Islands—Samoa, French Polynesia, New Hebrides—except for the fact that distances are so tremendous in that part of the world that a long-term or permanent residency there means accepting a very high degree of isolation, unless one is equipped with a very large pocketbook, which certainly was not our case.

Along here someplace—I think it was just before we let Jane in on the deal—one of us got the brilliant idea that rather than selecting a heaven on earth ahead of time, we should buy a live-aboard-size sailboat! We could live on it here for a few years, which would give us a chance to make our plans and get our marbles together, and then after proper planning, crewing, et cetera, we would commence a leisurely cruise of those places in the world we wanted to consider, maybe including a few more places that we might hear about along the way. After two or three years of wandering and comparing and analyzing, we would pick our dream spot, and *then* settle down.

At first, in all these dream plans, we had thought that we would sell the boat once we picked the place. But as our thinking progressed, we considered more and more the wonderful freedom a boat would give us—the mobility, the fun and the sport of sailing and cruising, even the earning potential of chartering or other commercial use if we were near resort or tourist facilities. Perhaps most important of all, we would be free to pull up the anchor and move on when we felt like it.

In short, the cart jumped in front of the horse. Why buy land and settle down when you can cruise the world with extended stops of weeks, months, even years for that matter?

There is a thin line between dreams and plans; when does a dream become a plan? However and wherever that thin line was, one day in early 1973, advertently or inadvertently, we stepped over it: our dreams became our plans. We decided to cruise the world; to be soldiers of fortune for a few years, or forever; to live off the fat of the sea.

It was time to tell Jane.

JANE

Carol and E. Jane White had met each other on the *S.S. New Amsterdam* crossing the Atlantic in 1965. Carol was returning home from Paris, where she had lived and worked for a year; Jane was making a pilgrimage from England, where she had grown up, to the United States, where she had been born.

Jane was the daughter of an English mother and an American G.I. During the war her mother and father had been married in England, where both were in service for their respective countries. After the war father had returned with new English bride to Baltimore, where Jane was born. The marriage broke up shortly thereafter, and mother and baby returned to England. Jane thus had her choice of a U.S. or an English passport. She chose the U.S. and was coming across (on the *New Amsterdam*) to visit the land of her birth before settling down to do whatever one settles down to do.

Carol at twenty-four and Jane at nineteen enjoyed together the usual shipboard gourmet food, special events, and so on, and by the end of the voyage had become good friends. On reaching New York both went their merry ways, Jane to see the U.S.A., and Carol back to Southern California. Months later, after ninety-nine days for ninety-nine dollars on leave-the-driving-to-us Greyhounds, a round of parties from city to city, Jane called on Carol in Los Angeles. Carol had had her first ski trip planned for the next day; naturally she invited Jane to come along. Carol fell and broke her leg (a spiral fracture that took twelve weeks to heal); Jane stayed on to help Carol in her time of need; and by the time the leg had healed, Jane had gotten a job and had decided she liked the States in general and Southern California in particular.

A few years later, when I came into Carol's life (or did she come into mine?), Carol and Jane had scraped their meager dollars and pounds together, had purchased a somewhat ordinary and bedraggled house in the Hollywood Hills, and had rebuilt and redecorated the house and grounds into a showplace. Each of them had above-average ability to create and to work with material things.

Jane was a no-nonsense, hard-working person, whether at work or play; she held herself and others up to high standards. Almost universally I have found that the person who goes through the English public school system (called public because it is really private) comes out with an excellent education. Jane was no exception. She was smart, articulate, knowledgeable. Perhaps not beautiful, but unquestionably attractive—blond and leggy, with a marvelous figure.

But she had never been on a sailboat in her life.

After Carol and I were married, instead of Carol and Jane as a twosome, it became Carol and Jane and Taylor as a threesome.

In 1970 Carol and I had purchased and moved aboard a Columbia 43, a forty-three-foot William Tripp-designed fiberglass racing/cruising sloop. We named the boat *Morgan*, a name we had left over when our firstborn turned out to be a girl.

Jane didn't move onto the *Morgan*, but she did spend a lot of time on the boat, both at dock and at sea. She and Carol took sailing lessons at a sailing school in Marina del Rey, and we all joined a sailing club known as Wind 'n Sea, where Jane especially pitched in seriously, taking full advantage of the club's excellent courses of instruction, daysails, and cruises.

When we again had a vicious attack of boat fever in 1973, it was only natural that Carol and I decided to let Jane in on our stop-the-world-I-want-to-get-off secret.

We told Jane about Grand Plan 75, or GP-75 as we called it. We were fed up with crime, narcotics, bullet-proof barriers in taxicabs, endless traffic jams, smog, phony politicians, the nine-to-five rat race. We would buy a sailboat, live and train on it, become the corporate dropouts I had mused about some time ago, and sail off to find a better place and way of life.

After deliberating for about thirty-eight milliseconds, Jane's reaction was as we had hoped and expected: "When do we leave?"

II

The Boat

Having Jane on board gave us some real impetus to get off of our duffs and do something. With her help and prodding we started planning much more seriously. We began compiling the inevitable lists and specifications of features we wanted in our boat, types of boats, sails, power, equipment, outline of voyages, timing, crew selection, even lists of supplies for the first leg.

And we started reading literature on various boats, drooling at the brokered boats in the back of *Sail* and *Yachting*, reading the "Sailboats for Sale" classified ads in the *Los Angeles Times*, and boat-looking in person. We had enough sea sense to realize that nobody in his or her right mind would buy a boat that was new. The smart money waits for the first or second owner to go through the agonies of shakedown, design bugs, factory bugs, bug bugs, massive dollar depreciation, buying all the extras that it takes to sail and live on a boat: fenders, dock lines, dinghy, liferaft, awnings, cushions, stove, fridge, generator, radios, depth finder, speed indicator, extra sails, storm sails, spare anchors, more anchor chain, anchor line—it goes on forever!

With the rapid, almost complete conversion to fiberglass in the small sailboat category—up to about fifty feet or so—and with the overwhelming preference of the buying public for fiberglass over wood, it was obvious that the place to find bargains in sailboats in the forty- to fifty-foot category, where we felt we had landed, was in older wooden boats. So this was primarily the area to which we devoted our searching time.

And a sobering thing happened over a two-weekend period of boat hunting. We had arranged ahead of time to examine in considerable detail a total of five boats that met our general specifications: forty to fifty feet in length, with accommodations for four to six persons, diesel powered, in fair shape; we didn't mind a fixer-upper if the boat had a good basic design and was well built in the first place. In three of the five cases, the boat had been purchased and outfitted by a couple for extended world cruising; each couple had previously sailed extensively; and each couple had been forced to call off the dream cruise for which they had planned for years because of the failing health or physical condition of one of the partners!

Running across these three instances of the best laid schemes of wife and man gang aft aglaye really put some imp into our petus toward avoiding there but by the Grace of God go we! Let's not wait until one of *us* peters out!

In an effort to get within our price range, we even looked at smaller production fiberglass boats and began to wonder why we sold the *Morgan,* our Columbia 43, which had lots of room, diesel power, sailed great. . . .

THIS IS THE BOAT?

During this time, whenever I traveled and had a few hours or moments to spare, I would look at boats. I was ever mindful of the great traditional boats that had started out as working boats, but over the years had become boats for pleasure, boats for living: the friendship sloops used off the coast of Maine, bugeye ketches in the Chesapeake Bay, pilot schooners, Hudson River freight sloops, sharpies, skipjacks, pinkies. So it was quite natural that when I was at St. Vincent in the Caribbean later in 1973 I looked long and hard at the indigenous Bequia-built ketches, one of the few sail-powered commercial cargo-carrying boats left in the world. All utility—husky, roomy, tough. Could one of these be converted into a sailboat for living and cruising?

Also on the Island of St. Vincent one star-studded night, while recovering from the overpowering beauty of a concert by a steel drum band consisting of twelve persons playing on thirty (count 'em, thirty) steel drums, featuring all the traditional Caribbean songs, I fell into conversation with a very interesting English chap by the name of Douglas Moxey. It turned out that Moxey had tossed into a cocked hat everything in his formerly very civilized stockbroker-type existence and had come to the Caribbean, where he lived on a thirty-seven-foot fiberglass sloop that earned him his keep by taking daytime charter parties for tours of the islands when his mood and the customers' desires happened to coincide. Like a couple of golfers comparing sand traps, we naturally compared boats of the present, past, and future that we had owned or longed to own. I told him of my desire to buy a boat and to do something not unlike what he had chosen, except in my case with family. I asked him how good the market was in the Caribbean for the type of boat I was looking for. He replied that it was excellent and that he would keep his eyes open for me.

Seldom does anything come of such a casual conversation, and nothing would have come of this one were it not for the fact that when I return from a trip, I try to drop a note to people who have helped or befriended me on my journey— and since I need a lot of helping and befriending, I write a lot of letters.

In this instance I dropped Moxey a note thanking him for his hospitality and for buying me a drink and saying, "By the way, if you ever *do* run across a real buy in a forty- to fifty-foot, well-built sailboat, drop me a line."

Nothing happened. Carol and I, with help from Jane, went about our reading, planning, and equipment-looking, even working at our respective work-a-day jobs once in a while.

And sure enough, about four months later, we received The Letter from Douglas Moxey.

A *William L. Hand!* If it's still floating it's got to be good! And any boat built in Boothbay, Maine, no matter who the designer, has to be great—even the name Boothbay instills confidence! And only $22,500 for a fifty-three-foot staysail schooner! When do we leave? Who goes? Why bother to look, let's just send money!

But calmness, or some pretense thereof, prevailed. Carol was between jobs, so in theory her time was free. I figured (mostly incorrectly as it turned out) that through some friends in the travel business I could get a bargain rate (like zero) for our three-year-old April and a low rate for Carol. And although I was probably the best judge of horseflesh in the family, Carol was by far the better business person and was no dummy about boats. Besides, before we bought we would have the boat surveyed, and when and if it looked like a real deal, I would come to St. Vincent, and Carol and I would sail west across the Caribbean through the Panama Canal and up the coast of Central America and Mexico to Los Angeles.

Neat!

Within a few hectic days I had contacted Moxey to put a small hold-it-for-us deposit on the boat; Carol and daughter April were ticketed via New York (which always seems out of the way, but usually makes better connections). Inoculations were checked and updated. I made arrangements for a surveyor out of New Orleans to fly to St. Vincent if Carol gave a green light.

Two days after she had left, Carol called from St. Vincent with nothing but praise about the *Evoe*, the William L. Hand-designed schooner. Absolutely beautiful. Traditional. Owned by the couple who managed the C.S.Y. Chartering Service in St. Vincent, an American with a Dutch wife. They lived on board and had kept the boat immaculate. In addition, they had the service of the C.S.Y. yard to keep the boat ship-shape and Bristol fashion, which it was.

There were only two flies in the ointment. One was nothing—some dry rot in the upper part of the mizzenmast. This was easy; the mast would be replaced. The other Carol felt was practically insurmountable: the boat had a huge cockpit that took up roughly a third of the cubage of the hull. Because of the relatively limited space below decks, previous owners had converted all the inner space into what amounted essentially to one large cabin. Great for a couple without

children. Not at all appropriate for a couple with two girls—
April, age three, and Laura, age twelve!

Goodbye *Evoe!* Hello *John Morley!*

THE *JOHN MORLEY*

*Darling, I've found an 83-foot ketch built in 1896 that I think we can
get for twenty thou'—either you'd better get down here and stop me or
I'm gonna buy it!*

On the theory that once she was in the water she might as
well enjoy the swim (or whatever), Carol had decided to come
back to the States by way of St. Lucia and finally Antigua
(pronounced An-*teeg*-ah by the English, who taught the An-*teeg*
-ans the same poor pronunciation). She chose Antigua because
it happened to be race week there, an event that attracts a good
percentage of the boats in the lesser Antilles, as well as from
Europe and the United States.

On Saturday 5 May 1973, Carol and April, accompanied by a
lovely elder statesman named Prescott Hubbard, who had
befriended Carol in Antigua, met me at the Antigua Airport,
to whence I had come to stave off the purchase of some old
wreck by Carol.

As usual, Carol practically owned the place after having been
there for three days. She had several boats lined up for me to
look at, but based on her prescreening there was only one
realistic possibility—if you can bring yourself to call a boat
realistic at age seventy-five.

Prescott took us to the local watering spot, the Admiral's Inn
of English Harbour, which was the home of Admiral Nelson
during his two-year stay in Antigua. The Admiral's Inn is one
of the spots you find throughout the world that has that certain
quality long attributed to the old Astor Bar in Times Square: if
you stay there long enough you'll see everyone on the island.
We had barely had time for the first one when in walked Per
and Andrew, the owner and crew of the *John Morley,* and we
were soon underway in the dinghy for our First Look.

Per was a Swede, twenty-seven years old, an expert sailor,
seaman, and mechanic. He had purchased the *John Morley* in

his native Sweden with the idea of fixing it up for charter in the
Caribbean and in the Mediterranean. As always, outfitting the
boat had cost Per more than he had planned. Charter business
wasn't good—local vested interests don't move over too easily
in these matters—and Per was simply running out of operating
money to keep the boat and himself alive. He would welcome
us in the morning at 1100 hours and we would have a great
sail!

And we did!

I couldn't believe the beauty and majesty of that boat! It was
a Brixham trawler originally built in England as a sailing/
working/fishing vessel with no auxiliary power. Sometime
before World War I its masts and rigging were removed, and
diesel power was installed. With the coming of the war and lack
of fuel, the boat was reconverted to sail during World War I,
then restored to power after the war. The same cycle followed
in World War II.

The engine room could have held twenty-five people. It had
two generators; a 240-volt electrical system for welding; plus
110-volt, 32-volt, and 12-volt systems; a dining room that could
seat 18; huge storage areas; I have forgotten how many
staterooms. And could she sail! The lovely Caribbean! Wind
always blows enough, seldom too much; steady in direction
and speed. We sailed for nearly four hours, tacking only once.
We powered out of English Harbour, secured engine, raised
mainsail, genoa, and a forestaysail. Then we sailed southeast
on a fairly close reach for a couple of hours with hardly any
need to touch the wheel. Per and Andrew, his young Scottish
crewman, just the two of them, handled the boat effortlessly.
Sails were not sparkling white, rather a gray heavy dacron, but
seemingly in good condition. Nothing shone, but nothing was
rotten or loose or dirty or needed fixing. The gunwales around
the deck were almost higher than April's head—certainly a
great safety feature, not only for children but for anyone. No
flimsy lifelines here!

And there was Lars! If Lars had come with the boat, I think
we might have made a deal, and our lives would have gone off
on an entirely different tack—probably bankruptcy! Lars was
the most beautiful, smart, obedient, and friendly German
Shepherd dog, or maybe the most beautiful (et cetera) dog of

any kind that I ever met. He had spent his whole life on that boat. It may be an old Swedish custom, but it was the first time I had seen this done: In order to take care of Lars's toilet needs, Per had an old heavy net piled up just aft of the mainmast. Lars used this for all purposes. Every few days Per would drag or hang the net over the stern for a few hours, and the wake or surge or fish life would do the rest.

Meanwhile, back on the port tack, after a couple of hours of zooming along at 10 or 12 knots or better in this septuagenarian, Per and Andrew swung the boat around to a reciprocal course on a starboard tack, heading back to English Harbour, to Lord Nelson's shipyard.

Other boat owners will recognize my feeling when I say that as we approached the rocky, narrow entrance to English Harbour I felt a little antsy and wanted to suggest to Per and Andrew that they might consider taking down some sail. But on the other hand, it's the other guy's boat, and his backyard, and he must know what he's doing. Nevertheless, I edged toward the little protected wheelhouse, where the wheel had been unattended for the past thirty minutes or so—amazing how well the boat held its course. Finally, Per asked me if I would take the wheel and head up into the wind while he and Andrew dropped the sails.

Would I!

I didn't want to overreact, so I moved the wheel very gingerly at first. There was considerable resistance to movement, and when I did grunt it over a turn or so, nothing happened. Another full turn. Nothing. That entrance rock was getting uncomfortably close.

"Taylor, can you bring her up into the wind now? She takes a lot of wheel!"

Yeah. I was beginning to find out!

Finally, after what seemed like ten turns and ten minutes, I could see the headstay start to move slowly to port along the shore where I now could practically see the whites of their eyes.

Per and Andrew got the sails down and furled with what seemed to be amazing ease. I am sure that much of this came from practice; the two had been on the boat for over eighteen months and had sailed across the Atlantic with only one other person on board.

As we eased gently into English Harbour, I could see that we were getting close to the moment of truth in the deal; I hadn't dared ask myself if we really had the guts and the lack of sense to do this thing. I could tell that Carol was in love with the boat—and it sure was lovable. I knew that it was too much boat for us, was too old, had incompatible equipment and machinery on it, would cost two legs to dry-dock, two arms to maintain, and the rest of our bodies in docking and insurance charges. But what a boat, and what a low price! What character! What accommodations! It would almost be worth it, just counting all the bugged eyes!

I guess the kick in the head I needed came from the anchoring episode. Per had brought the boat easily into the harbor and dropped the hook. Just about the time the anchor was set and holding, someone from the local equivalent of the harbormaster's office came to advise Per that we would have to move because our position would interfere with a small boat race scheduled for the next day. We were in considerably deeper water than we had been when we weighed anchor at the start of the trip, so raising the anchor this time was a long, laborious task, with Per and Andrew taking turns at the manual windlass. They refused my offer of help, probably because they didn't want me to feel how hard it was. I was embarrassed for Per.

The episode gave Carol and me a chance to pro and con the situation; wisely and almost tearfully, we decided that we would pass up this golden opportunity.

We were learning. A little.

AS LONG AS WE'RE HERE . . .

After all that travel, culminating in disappointment as we turned down both the *Evoe* and the *John Morley,* and feeling foolish for having spent money chasing rainbows, we decided to take advantage of the situation and stay around Antigua for a week's vacation, subject to a check with the office to be sure that the world wouldn't collapse if I knocked off for a few days.

The Admiral's Inn, where we were then staying, was quaint and lovely and very hospitable; however, it was also pretty noisy and raucous as the center of all the yachting activity on the island. The Inn had no beach facilities; it was not the place for us to relax and unwind with our three-year-old.

Anyway, let's have a good lunch here and think about a place to stay.

Our companions for lunch were Prescott Hubbard, his friend Anne Wilkinson, and Pat and Jack Henderson. It turned out that Pat and Jack had come to Antigua several years before, had fallen in love with the place, and had bought a large tract of land surrounding a picturesque cove just inside the entrance to English Harbour, where they had built a beach resort, somewhat reminiscent of Kona Village on the island of Hawaii. They had constructed a central clubhouse and had plunked down separated and isolated cottages at strategic spots, each overlooking beautiful Galleon Beach.

At Pat and Jack's invitation we joined them in their Boston Whaler to putt-putt from the Admiral's Inn to Galleon Beach to have a look. We looked; we liked; we stayed.

And unwind we did. Long swims. Long walks on the beach. *This* is the place! And it well could be. There were always sailboats anchored in Galleon Cove. Their graceful lines added to the beauty of the place and continually filled me with longing and hope. There was Bob MacPartland's forty-four-foot lean-looking but beautiful black German sloop, with portholes spaced regularly in the hull with prim precision. There was a sparkling white trimaran from Canada whose owners were planning to sail her to England in July.

We rented a mini (like a jeep, but the runt of the litter), explored the island and joined the fun of Antigua's Race Week.

Swimming in the Caribbean is about as good as swimming can be any place in the world. The water is always a pleasant temperature, never too cold as it can be even in Southern California, never too hot as it is in the Persian Gulf and at the Casper Country Club. There are relatively few things that bite, sting, or scratch (although I did have a horrible experience a hundred years ago when I inadvertently stepped on some black sea urchins while going into the water at Curacao). I had brought my trusty fins and prescription face mask with me and enjoyed at least one or two swims each day.

Whenever a new cruising sailboat appeared in the harbor I had to get out there right away and sniff my way around it. One day there appeared in Galleon Cove a beautiful white ketch that turned out to be a Northstar 48. I circled the boat a couple of times and started to swim away, when the owner tossed out a cheery "Good morning!"

We exchanged the usual how's-the-water; where-are-you-guys-from; you-sure-have-a-beautiful-boat.

I turned again to swim away when the owner asked me if I wouldn't come on board. I welcomed the chance, climbed up the swimming ladder, and was greeted by an attractive gentleman sporting a trim speckled-gray beard.

I took off my mask and was greeted by my own name: "Taylor! Taylor Hancock!"

It was my brother-in-law! Well, maybe my brother-in-law once removed.

Jim Power and his wife Liza had purchased their Northstar 48 in Ontario and had been cruising the East Coast of the United States and the Caribbean for a year or two. I eagerly ate up everything they had to say and to show us.

I was like the proverbial blind dog in a meat house, going over the boat inch by inch, getting all of Jim's and Liza's ideas about how they would do things differently if they were doing them over again, learning what can go wrong, and what does go wrong.

One point that had a lasting and devastating effect on our Pacific voyage was Jim's unhappy experience with plastic tubing. After a series of failures in the material, Jim replaced virtually all of his hydraulic system with copper tubing. He was adamant in his recommending that we not accept plastic; we should insist on copper tubing when we made *our* big step.

We left Jim and Liza in Antigua, saying goodbye among the ruins of the fort built by Admiral Nelson, which at one time guarded the entrance of English Harbour. The trade winds were blowing the girls' hair and the waves of the Caribbean were crashing on the rocks a thousand or so feet below.

One could feel the ghosts of Admiral Nelson and Lady Hamilton flitting in and out of the ruins.

THIS *IS* THE BOAT!

Back in Marina del Rey on Saturday 19 May 1973 we saw for the first time a Force 50, a William Garden-designed heavy-displacement fiberglass diesel auxiliary ketch. A typical Garden design, the boat carried its fairly broad beam deep below the turn of the bilge, resulting in a very roomy interior. This construction enables Garden to do a rather spectacular design job. When going below on many boats, one has the feeling of crawling down a ladder into a basement. On the Force 50, however, one walks down a curving staircase (not very nautical, but very descriptive) to a large combination pilot house–salon, and then down another curving staircase to get to the forward staterooms or, in the other direction, to the aft master cabin.

We were soundly and favorably impressed by the boat—hell, we were knocked out! The design of the Force 50 and its general features became the criteria by which we judged other boats, and we couldn't find any boat to fit our own likes so well.

Rather than having a navigator's station tucked away in a cubbyhole, the galley tucked away, a separate dinette, and a separate inside steering station, Garden had placed all of these functions in a commodious pilot house–salon that could be compared only to something on land—the old farmhouse kitchen or the modern family room.

Aft of the family room was a master suite with a double bunk and a private head complete with basin and shower. Forward of the family room was a double stateroom laid out so that it might be (to use another unnautical term) a sitting room by day and two separate staterooms by night.

Forward of the sitting room was a head to port with a basin and a separate shower/tub combination and two more private staterooms, making a total of six fixed bunks, two of which were doubles.

Ready to sail, but with an absolute minimum of equipment, the boats were selling for $80,000—certainly beyond any of our wildest dreams.

In June 1973, I went to Taipei, the capital of Taiwan, on

company business. When I realized I was going there, I think I had in the depth of my little black heart that I would take a look at the Robert Perry-designed CT 54, which had recently been advertised as being built by the Ta Chiao brothers of Taiwan, and also, since I would be there, at the Force 50.

We had earlier looked at a CT 41 center-cockpit ketch that I had liked very much; consequently, I had a good feeling about the Ta Chiao yard. And since the yard is not far from downtown Taipei, it was easy to get there to see the CT 54. It appeared to be a great boat. However, all that had been built to date was a male plug, which is a mock-up of the outside of the boat constructed for the purpose of building up a female mold, which in turn would be the womb for building an unlimited number of production CT 54s.

A couple of days after seeing the CT 54 male plug, I looked up the man whom I understood to be the builder of the Force 50. We'll call him John Smith. He was an easygoing, affable, soft-spoken, and most likable individual. He operated out of his residence, where I called him. His home was a lovely old house within walking distance of my hotel, the Imperial, in downtown Taipei.

Smith offered to take me out to the yard where the Force 50s were built, and a couple of days later when I had a little time, we drove out. The plant was located on the coastline, but not near any launching facilities. However, this was not particularly important, as practically all the boats produced in Taiwan are shipped out by freighter.

One hears adverse information about construction material and construction methods used by boatyards in the Orient— Hong Kong and Taiwan in particular. So even though I don't feel myself qualified to judge boatyard construction methods or material, I nevertheless looked forward eagerly to my first exposure to an Oriental boat-building operation.

Again, I was bowled over by the Force 50. Everything I saw I liked. The massive molded cast-iron weight for the keel, the generous thick fiberglass construction, the lavish use of teak, the hefty fittings and hardware—it all looked mighty good to me. Smith took me through several boats in various stages of construction, at which time I first learned that it was possible to a considerable extent to have a boat customized at no particular extra expense.

I was in love with something I couldn't have!

Unrequited love's a bore.

Driving back to Taipei, Smith asked me, as if he had just thought of the question for the first time, "How do you like the boat?"

"Hell, John, I think it's the greatest thing since powdered milk. I'd give anything to have one."

"Why don't you buy one? Hull number 17 is open."

"John, there's just no way I could come up with that money at this time; but if our financial picture improves, and I have good reason to think it will, we'll be in the market, probably in a year or two."

"I'd really like to make a deal to sell you a boat. It would help me right now, and I could make you a very attractive price. Could you take delivery someplace other than the States?"

"Well sure; I could take delivery almost anyplace and sail it to California, but that doesn't solve the problem."

"It just might solve the problem. If you could take delivery outside the States I could sell it to you now, say in Hong Kong, for $55,000; how about it?"

"Well, that's a pretty attractive price, John. I'll take that back and discuss it with Carol. You can be assured we'll give it serious consideration."

"I rather thought we could make a deal while you're here, Taylor."

"Good God, John! You can't expect to pressure a guy into making a quick deal on a $55,000 sailboat the same way a suit salesman pushes a suit of clothes onto a prospect, can you?"

"Well, Taylor, you may never get another bargain like this one."

My heart was pounding; it pounded for the next twenty-four hours—and maybe ever since.

When faced with a major or hard decision, Carol and I follow a practice (which I am sure is followed by millions) of putting all the pros or pluses on one side of a piece of paper and all the cons or minuses on the other side, tossing in everything that comes to mind. Sometimes on close calls we even go so far as to attempt to assign weighted values to each of the pluses and minuses.

In trying to overcome my unreasoning desire for that beautiful hull number 17, which was not even in the mold yet,

I pro'd and conned far into the night. The trouble was that the pros kept coming in way ahead of the cons. The following is just as I wrote it down on the night of 17 June 1973, unexpurgated:

Pluses

Big, heavy, rugged, strong

Ketch rig

Club-footed jib—easy to sail alone with three sails

Full-length keel—dry-dock on beach in emergency

Heavy fiberglass—no sandwich construction below water

12,000 pound iron *inside* ballast

Two steering stations; one inside

Big single cabin (pilot house)—all things to all men

Five (count 'em five) staterooms

Three w.c.'s, two head compartments, two showers, one tub

Good storage and lockers

Anchors carried outside and ready to go

Full ground tackle included

Light and airy (*24* openings for ventilation)

Good workmanship

Much teak, but not overpowering

Certain amount of customizing possible

Great fabrics and selection

Rigging would be done by builder (big advantage)

Sleep up to 12 in regular facilities

Tremendous deck space

Teak cabin sole

Private master cabin and head for C and T

Showers and head have separate sumps

Heavy sails

Heavy cabin doors (not bin boards)

Screening feasible

Only boat with gentle stairs, minimum of level change, curved for convenience and grace

Absolute minimum of protrusions, corners, *bumpables* on deck

Copper piping available

Three bilge pumps

Good deck storage space for Avon, hammocks, liferaft, bicycles, scuba gear, sunbathing

Simple and flexible rig and rigging

No running backstays

Beautiful!

Dream come true and all that

Heavy enough to be stable in most seas, but still readily handleable by five foot two inch girl

Good headroom inside

Headroom at outside steering station sufficient for sunshade

Good anchor-handling gear arrangement

Water and fuel inputs on deck

Fate!—now or never, and all that *(muy importante)*

Very heavy deck construction—good nonskid surface

Wild chance might pick up Amah or boat boy—foc'sle would be ideal for same

Opportunities fantastic for charter in Caribbean or elsewhere

Minuses

Lotsa necessary electronics are not included in base price (but many goodies *are* included)

Steering is aft instead of midship (but we'll go autopilot anyhow)

No walk-in engine room (but modern diesels seldom need checking—and access good when hatches are up)

Aft bunk not entirely open (but not sure this is a minus)

May be no room for water maker, and washer/dryer (but let's live without, and see how it goes)

No built-in holding tank or tanks (but can put one in ourselves—or recirculate)

Spars and rudder are painted wood (but easier to work on, and are replaceable)

It isn't too difficult to see which way the tide was running. By ten o'clock that night I had figured out a way that I thought might work: to beg, borrow, and sell in order to finance the boat. I placed a call to Carol and ran the whole deal past her.

She asked me the crucial question: "Are you telling me you'd like to buy that boat right here and now?"

"Yes."

"Well, you know how I respect your judgment, dear. If you're convinced that it's a good deal, and that we can somehow pay for it, you've got my okay."

I had an old battered Remington typewriter in my room which I had borrowed somehow. I sat down and whomped out an outline of an installment purchase agreement along the lines of an on-land construction contract: so much down payment; progress payments at fixed stages of construction; followed by a final payment upon delivery and acceptance of the boat.

It seemed like a good idea at the time.

The conventional way to purchase a boat under circumstances of this nature is to sign a sales and purchase agreement with the entire consideration to pass to the seller-builder upon completion and delivery, and with the buyer putting up a letter of credit to back the purchase price and thus protect the seller. I couldn't go this route because at that time I didn't have the wherewithal to back a letter of credit for $55,000. But I was reasonably confident that I could raise the necessary funds over a period of time and thus meet the progress payment arrangement. I recognized the risk and accepted it. Well, I *thought* I recognized the risk; as it turned out I only recognized a part of it. I very clearly saw the tip of the iceberg.

John Smith and I closed the deal on a handshake basis, then signed a document banged out on the old Remington by me. Taking advantage of the international date line, that very same evening I was home telling Carol all about the deal. From that time on our GP-75 plans really got into high gear.

THE *ISLANDER*

Now that we had signed on the old dotted line, with delivery scheduled for November 1973, we felt a great emptiness in that we had never really taken a good look at the finished product we were spending all that money for. True, we had made one quick inspection of a finished Force 50, but without the real critical look that one would have made before buying since we had no intention of buying a boat as big (and expensive) as the Force 50 at the time we had taken a quick run-through. And in Taiwan I had seen nothing but boats in various stages of construction, none of which were near completion.

Since we were not buying through a dealer, we did not feel right about posing as prospective buyers and looking at a dealer boat.

Patsy and Jack Mullen to the rescue!

We had noticed a Force 50, apparently in private hands, not too far from where we were living in Marine del Rey. I cannot remember our first approach to the owner. It was probably no more imaginative than: "Hello. That sure is a good-looking boat. Do you think we might bother you to have a look?"

In any event, we got to know Patsy and Jack Mullen. They, like an ever-growing number of people, were giving up life ashore, were living on a boat, and planned to cruise extensively. So not only did the Mullens think as we did; they had the same boat. And they were fantastically good boatkeepers. Their boat, the *Islander,* was immaculate. The two of them had done almost all of their own work, including Patsy's painting the deck and Jack's installing a generator. Naturally I told the Mullens that we were buying a Force 50.

We told Jack we planned to fly to Hong Kong and sail the boat back to California. His mouth dropped several inches.

"You mean, just like that? Just like that, you're going to take a plane to Hong Kong, get on the boat, and sail back?"

"Well, it's not quite *that* simple, Jack; but essentially, yes. I'm sending some of my crew over ahead of time to outfit the boat. We'll have a series of shakedown cruises out of Hong Kong. We plan to assemble the crew here in the States, and we'll do a lot of planning and studying; but, yeah, we're going to fly over, pick it up, and sail it back."

Jack was still speechless and unbelieving. It was a little bit as if I had announced that I was taking the 0516 flight to Mars.

We hated to impose too much on the Mullens' hospitality and would limit our visits to the *Islander* to once or twice a month. In the meantime, I would drive by or sail by their boat every chance I got. Sometimes I would just sit in the distance and stare at it; other times I would try to appear to be casually walking by and stop to study the boat's detail. When Jack would ask me to come aboard, I would usually decline, but almost always I had some question to ask him about a feature of the boat that had come to our minds since our last meeting.

Thinking back, I would have been a lot smarter to have asked Jack if he would be kind enough to devote a full day to going over the boat inch by inch with me, explaining each bug and problem that he might have had, or that he had avoided.

THE LONG WAIT

On my return to Los Angeles from Taipei in June 1973, I found myself caught up in a deluge of business and personal matters that forced voyage planning into the background. A couple of months later I woke up to the fact that we hadn't heard word one from Smith. Good god, he didn't take my $5,500 and run, did he? My concern was heightened in early September. I had asked another fellow with our company to look up Smith if he had time while he was in Taipei. My friend had reported that Smith was no longer at the address I had; nor at any of the telephone numbers that I had given him.

On 9 October, realizing that a progress payment was to have

been due on a date between 15 August and 15 September when the hull was to be out of the mold and bonded to the deck, I sent a wire to Chuck Berry of the First National City Bank in Taipei, asking him to contact Smith and advise me of the status of hull number 17.

Chuck had been reassigned to the Bangkok branch of the bank, but someone else was kind enough to check with Smith and advise me that he had just returned from abroad and had promised to call me.

III

The Preparation

On 13 November 1973 we held the first meeting of our prospective crew at our apartment in Marina del Rey. Of the thirteen people in attendance, seven then intended to participate in the voyage. All of us were members of the Wind 'n Sea Club; all seven who planned to participate were good sailors; none was a master mariner. Our calculations at that time were based on maintaining an average speed of five knots, making up any deficiency of speed under sail by utilizing our diesel main engine as necessary. Our intended route from Hong Kong to Guam to Ponape to Majuro to Hilo to Los Angeles covered a distance of just under 8,000 miles. Allowing for four days in each port, the elapsed time was just over eighty days.

We got down to the nuts and bolts that each member of the crew should be taking care of: physical exams (this cost us one potential, whose doctor advised against making the trip); clothes (we urged each person to bring at least one complete white outfit so we could line up impressively at the rail coming into port); flashlight (to each his own; otherwise you never can find one); sleeping bag (same); suitcase (sorry, absolutely verboten; no place to keep when empty); travel (I recommended Pan Am flight #1, which leaves LAX at 0825 every morning en route to Hong Kong).

I wanted to be as sure as I possibly could that each member of the crew was fully aware of our plans, intentions, philosophy, expectations. I wrote a series of Crew Bulletins that could form the basis of our discussions at crew meetings. Prior to our first crew meeting, I had written:

We chose the Hong Kong-Guam-Ponape-Majuro-Hilo-LAX route primarily for safety, both from the point of view of each stop being on one or more international airline routes in case of emergency, and for navigational safety purposes. I was also influenced toward Ponape because one of my good friends spent considerable time in Ponape (the occasion was accepting the surrender of 26,000 Japanese) and says it is a great place.

Anyhow, my point right now is that as I look into the places we are planning to stop, they all really look to be great. Hong Kong probably has the most beautiful harbor (harbour) in the world; politically intriguing nearby Portuguese enclave of Macao; well, this is not a travelog I guess. Guam, while military and all that, has much charm—enough to be the big center for honeymooners from Japan these days. Ponape is really exciting—volcanic, with highest elevation over 2,500 feet; population about 45,000; streams, waterfalls, ruins, charm. Majuro is the opposite; low-lying typical Pacific atoll with large inner lagoon; starting to be developed by Continental Airlines and others, but still pretty unspoiled. Hilo, well, it's a pretty spectacular place, too. We finally decided on Hilo over Lahaina in spite of Lahaina's old whale-town charm simply because the shore base facilities at Hilo are better than those at Lahaina— and the benefit of direct flights between Hilo and LAX. I've been poring over the charts, Sailing Directions, facilities lists— and like a kid with a new toy, really enjoying it. Entering harbors at Ponape and Majuro will be tricky—but local pilots are available in both places, which we will use.

Maybe none of the following needs saying, but to be on the safe side I'd better say it now: our main purpose, in a nutshell, is to bring the boat back from Hong Kong to LAX and to have fun in the process. As a part of bringing her back, it naturally follows that we want to bring her (and all of us) back *safely;* and thus safety will be the key word, by-word, over and above all other considerations.

As part of both the fun and the safety elements, we intend to run a very well disciplined ship: regular watches will be stood at all times, with a watch captain in charge of the watch; we will intend to have two on watch during hours of darkness, bad weather, or any emergency. We intend to maintain a daily routine of cleaning and maintenance in addition to regular rotating assignments of specific duties; each person will be responsible for and expected to clean up after himself or herself (heads, galley, bunks) as soon as use of the facility is completed; we will stress the old cliche, a-place-for-everything etc.; otherwise the boat becomes a shambles, and not only is pleasant living jeopardized but so is safety.

We will maintain a regular log into which will be entered hourly weather and sea observations, wind speed and direction, course (natch), barometric pressure, daily maintenance routine, and measurement of water and fuel. We will hold lifeboat drills, person overboard drills, and the like. Gee, I guess I'm belaboring the obvious here . . . but I felt perhaps it might help to set the scene at an early date.

We discussed and reviewed equipment, outfitting, shakedown, the voyage route, and of course personnel, far into the after-dinner wine. There were many suggestions for added equipment and supplies. In fact there was *no time, no port, no day at sea, no day in port* for which someone didn't have suggestions for added equipment and supplies!

GENERATION GAP

To generate electricity we had originally planned to install two small 3.5-kilowatt generators that John Smith had recommended. I have always been enamored of the idea of having two small generators driven by separate engines, as opposed to a single generator. Not only do you have a backup, but in emergencies you can rob parts or components of one generator for the other. However, the sales manager for the company handling that particular generator (who fortunately was familiar with the Force 50) advised that in his opinion the engine compartment wasn't large enough to handle two 3.5-kilowatt generators.

Inasmuch as it was necessary to have more than 3.5 kilowatts to handle the electrical equipment we planned to have on board, I looked elsewhere, compared various generators, and decided that the Kohler 7.5-kilowatt generator would do the trick.

I wired the dimensions of the Kohler 7.5-kilowatt to Smith to be sure that it could be fitted into the engine room.

Having received an affirmative reply, I proceeded to put in a purchase order for the Kohler 7.5-kilowatt unit. In checking out the specs in the Kohler literature, I noted that the 10-kilowatt unit had the same exterior dimensions and was only a couple of hundred dollars more. I took this matter up with my marine equipment agent, Bill Druitt, who told me, "Hell, Taylor, for a couple of hundred dollars more you can have the 12.5-kilowatt, which is *also* the same size as the 7.5 kilowatt!"

Boy, the money I was saving!

The Kohler equipment proved to be very reliable and quite satisfactory. I pulled one bonehead error here, however; the Kohler is powered by a Perkins 4-107 four-cylinder diesel engine. If I'd had my head screwed on straight, I would have arranged for both the generator engine and the main propulsion engine to be the same make, preferably the same model. This would have saved considerably in spare parts and equipment, would have improved our learning curve in care and maintenance of engines, and would have provided extra spare parts for cannibalizing in emergencies.

Also, in the wouldn't-it-be-nice department, if I had it to do over again, I would mount the main engine and the generator engine in such a way that power could be transferred in either or both directions, particularly from the generator engine to the propeller shaft. And, of course, if I *really* had my way, I would go to three smaller engines, any combination of which could be used for direct current, for charging current, for turning two drive shafts through two electric motors, or any one or more of the above.

Dream, dream, dream.

FIRST PROGRESS PAYMENT!

In mid-November, shortly after our first crew meeting, we finally received word that construction of hull number 17 had reached the point at which not only the *first* progress payment but also the *second* payment was due: hull out of mold and completely bonded to deck, basic woodwork completed, water tanks installed, and pilot house installed.

We had sold our previous boat, the Columbia 43, under an oddball arrangement in which we were to receive a final balloon payment. Happily, this balloon payment had recently blossomed, and somehow we were able to find the money to send to Bob Phillips of the American Bureau of Shipping in Taiwan, who acted as an escrow holder, with instructions to deliver the check to John Smith when Phillips was satisfied that the qualifying stages of construction had been reached.

A NAME IS A NAME IS A NAME

Carol and I look upon names—children's, pets', cars'—as being very important. If you name a kid Joe Blow, that's all he becomes; if you name him Nathaniel Hereshoff, he grows up to design classic boats.

We were getting pretty far into the planning of the voyage and still hadn't come up with a name for the boat. One day while sailing with a friend at Marina del Rey, we came upon a medium-size cruiser that neither of us had ever seen before: the *John Galt*. We both did a double take. John Galt is the principal hero in Ayn Rand's classic book, *Atlas Shrugged*. This book and its philosophy of objectivism was already a way of life, a Bible, for Carol when I first met her. A couple of years later, when Carol finally got me to read the book, I became just as avid a follower as she was of Ayn Rand's philosophy.

The heroine of the book was Dagny Taggart. We couldn't

use John Galt, because someone else had used *that* name for another boat and besides, sailboats, like hurricanes, must be named after females (it's in the rules someplace). *Dagny Taggart* . . . why not!

DIESEL POWER

A conventional sailboat or cruiser powered by an enclosed gasoline engine is at all times a potential bomb. All three right (or wrong) ingredients are present: confined space, powerful explosive, and ignition source. Naturally, by following good safety practices, and by having properly designed equipment and safety devices, this risk can be minimized. But I am a firm believer in Murphy's Law: that which can go wrong, will. I certainly am not alone in this concern, but the feeling may be a little more intense in me than in others since I have been involved in several fires at sea, the most serious of which was a gasoline fire in a family cruiser in the Santa Catalina Channel when I was in my teens, which nearly killed all of us. But that's another story.

As it turned out there really wasn't much of a choice to make in the diesel-versus-gasoline department. We wanted diesel power; Smith offered a choice of two engines, both diesel: a Perkins or a Lehman Marine conversion of an English Ford diesel truck engine. The choice was tough since they both have excellent and well-deserved reputations. Although both are found throughout the world, I reasoned that the parts for a Ford engine might be more readily available, or adaptable from something else, in some of the remote places where we might find ourselves. I simply didn't think about the matter of matching the main engine with the generator engine. Better wisdom next time! I hope.

The Lehman Ford was available in either a four-cylinder 80-horsepower model or a six-cylinder 120-horsepower model. I figured that the better fuel economy of the 80-horsepower model would be more valuable to us than the extra speed and power of the other.

So we ended up with the four-cylinder Lehman Ford diesel engine, about which I knew practically nothing by way of maintenance and repair. It was a severe blow when potential crewmember Harry Garside informed us that he was not going to be able to make the voyage as planned. Harry was the most mechanical member of our proposed crew. Even when we were counting on him to come along, I had firmly resolved that I would take a vocational course in the care and feeding of diesel engines. When we lost Harry, and had no other competent diesel mechanic either in the flesh or in the making, I renewed my resolution to get with it and take a course.

I no longer permit myself to use that self-deceitful phrase: I haven't had the time to do thus-and-so. What we really mean by such an expression is that in our personal order of priorities other items are more important to us in allocating our time.

Apparently other items were more important to me than taking a course in maintenance of diesel engines. In any event, I didn't take any such course. This was a mistake in the allocation of time that was nearly fatal.

I did write to Lehman Manufacturing Company in New Jersey, the company that converts the English Ford diesel for marine use under the trade name of Econ-o-Power, asking whether they could recommend any diesel schools or courses on the West Coast that would be particularly appropriate for the Lehman Ford conversion or whether they had any course of instruction at their facility in New Jersey. I also asked for all available literature, including complete instruction and repair manuals, and an estimate (or even a guess-timate) of the fuel consumption to be expected while cruising at moderate speed.

Bob Smith, the sales manager for Lehman, put the handwriting on the wall bold and clear in his letter of 16 July 1973, responding to my inquiry. The company, he said, "must honestly admit that we have never paid strong attention to the new Force 50." The enclosed copy of the 4C61 Owner's Manual and Handbook contained most of the important information on servicing the Lehman Ford, but "unfortunately, the book cannot make a mechanic; it can only inform and advise procedures to be followed by a competent mechanic. Should your desire be the development of mechanical skills, we recommend the enrollment in a Vocational School program given in the evening."

Furthermore, he wrote, the estimate of fuel consumption is very difficult to pinpoint but should be less than two gallons per hour under normal circumstances with proper propeller wheel loading.

I should very carefully point out that while we had diesel engine problems, we had no problem with the diesel engine. The Ford Lehman conversion was an absolute dream. It took punishment that no engine should ever be asked to take and came through beautifully.

We just didn't feed it very well!

THE RED DUSTER

Except for a toy boat, and except for a boat that you might build in your own backyard and sail on your own private lake, a boat must be formally registered with the correct bureau or agency of an appropriate governmental body. Without such registration it is difficult, in most cases impossible, to move from port to port, or from country to country, or to put up the boat as security for a loan. In California and many other places, navigating an unregistered boat will result in a citation and fine by the local authorities.

We considered long and hard the choice of state or country of registration and finally decided on British registration.

One of the primary reasons for choosing the British flag, affectionately known as the "Red Duster," was that British registry and the Red Duster are widely recognized and accepted throughout the world. Old Britannia rules the seas. There is also a somewhat more subtle advantage in that the British aren't subject to quite as much prejudice throughout the world as U.S. citizens sometimes are. And, sad to say, both my direct and vicarious experience had indicated that the services available from British consular offices are better in quality, and are more readily available, than comparable U.S. services.

There was still another reason for going British, or for not going U.S. It hurts me to say it or to think it, but somehow we Americans, with what we conceive to be our good-neighbor policies, seem to have become a hated people in a great many countries.

And, of course, our plans called for taking delivery in the British Crown Colony of Hong Kong, where all the registry facilities were British. It seemed like a natural.

All we had to do was form a British corporation (to be called The John Galt Line Limited), clear the proposed name of the boat with the Department of Trade and Industry in London, have the boat surveyed for British registry in Hong Kong, supply the usual reams of paperwork (declarations, builder's certificates, bills of sale), and have the boat's documentation number carved on her main beam, and we were in.

HOT STUFF

Selection of a method of cooking food aboard a boat must start with selection of the fuel that is going to be used in the stove or other heating device.

All stove fuels seem to have one thing in common: there is something wrong with each of them.

Wood, coal, charcoal: Too bulky, and usually too dirty.

Alcohol: Too expensive, often hard to find, takes a special license to purchase in some ports.

Kerosene: One of the best. However, kerosene has a fairly high ignition point, and therefore is difficult to light in most types of stoves. Many kerosene stoves require priming with alcohol for initial light-up, which is certainly a bore. And kerosene also has an odor that is offensive to some people.

Propane and butane: Almost ideal, except difficult to find in out-of-the-way ports, and may be very expensive. Most important there is a potential hazard of explosion due to a leak, inasmuch as propane and butane are both heavier than air and tend to sink to the bilge, making a giant bomb.

Gasoline: Too dangerous; no way.

Diesel fuel: One always hears that diesel stoves are used extensively on commercial fishing boats, and it certainly makes sense. The big advantage of a diesel-fired stove is that it utilizes the same fuel that is already on board for the ship's propulsion engine or engines. In addition, diesel fuel is about the most universally available fuel and is less expensive than the other fuels mentioned here. The disadvantages of diesel fuel for cooking are that igniting it may be a problem, and, like kerosene, diesel fuel burning may have an offensive smell.

Compressed natural gas: To us nontechnical people, compressed natural gas is the same as propane/butane in every characteristic except one; compressed natural gas is lighter than air, and therefore does not pose the same safety hazard. But unfortunately, compressed natural gas has one big drawback; it is not universally available. Perhaps its time will come.

It would appear that diesel would be by far the first choice as a cooking fuel if it were not for the fact that it allegedly offends some people by its smell or smoke when burning. But, ah ha! There's a way to cook with diesel without burning the fuel with an open flame. Just feed the diesel fuel into an internal combustion engine where it is burned *internally,* and convert this energy into electricity. The electric cooking itself is clean and neat. All the fumes from the heat and burning of the diesel fuel go outside via the exhaust. And since on a vessel with even a small amount of electric and electronic equipment it is necessary to run the generator periodically to charge the batteries, it is quite logical as well as practical to cook with electricity two or three times a day, at the same time the generator is recharging the batteries.

In order to minimize generator time, one should consider methods of cooking by electricity that take as short a time as possible. As far as we could ascertain, this seemed to boil down to microwave cooking, and the Corning Gourmet Cooktop system.

I mention in passing, with a laugh, that Carol got the wild idea that we might be able to persuade the Corning people to supply us with Corning cooking equipment at no cost if we in turn let them use our name, take pictures, and describe the successful use of the Corning equipment on a voyage across the Pacific for advertising purposes.

I explained to Carol that we would be wasting our time; that things like that happen only in the movies.

I had obtained Corning literature covering stoves and ovens. It was not completely clear to me which units required 240-volt current, and which could be operated on 120-volt. I placed a call to the Corning people and eventually ended up talking to their Southern California sales manager, Randy Barker. Somehow, before I could tell *my* story, Randy had related to me that he had just returned from Honolulu in connection with the installation of Corning equipment on a forty-foot cruiser. I then took his time and mine to give him a four-minute rundown on our plan to install the Corning equipment on our fifty-foot boat and then to sail it from Hong Kong across the Pacific to Marina del Rey.

I thought that the line had gone dead, because there was complete silence on the other end for a period of time. Then: "Mr. Hancock, by any chance would you and your wife consider the possibility of allowing us to give you the Corning equipment of your choice, free of charge, in return for allowing us to use your boat and the Corning installation for publicity purposes, with the right to take pictures of the boat on its return to California?"

There followed a period of silence on *my* end of the line!

TAKE THREE ASPIRIN; PUSH LIQUIDS

No one in our prospective crew could have been considered to be a medic. All of us had had some first aid training at one time or another. My biggest exposure was when I was in the Coast Guard in World War II. Carol had done some medical and lab work and was reasonably proficient. And crewmember Harlan was highly knowledgeable in the field of physiology. But we didn't have any experts.

Our good friend Earl Rubel, the fleet doctor in our Wind 'n Sea Club, was extremely interested in the trip—would that he could have come along! Earl spent the better part of a weekend going over with us all the things we might expect to happen and what to do about them. This was a most valuable session. Earl also gave us a list of drugs and equipment, divided by sections and arranged in such a way that it amounted to a miniature chart on what-to-do-until-the-doctor-comes in various medical situations. He even ended up taking the list to his own prescription pharmacy and getting all the drugs and equipment for us. All we had to do was pay the pharmacy.

CHUCK

Of our nonfamily crewmembers, the one who was closest (after Jane) to being a member of the family was Chuck. Carol and I first met Chuck in the summer of 1971 when son Bob was home from Oregon on vacation. We had invited Bob and some of his college friends to spend a week with us on the *Morgan* as we cruised from cove to cove around Santa Catalina Island.

We spent a day or two at the Isthmus—lovely old place—and then day by day we worked our way around the island counterclockwise; Cherry Cove, Emerald Cove, Parson's Landing, Catalina Harbor, Little Harbor, and finally around the east end of the island past the seals on Seal Rocks and on to Avalon. There was no room in Avalon Harbor itself, but around the corner in Descanso Bay there was good anchoring space.

We had a great couple of days in Avalon. Then a funny thing happened on the day that we were scheduled to leave—a thing that never happens in sunny California. There, smack dab in the middle of summertime, a quick storm came up. We had been about the first boat to anchor in Descanso Bay for the holiday weekend. By the time we were arranging to leave there must have been *eight dozen* boats in an area that normally would accommodate *one dozen*. We had anchored, quite properly, bow and stern with a good deal of anchor chain out on both anchors. Those who had come in later had anchored bow only, and mostly with short scope. Consequently, when the squall hit, our boat was sitting there like a rock, but the other boats, mostly smaller, were swinging 360 degrees around their anchors and banging into our boat on the way.

It wasn't good.

Our best deal was to get the hell out of there. But this wasn't all that easy, since our careful seaman-like job of anchoring also meant that we had to go through a careful seaman-like job of retrieving our anchors and chain.

And wouldn't you know it—our stern anchor had become entangled with some other boat's anchor gear!

About the time the winds were howling at maybe thirty or forty knots, and a pretty fair chop had built up, some crazy thirty-foot cruiser came roaring down on our bow like gangbusters. Chuck and I ran forward to fend off and barely managed to avoid any serious damage to the boats or injury to ourselves.

The cruiser owner was desperately trying to haul his anchor in so he could get away from all this, but *his* anchor line was fouled around *our* anchor chain in some ridiculous fashion. Since our dinghy was in the water, tied alongside our boat, I asked Chuck to jump into the dinghy and free this jerk's anchor line from ours so that both of us could get out to sea and away from all of these foreign entanglements.

Chuck wanted to be sure that he understood what I was asking him to do; but when he *did* understand that I wanted him to jump into the dinghy and free up the anchor line of the guy that was by now pounding into our hull, Chuck by-God jumped into the dinghy! I hadn't considered the fact that Chuck and I were currently standing on the highest point on the *Morgan*, at least ten feet above the water! Chuck didn't really jump—he swan-dived, beautifully, right on top of the dinghy. The dinghy, light little thing that it was, squirted away from him, leaving Chuck in the water and the dinghy torn from its tether by the force of Chuck's 180 pounds.

The skipper of the other boat meantime was racing his engine fore and aft, like someone who gets stuck in the snow for the first time, and managed to suck the now-free dinghy painter right into his prop.

And there we were: wind howling, Chuck in the water, another anchor line entwined with our anchor line, powerboat hull bouncing off of our bow with our dinghy's painter firmly wound around its propeller shaft.

I can't even recall exactly how the whole thing worked out, but we fortuitously found a bevy of scuba divers who obligingly retrieved our stern anchor for us. What I'll never forget is Chuck's great straightforward approach: You want me to jump in the dinghy; so, sure, I'll jump in the dinghy!

Years later, on the great cruise of the *Dagny Taggart,* I had many occasions to remember that cruise and Chuck's supreme swan dive. He was always that way; as long as he understood the situation and the request, he'd fulfill it if it killed him, which it nearly did more than once.

FAREWELL COLUMBUS

In preparation for a big event, no matter how brave and true and moral and helpful to mankind the event might be, eventually if the preparation goes on long enough Mo's Law takes over: the planning becomes a chore, and the people become a bore.

As exciting as the whole prospect was—this once-in-a-lifetime high adventure, this ultimate challenge—day after day and night after night Jane and I found ourselves on our knees, literally and figuratively, sorting and arranging and packing and documenting and making checklists. God, will we *ever* get through these damned checklists? We need a checklist to cover all our checklists! (And eventually that's exactly what we had!)

Not *another* unbudgeted expenditure!

Jane was a real rock during this preparation period; in fact, Jane and I worked together so much that Carol began to feel left out of the project. I had serious fears of Carol's losing interest in the entire enterprise, even including GP-75. This would never do!

By the time we sent out Crew Bulletin number 6, the crew had stabilized at good friend Jane, son Bob, Bob's friends Chuck and Randy, and fellow club member Harlan—each signed on for the whole trip. Carol and I would take partial but separate parts of the voyage. And shortly thereafter a new crewmember was added: Jim—another Wind 'n Sea member. While Jim didn't fit my mold as to lifestyle or hairstyle or dress style, he had a tremendous desire to join us. He had had a year at Annapolis, had good skills, and was willing to pitch in and to do whatever work was necessary.

We made plans for Jane and Bob to island-hop across the Pacific to check out facilities at as many of our planned stops as possible, and then to work with the builder on the final rigging, outfitting, and finishing touches in Taiwan preparatory to sailing the boat from Taiwan to Hong Kong.

As master of the vessel I supplied each crewmember with an affidavit stating that the holder was a crewmember on the *Dagny Taggart,* which would be leaving from Hong Kong to cross the Pacific, and therefore the person had only a one-way ticket rather than round-trip. This was important, since some countries will not allow a person into their jurisdiction without possession of the means to leave the country.

On 21 January 1974, we received a cable from John Smith:

CARPENTER WORK FINISHED, PLEASE SEND US$10,000.

By this time I was pretty numb. I dug up the US$10,000 somewhere and mailed a check. I also advised Smith of our scheduled crew itinerary, which at that time was for Jane and Bob to arrive in Taipei on Sunday 3 February. When Smith had been with us in Marina del Rey in December 1973, we had talked about the possibility of Jane working for him while in Taiwan—thus at least earning living expenses for herself. I reminded him of this and also asked if he might possibly find a place for Bob in his operations for a few weeks or months.

On Monday 28 January Jane and Bob had finished their last-minute rushing about. They had cleared their ticketing/visas/ shots; had done their sorting/storing/packing; and were on their merry way!

A happy group from the club, bringing their own champagne, by God, joined us for a farewell party at the Clipper Club at LAX International. Great goodbyes. Great see-you-in-Hong-Kongs.

During their stay at their first stop, Honolulu, Jane and Bob concluded that neither Lahaina nor Hilo would be practical as a pit-stop for the type of maintenance, repairs, and supplies that might be necessary for the trip we were planning; Honolulu was the logical and only choice.

Our dynamic duo left Honolulu en route to Guam on

Thursday 31 January. This was Bob's first trip across the Pacific; his diary entry for Friday 1 February:

Due to International Date Line did not experience this date!

They began their first day in Guam playing cribbage for three hours at the spectacular Guam Airport waiting for 0800 hours to arrive so that they could start calling their various contacts.

The following is from Bob's diary on 2 February:

Turned out to be a most successful and long day. We hitched a ride to Marianas Yacht Club quite easily. Met Jim McFarren and Bob Urbohl. Told us much of what we wanted to know. Incredible! Fed us and gave us a beer. Went sailing in Apra Harbor on Jim's 16-foot Hobie Cat. Excellent for Jane and me, 'cause we saw not only from charts, but from up close, the reefs, ranges and buoy markers, gas dock, and anchoring spot.

Realistically, we now feel we have a good idea of how to sail into Apra Harbor. Also went to the Trust Territory office and picked up entrance forms and proceeded to go back to the hotel and then down to Tumon Bay and resort hotels. At Hilton met Denise and Robbie Kaplan. Robbie is a mechanic on the island for Mobil, with diesel experience. He would like to sail with us, but offers his services if we need them while in Guam.

One interesting note—one fellow we met, at the Marianas Yacht Club, had known Smith from Japan. Nothing good to say about him. Told us to watch him carefully.

And Jane's final diary entry for the day:

What a great day!

Pretty good beginning!

THE ANCHOR WINCH

Isn't an anchor winch simply an anchor winch? Unfortunately, no.

For one thing, perhaps more than with other mechanical

equipment on board a boat, there seems to be no upper limit to what one can pay for a good anchor winch or to the amount of trouble one can have or get into, with an anchor winch that doesn't operate properly. I read one boat builder's advice that in building a boat the first thing to do was to buy yourself a good anchor winch, nail it to a fence post, and then build your boat around it.

As always there is the Quality Pitch: you can't compromise on quality; you get what you pay for; you need the best; safety of life at sea. But all that quality pitch can go just so far. You simply can't build or buy the QE2.

On previous boats I had struggled for so long, pulling up anchors hand-over-hand, with resultant sore back and scraped knuckles, that I had my mind firmly set that we must have a winch, and it must be electric. We were going to have a fantastic amount of electrical power available; shouldn't it all be used? But the anchor winches meeting the specifications that I wanted cost a thousand or even thousands of dollars. This simply wouldn't do. Somewhere I ran across an ad by Beejay Marine in Marina del Rey, not far from where we were living. It looked like a little one-man outfit, and it was. But what a man!

B. J. did most or all of his own work. He bought surplus electric motors and other parts as far assembled as he could get them, and as cheaply as he could get them, and put them together to make what seemed to my semipracticed eyes to be a pretty good winch.

I had the luxury of literally custom designing the winch I wanted. It was powered by a 12-volt electric motor, controllable from a switch near the winch itself; it would take either a chain over a gypsy or rope over a wildcat and could handle an anchor on either the port or starboard side. The magic day came in November 1973, when we picked up the eighty-eight pounds of metal and equipment, for which we paid a bargain price of $265. And we had ourselves a winch!

And to my great delight, it worked like a charm. We did have a little trouble with the friction brake, but nothing insurmountable. As was true of most of the mechanical items on board, son Bob proved to be boss man when it came to the anchor detail. The main pieces of auxiliary equipment utilized were a large hammer with which to release the brake; a piece of teak, of which we always had plenty, to protect the chrome-plated brake handle from injury by the large hammer; and a homemade-looking handle affixed to a ratchet arrangement, which was intended to be used in an emergency when the electrical power or electrical drive went out, but which proved to be necessary in order to control the speed of the chain as it was being payed out for anchoring.

What the hell, doesn't everybody anchor with a large hammer, a block of teak, and a homemade lever with ratchet affixed thereto?

IN ALL HER GLORY

At last—on Monday 4 February 1974—one of us finally saw, *in all her glory,* the hull of the *Dagny Taggart.* Arriving at Taiwan from Guam by way of Okinawa, Bob wrote in his diary:

> Number 17 appears in good order—didn't catch any flaws, but can you expect any before sailing? Smith very congenial—lunch, tour of bustling, frenzied Taipei. Number 17 should be launched approximately 20 February. Plan to leave for Kaohsiung with Smith.

> New boat equipment hang-ups—but still promised launch on time. To me it would be doubtful right now. She looks wonderful: tough, beamy, heavy, sturdy, thick masts. Smith sails by the seat-of-his-pants—this ought to be interesting!

While waiting for the boatyard to finish hull Number 17 to the point of launching, Jane and Bob drove with Smith to Kaohsiung, where Smith was setting up a new plant and office. Jane worked for a while in his office. She wrote:

> It's still hard for me to work, with cocks crowing, kids screaming, cars careening, scooters scooting, and workmen everywhere.

After a few days the duo became a trio when Chuck came down from Japan and joined Jane and Bob in Kaohsiung.

Dagny Taggart's *hull being winched out of a shed at Hudson Shipyard, Keelung, Taiwan, December, 1973.*

They had a little time for sightseeing and cultural exchange. Bob wrote:

> So lucky to be able to see this side of the world . . . saw magnificent Buddhist shrine, and ran into T'ung Chen and family. Must remember to send his wife a Levi jacket and pants outfit.

By Friday 15 February, oriental tranquility had descended upon both Jane and Bob. Jane wrote in her diary:

> I feel strangely happy—unhurried for a change, and happy to let the day go by without having to accomplish anything much.

The next day, all of the inactivity and tranquility and relaxing bore fruit. Jane wrote in her diary:

> Woke early and decided we are wasting our time here; also I am not really doing much for Smith; plus I have not checked the boat to see if all is going per contract. Must talk to Smith—go through contract and equipment. Called Smith and he invited us to dinner tonight. Tried to call Taylor to discuss the matter. I feel I should go to Taipei and watchdog the boat; check that they are doing it right; no point in having boat taken to Keelung and put in the water if there is a lot to do at the yard. The yard is miles away from Keelung.
>
> I am anxious to do the job I'm here for. I believe we made a mistake in making a deal with Smith for me to work for him, as it puts me at a disadvantage. Had enjoyable pre-dinner drinks and chat at John Smith's house, followed by a great Chinese dinner, but he flew into a temper when I started to talk about going over the contract. Hard to understand him. Felt I didn't deserve it. He took us home immediately. Was able to calm him a little, and will leave tomorrow.

About the same incident, Bob wrote:

> The next day, however, all was normal again. Jane and Smith reviewed the equipment on the boat and the status of construction, and Smith was agreeable to Jane's returning to Taipei.

The trio set out for Taipei on a bus via Taichung on the

scenic East/West Highway. Bob wrote in his diary on 19 February:

> After spending the night at the Fun Chuan Hotel in Taichung, and waiting for Chen at an extremely cordial neighbor's home, where we watched "The FBI" and "The Rookies" and drank tea, we took off at 0715 hours for Taroko Gorge by way of a long bus ride over mountains ranging up to twelve thousand feet high.
>
> That drive was possibly one of the most fantastic I've ever seen; the River Taroko cuts through almost solid marble canyon wall—straight up and down (the wall, that is) for about fifteen hundred or two thousand feet. Absolutely incredible! The bus ride truly enhanced our stay in Taiwan, showing us that she is more than cities and farmland. The hard cut road over the hills and down through the gorge is a remarkable engineering feat. But it is dwarfed and dominated by the Lord's beauty in which it runs. Solid marble boulders as big as tractors and buses.
>
> Beautiful warm weather, and clear running river. The third paradise I've seen so far. I do hope to return to Taroko someday. But it's on to business and our boat tomorrow, which means Taipei.

Finally, on Thursday 21 February, our trio got out to the Hudson Yard where hull number 17 was more or less nearing completion. Jane reported in her diary that the *Dagny Taggart* looked great but would not be in the water for another ten days. Bob concurred that number 17 was coming along fine.

These times were frustrating both for us in Los Angeles and for our trio in Taipei. On Monday 25 February Bob wrote in his diary that the boat wouldn't be done for at least seven more days—probably more. The weather had turned bitter; he had the worst cold on record; and the night before he had gotten so mad he screamed, startling the hair off Jane and Chuck.

And again, on 26 February:

> Bad day at Black Rock. Number 17 won't be done for another 14 days. Cold, bitterly damp day, making me wonder if we will *ever* get out of here.

GATHERING IN THE SHEAVES

December 4, 1973, had been a red-letter day. On that day we shipped to John Smith in Taiwan on the ship *Japan Mail*, ETA Keelung 25 December 1973, one Kohler 12.5-kilowatt marine electric plant, one Norcold refrigerator, one Wood Freeman automatic pilot, two Repco marine air conditioner/heaters, one Beejay anchor winch, and one plastic tool kit containing miscellaneous equipment removed from our previous boat, all itching to get back to work.

Along about mid-February it became clear to Jane and Bob in Taipei, and it was relayed to me in the States, that our current main obstruction and hurdle looming larger and larger was the difficulty of getting the above principal shipment through the customs service in Taiwan. This shipment was our first one. It contained a great many crucial items, each of which was vital to us. Even more important, each was scheduled to be installed at the yard in Taiwan before the boat was launched and was to leave for Hong Kong. We couldn't get going without that first shipment.

One of the advantages (or so we had thought) of having Jane and Bob in Taiwan early was to enable them to check on the exact manner in which invoices and other customs documentation should be prepared. They had done this and had telephoned the information to me: Do *not* unit price the miscellaneous shipment; price only the major items for which you have commercial invoices; the miscellaneous items should be listed as:

Skin Diving Equipment . . . . US$4,000

I followed their instructions to the letter.

After many delays, on 27 February the Taiwan customs authorities rejected all our invoices, reversed themselves, and insisted that each item be *unit* priced. Bob and Jane worked into the wee small hours for two nights, unit pricing each item and getting the grand total to match what had previously been given to customs. They turned in the papers, hoping they would be successful this time.

The estimate of boat completion, except for the customs shipment, was now 7 March. On 5 March we were told by Smith's superintendent that he had received the all-important import license on our equipment that was stalled on the dock in Keelung, and that the necessary certificate was being prepared. We were also told that a present had been involved in getting our shipment cleared. I was of course aware that the giving of small presents and favors—cigarettes, or a pen, or a bottle of whiskey—is a fairly common device throughout the world (including Houston, New York, and San Francisco). Therefore, although I didn't like the idea of giving *anything*, I considered the matter so routine, and I was so relieved to hear that the bottleneck was unbottled, that I was not particularly concerned about the morality of the transaction.

But even with the present, more delays were encountered. It took time to type the certificate; the day Jane was to pick it up, the customs office had lost the file.

Finally, on Wednesday 13 March, they got the certificate and took it to the customs bureau, where they were told they should be able to pick up the shipment Saturday. "Hooray," wrote Jane, "Bob and I had ice cream by way of celebration!"

Everyone was amazed at the size of the Kohler generator and the Perkins 4-107 diesel engine that drove it. Even though John Smith had checked the dimensions, it turned out to be a tight squeeze. The yard had to mount the generator athwartship rather than fore and aft, which was to give us some problems later.

Back in Marina del Rey, by 13 February I had assembled all the gear for a second shipment, which we were sending to Hong Kong to be picked up by the *Dagny Taggart* when she got there. This shipment included over 200 miscellaneous items, from hose clamps to safety harnesses; from solderless ring terminals to a strobe-lighted man-overboard pole; a Lehman diesel spare parts kit; a surplus WW II hand generator; chronometer; barometer; navigational publications; shotgun, rifle; tools; our medical drugs; six or seven radios of various types and purposes; ten plastic drinking glasses.

Making a shipment of this nature is far from simple. After buying, gathering, and temporarily storing someplace (unless you are an expert packer with facilities to build custom packing boxes), the equipment must be delivered to a packing company. After building a special box, the packing company packs the stuff and turns it over to another outfit, a forwarding company, who delivers the box dockside, where it is identified as waiting to be picked up by a particular vessel.

There was a slight communication failure between the packing company and me. I had made the error of delivering our supplies and equipment in two batches—simply because the pickup truck I had borrowed wouldn't hold everything on one trip. A couple of days later I delivered the second half. Lo and beheaded, the packing company had built a box for the first load already, and it was packed and nailed shut.

"No problem, Mr. Hancock; we'll just build a second box."

But that worried me; I dreaded the possibility of the second box getting lost or not getting unloaded, or something.

"But Mr. Hancock, there is nothing to worry about. You must realize that these matters today are all programmed to avoid errors; everything is computer controlled."

Yeah, that's what's worrying me.

At my request each box was prominently marked with the fact that it was one box of a two-box shipment. And when I learned that the second box had been completed, I traced the shipment to the dock warehouse where the boxes were to be picked up and loaded on the ship. Sure enough, big as *Life* magazine, there they both were, sitting right next to one another, and each plainly marked: *One Box of a Two-Box Shipment.*

I felt better.

CAROL JOINS OUR CRACK TEAM

In the fall of 1973 Carol and I felt that she had at last found her niche in the business world. She had accepted a job as office manager of a medium-size law firm in Century City. Carol's background in both legal matters and office management seemed to make this a natural for her. And so it went, until Friday 1 March 1974, when Carol was told that the firm had decided that the firm and Carol would part company.

I have no use whatsoever for any of the so-called occult sciences—astrology, graphology, numerology, and so on. And yet I have to concede, inconsistently, that I *do* look for Signs; or at least I am receptive to Signs in somewhat the Old Testament fashion.

When Carol lost her job right at this critical time in our lives, it struck me as a Sign. It seemed suddenly to make all the sense in the world that we should step up our pace. There wasn't really any compelling reason for Carol to stay behind now; in fact, why not have her come along for the entire trip? This was a particularly attractive proposition for me, since we could have the Great Experience together; and, most important, Carol had expressed concern more than once that the whole outfitting and voyage planning had become a Jane and Taylor affair, with Carol on the outside looking in and not feeling very wanted. Carol's coming along should completely solve this serious matter of her concern.

Daughter Laura was spending the current school year in Miami. We could take daughter April with us. Having Carol on the entire voyage meant we could give up our apartment, saving unnecessary rent and maintenance costs.

We gave notice under our lease, started planning garage sales, and passed the great news in re Carol to the troops in Taiwan.

WILL IT EVER GET LAUNCHED!

On Friday morning, 4 March, Superintendent Tsai called Jane and Bob in Taipei to tell them that the boat would be finished on that same day. Bob wrote:

> We laughed, but the latest report is that the mast is to be stepped on Sunday. Jane and I rode out to the yard. The boat has come right along and it looks like seven days or so until completion. T'ung Chen showed up with his friend Captain B, and we all had lunch together. Captain B is such a joy to be around. He brought a TV-type friend with him who owns

horses near Taichung, and water skis at Sun-Moon Lake. If I have time he will take me there—free; more hospitality. Captain B also wants to put our boat launching and our leaving Keelung on the Chinese TV network. That will remain to be seen. Smith arrived in Taipei today—something may happen. We also got mail. I feel better.

The next day Randy joined them, so we had four in Taiwan.

GENTLEMEN, START YOUR LAUNCHING!

Jane first saw the launching area on Sunday, St. Patrick's Day, 1974. She and Bob and John Smith had driven up to Keelung from the boatyard:

Very picturesque drive by the coast and mountains. We looked in Keelung for a place to tie up the boat; we saw where they would launch the boat—am scared to death. Cannot imagine how they will do it. The road ends, and there is just a track to the launching pad.

And Bob had this to say:

The harbor is filthy with a thick film of grease floating on it. The facilities are primitive. Jane and I really feel that if the boat gets launched without any mishaps and in full working condition, it will be nothing short of a miracle. The conditions here are incredible in regards to boat building. It's so new that Smith and his assistant must instruct the people at the yard on how to do everything. The whole thing seems preposterous. I won't believe that the boat will make it into the water until I see it.

In retrospect, I think that Jane and Bob did me a service by *not* communicating their trepidations to me in connection with the forthcoming launching. If they had told me their fears I couldn't have done a damn thing and I would only have agonized.

On Thursday 21 March, the launching date was set for Tuesday 26 March, and the butterflies started to jump.

APRIL

What do you do with a three-year-old daughter while Mommie and Daddy go off to sea?

Living with a baby on a boat, as we had on the *Morgan,* isn't as awkward as it might seem at first blush—in fact, its advantages just about balance its drawbacks. Our primary recreation and pastime was sailing. Unlike golf or tennis, there was never any question of what to do with the baby; she just naturally came along. It was similar with evening entertaining; it's hard to figure a nicer evening than a cocktail cruise around the harbor followed by dinner at one of Marina del Rey's restaurants or clubs, with a boat tied up at the dock in front of the restaurant; baby by this time sleeping it off.

And living with an older child on a boat is even better. There is always something to do, particularly if the boat is moored or anchored in a recreational area. Friends are easy to make when the kids at school find out that Laura lives on a boat. Friends are eager to visit Laura's home, and they are intrigued when they get there. Living on a boat is *in.*

However, between the baby and older-child stages is an awkward time, unless the parents are much better swimming instructors than we were. When April could only crawl, or barely toddle, the boat was one big playpen for her; we felt very secure insofar as baby-overboard was concerned. But when she became a real walker and a climber, but hadn't yet learned to be a good swimmer, it was hell. For this and other reasons we moved off the *Morgan* in mid-1971 and sold it about nine months later.

April had lived with us for almost a year on our Columbia 43. She was agile and extremely good-tempered. We hated the thought of leaving her behind, and we didn't have anyone to leave her with anyway; therefore, right after we decided that Carol would make the whole trip, we decided to take April with us.

That was before Jane straightened us out. Taking April, wrote Jane, not only would risk the life of a human being who had no choice in the matter, but would greatly endanger the lives of the crew. Neither Carol nor I could possibly be a constant twenty-four-hour-a-day watcher; and no matter what, the rest of the crew would be concerned for her safety and might even risk their lives to save her.

Further, wrote Jane, a child's inevitable whining and crying would only aggravate nerves that were bound to be tense on a voyage such as the one we were undertaking.

"What I'm going to do is ask you both to look at it objectively; and I feel sure, with all the dangers and risks inherent in all trips of this type, that you will make other arrangements for April. Could you reconcile her death or the death of a member of the crew in your own minds? I think not."

Under date of 16 April 1974, just before my departure for Hong Kong, I wrote to April's various grandmothers, informing them of our decision to leave April behind (thanks to Jane's well-put words of wisdom) and to assure all that she would be in the best of care, and in a most happy atmosphere:

> April is very happy staying with Mrs. Figge, our chosen temporary-guardian, and her daughter Alexandra. The two girls are exactly the same size; although Lexy (can't you just hear it now, in teen-age language: Sexy Lexy?) is about six months younger and talks maybe a little better. They really do enjoy and love each other and have a wonderful time together. Very well behaved—both get gold stars at the Small World, their day school. Mr. Figge (who seems to be around an awful lot for a divorced Daddy—which is fine)—always takes April with him when he and Lexy go to dinner or to the beach or movie or what have you—so April is having the time of her life.
>
> I am distressed that both Carol and I, and especially Carol as it is now planned, will be away from April for such a long time—but I think there is a big compensating factor in April's having the experience of living with another person her same age and size, particularly in such a fine atmosphere as is maintained by Mrs. Figge.

OUT OF THE YARD

As the magic launching date of Tuesday 26 March approached, Bob wrote:

First long day of working on the *Dagny Taggart*. Randy, Chuck, and I spent at least 10 hours doing all sorts of things; check-up maintenance, tightening bolts, etc. So much hustle and bustle going on—almost every Chinese in the whole yard was on our boat doing something. As it turned out they had to work until 0200 hours, and the next day, and still didn't quite finish, but started to truck her to Keelung anyway.

On the Great Day, Bob wrote:

The *Dagny Taggart* was moved from Shao-Keelung to Keelung early this morning. Must have been quite the harrowing drive; thank the Lord we didn't see it. This morning we loaded a taxi with Jane's and our equipment, and it was so long to screaming Taipei, and hello to rainy Keelung. Boy, it's cold here compared to Taipei.

Besides splitting the forward dock line posts, scratching the hull, and dropping the boat, the move from the truck to the trolley (and launch position) was uneventful. Jeeze! it could give a young lad like me a heart condition. There's still much to be done (and, now, to be repaired); but it's all systems GO for tomorrow morning. Our first night on the *Dagny Taggart,* with one light to save battery power. Looks like tomorrow could be *Dagny Taggart's* birthday. The kids are here to patch the rudder.

To the *Dagny Taggart:*

Best of luck on your life at sea
   May the sweet Lord protect you and yours
And may you show those you carry
   The wonderful world we live in.

The Great Event occurred on Wednesday 27 March, approximately two months after Jane and Bob arrived on Taiwan. Jane wrote:

I got up at 0700 hours. Everything is in a mess, so it's hard even
to dress, let alone wash. Hudson yard crew came about 0930.
Everyone working madly. Took wood off mast; installed sheave
for burgee halyards. Working on engine and generator. Also
finishing off teak in pilot house. We had sandwiches for lunch.
Work continued into the afternoon, and then suddenly, they
said we are going to launch in a minute. Thirty seconds later,
we were running down the ramp. Scared me to death, but fun;
like a roller coaster. They lit firecrackers.

Ho, from the Hudson yard, at the helm nearly ran into a
fishing boat. Powered *Dagny Taggart* around and eventually tied
up next to the crane. They hoisted both masts—a bit tricky—we
put coins under each mast. Rope on crane broke on mainmast,
but we had mast on the deck at the time, thank goodness. We
spent the evening cleaning up the deck, removed loose wood,
and swept fore and aft. Looks like a boat at last. We ate some
bonito sandwiches; all of us very tired. Sat outside for a while.
Quiet evening. Checked lines about every three to four hours.
So good to be afloat! Can't wait to sail! Fair winds and God
Speed, *Dagny T*.

Jane, God bless her, started the official ship's log on 27
March 1974 with this entry:

Dagny Taggart launched from Awa Nan's yard on Peace Island,
Keelung, Taiwan, at 1430 hours; a typical Chinese launching,
with firecrackers and great disorganization.

The next several days were spent painting, rigging, attaching
booms, sorting lifelines and sail slides and tracks, installing
anchor winch, cleaning, finding and repairing leaks, cleaning
the bilges. Jane continued with her initial shopping for
supplies, to turn the boat into a living thing with living people
on board.

Another big event: on Sunday 31 March, Bob and Jane bent
on the mainsail and ran it up the mast. Everything worked
fine!

BOB

Son Bob, twenty-three years old at the start of the voyage, proved to be my strong right arm—the most conscientious person on board when it came to the boat, the machinery, the bilges, the water supply, the fuel, the safety of the boat and crew.

You might say that Bob and I have the ideal father/son relationship. Great mutual respect; great love one for the other; completely uninhibited communication. Each recognizes and accepts the other's weaknesses as well as strengths.

When Bob was thirteen, and I was what?—forty-three—we were fooling around with some neighbors on the front lawn and by chance found ourselves in an impromptu boxing match with someone's new Christmas boxing gloves. I think we had a series of three-minute rounds, and I think we had a referee. I know that neither of us would give up, and I know that we boxed and boxed and boxed until each of us simply fell on the ground completely exhausted, unable to move. And I know that out of that playtime physical combat came an even stronger cementing of the bond between us.

Bob is blessed with the body of an O. J. Simpson and the compassion of a Salvation Army nurse. He has his mother's quick physical grace and coordination; handsome without being aware of being handsome. In the entire two years of planning and voyaging Bob was the only one who made a point of thanking me for making possible what he felt was the greatest experience of his life.

In mid-March 1974, Bob wrote that he and Jane were ready to get moving:

> It's been a long time now since we've actually felt something was getting done; and although with the delivery through customs of the shipment from Dad, we feel somewhat relieved; but nervous. Jeez! we've got the jitters; and we're not even sailing yet.
>
> Speaking of fear, I wonder how I'll respond in the face of it.

Or, should I say, I wonder how I'll respond in the face of death. How will I react with 50-foot waves rolling the bottom out from underneath the boat? I think this is one of the reasons I'm here: to test this. I know I don't panic in crucial situations, but I clearly want to be as mentally prepared as possible for the critical parts of the voyage. I want to be able to gut-up-and-belly-out when the time has arrived. It's real. Can I face death and spit her in the eye? The next four or five months could very well tell the story. It's time in my life to test my courage.

As D-Day approached, Bob wrote to Carol and me from Keelung:

Jane and I really want you to know that this is no daysail. This is why we were so tremendously concerned over the situation with April. You two are in command, and must set a realistic example for the rest of our green green crew. You should also respect the knowledge that Jane and I are going to have about the boat. Hell, do we all realize what we're doing? I feel extremely confident that I know what I'm getting into, and Jane does also, but does everyone else? Both she and I have worried about the long ocean-sailing from Keelung to Hong Kong in a brand new boat with only an RDF—to me that's wild. But I want to do it, and so does Jane; however, we really want everyone else to be willing to take such chances too. Because a situation like that may just happen.

We had no choice but to send certain of our equipment to Hong Kong rather than to Taiwan. It was not possible to ship into Taiwan any equipment or material that might even remotely be construed as an instrument of war. The concept of being an instrument of war would naturally have encompassed our shotgun and rifle, but also, by Taiwan rules, would have covered all of our radio and other electronic equipment. We in the Western world do not ordinarily think of the relationship between Taiwan and the Chinese mainland as being that of a state of war, but, at least as of 1973/74, the two sides were still shooting at each other daily across the one mile of water between the mainland and the fabled Islands of Quemoy and Matsu that figured so prominently in the Kennedy/Nixon debates during the presidential election campaign of 1960. While we were there, fortunately, it was a fairly civilized war.

THE BEGINNING IN SIGHT!

After two or three days in the water, things finally started to fall into place. On Sunday 31 March work was finished on the main and mizzen sail tracks—both sails could be raised and lowered. The next day the ship yard crew got the fresh-water pressure system operating and repaired a leak in the generator riser. Environmental conditions were pretty hectic. Our boat was nested in a group of fishing boats and work boats; that is, one boat was tied to the dock, another boat was tied alongside that boat, another boat tied alongside *that* boat, and so forth. This meant that crew and workmen serving the boats farthest outboard were continually crawling across our boat; and we had to cross several other boats, varying in number from time to time, to get to and from our boat. It also meant tremendous pressures against each side of the boat caused by surge and wakes. And each time one of the boats in the nest would leave or return, there would be rearranging of lines and general pandemonium. All this resulted in frequent bumping and scraping. The other adverse element of the environment was rain, day after day, or parts of all days, that made working topside either unpleasant or difficult.

On the other side of the world we four (Carol, Taylor, Harlan, and Jim) were chomping and stomping at the bit— making reservations, breaking reservations, making them again, calling Taiwan, getting calls from Taiwan; writing letters; meeting; planning. When the hell do we get this show on the road?!

There comes a time when action is the order of the day. Waiting becomes a tyrant. *Any* action is better than no action.

On Saturday 30 March 1974 at the Imperial Highway Charter Flight Terminal at LAX International Airport, Carol's mother, Carol's grandmother, Carol's daughter, and I, Carol's husband, met to bid a tearful farewell to Carol, our intrepid seafarer. And Jim and Harlan were likewise off, Jim leaving his girl friend behind, and Harlan taking Frances with him for the

Hong Kong Is tour and return. This left only Taylor in the States—everyone else in our prospective crew was now either over there or in the air!

And one more gigantic step toward our goal was taken.

The start of the voyage from Keelung to Hong Kong was now being delayed by the age-old enemy of captains and crews who are in port and want to get underway. The last minute just-one-more-thing—this plagued Nelson and the Phoenicians and still plagues the captain of a modern aircraft carrier. On 5 April Jane wrote in the log:

> Started out a beautiful day. We cooked up some porridge and had coffee for breakfast. Bob went up the mizzen and installed the shrouds to the spreaders, and attached the baggywrinkle to stop sail chafe. Discovered a leak in the engine salt-water intake—this became very serious when a fitting came off in Chuck's hand. Water gushed into the boat. We finally put a wooden marlinspike in the hole which held very well. We could not contact Smith all day. Maddening.
>
> Bob finished up on the mainmast, installed club forestay, and also wired and attached baggywrinkle. We finished sanding the teak above-decks; ran out of oil in the cockpit. Chuck and I cleaned out the forward and aft bilges. Later went to town to buy—no luck—a pump to get oil and water out of the middle bilge directly under Ford/Lehman. Had dinner; noodles, in the cockpit—almost a full moon; a balmy evening.

Later they borrowed a crude hand pump and pumped the water and oil from the engine compartment bilge. Then, while cleaning off the pump with salt water, Chuck dropped it in harbor. He went over the side to try to retrieve it, but couldn't in all the muck. It was eventually retrieved by divers.

The next day Smith told Jane that he expected to get the export license for the *Dagny Taggart* on the *next* day, 9 April. The *big* problem, however, had now become that Smith was having trouble getting *his* personal visa, and that whatever this problem was, it would take four or five days to clear it up before we could leave. Oh what tangled webs we weave! This later development presented a personal visa problem for Bob and Jane, inasmuch as *their* various extensions were scheduled to expire on 10 April, before Smith's visa was due to be okayed!

On that same day, the fuel barge came by and pumped in 200 gallons of diesel fuel, revealing a leak in the cleanout plate on the starboard fuel tank. Another repair.

Jane went to the Police Bureau the next day and was successful in getting one last ten-day extension on Bob's visa and hers. Having arrived later, Chuck's and Randy's were still okay.

Part of the log entry for 10 April:

> A whole raft of logs jammed up against us, and we had to move the boat. It always seems to be a federal case, moving around here.
>
> Bob and I called T from town at 2300 hours. He is not coming here but will go direct to Hong Kong. We had a good talk with Smith, except he says he does not want Randy along on the sail to Hong Kong! Trust Smith to make additional problems. We hope it works out so that Randy can sail to Hong Kong with us.

Smith had written to me saying that Randy could not sail with him to Hong Kong. He had also telephoned to tell me the same thing. In the phone conversation Smith wasn't able to explain his reasons for not wanting Randy on the trip. About all I could get out of the conversation was that Randy broods a lot, and looks menacing. Sounded like Wilt Chamberlain. I was at a tremendous disadvantage to argue; we simply had to get the boat to Hong Kong. Any further delay was fatal; I use the word advisedly. I figured that if Randy had to fly from Taipei to Hong Kong it wouldn't be the end of the world. Annoying, but not the end.

The next day, 11 April, saw a lot of things accomplished. The yard sent two men to replace cracked windows in the aft cabin. The mechanic moved the fuel filter up and worked on the autopilot. Bob replaced the rubber gasket on the fuel tank cleanout plate and drilled new holes. Randy ran the anemometer wiring. Chuck did polishing, labeled switches, tightened latches, put brass set-screws on the coupling from engine to drive shaft. Jane retaped the mast and changed the line in the mast boot to make it more watertight.

Smith and Randy had a little talk on 12 April, and it looked as if Randy could go to Hong Kong with the boat after all.

By Tuesday 16 April nerves had become even tighter, and tension had mounted in Keelung Harbour, because everyone felt they were just sitting around. Finally Smith showed up and said the export license was okay and that the *Dagny Taggart* could leave within the next day or two. The next day the customs man came and appeared to clear everything; but the crew ran out of time to complete all the formalities and still have some daylight. They busied themselves with shipboard chores and turned in for still another night in Keelung.

LUXURY TOUR

The fare to Hong Kong by plane was no small matter. We checked around to see if we could find a bargain rate. There was an outfit in San Francisco called Creative World Travel who had advertised in the *Wall Street Journal*, citing a price of $310 for a one-way trip to Hong Kong. Unable to make contact by telephone, I stopped by the advertised address while I was in San Francisco on other matters. I talked to a landlady who told me that yes, there had been a man there in an office, with a chair and a desk, but nothing more; and that he had left some time ago.

For several months I had been receiving advertising brochures under the title Hong Kong Is. This was a two-week, all-expenses-paid tour worked up by an imaginative travel agency who sought and successfully secured sponsorship by various business and professional groups. At first I didn't pay much attention to the advertising, since we were not looking for a round-trip arrangement, nor for expenses paid while we were in Hong Kong. However, one day after the San Francisco Connection and all other avenues had proven nonproductive, and after I had priced conventional airfare, I finally got around to looking at the cost of the Hong Kong Is tour. I reached the conclusion that we could buy the whole tour, throw away the return ticket, and still save money over one-way coach fare.

As it worked out, Carol, Harlan, and Jim did sign up for the Hong Kong Is tour; and they did throw away the return ticket; and they did live high on the hog in Hong Kong for ten days; and they did save money over the cost of a one-way coach ticket!

Back in Los Angeles the first word I received from Hong Kong was pretty discouraging. Everything was fine as far as what might be called the tourist part of the trip was concerned. The flight was great; the accommodations were excellent; food was good; met some nice people; and all that. Carol explained in a very subdued and almost tearful voice on the phone that so far Hong Kong was frustration city. There was no trace of our shipment to Hong Kong on the *Trein Maersk* and she had no idea what was going on in Taiwan since she couldn't reach Jane or Bob. And a swarm of locusts had come through the city and had eaten up all the yachting and boat supplies!

The swarm of locusts was not a figment of her imagination. The South China Sea Race from Hong Kong to Manila had brought boats to Hong Kong from all over the Far East. Carol had discovered that many yachtsmen in that part of the world deliberately delay buying equipment over the two-year period between South China Sea Races and replenish their supplies when they get to Hong Kong in preparation for this race.

My first message to Carol, which I sent by way of Coopers & Lybrand's Hong Kong office, was the first of many:

BOB HANCOCK CALLED MONDAY AFTERNOON LAX TIME. BASICALLY GOOD NEWS. BOAT IN WATER 27 MARCH 1974. PRESENT ETD KEELUNG SUNDAY 7 APRIL. ETA HONG KONG 12 APRIL. THESE ETD AND ETA FAIRLY REALISTIC BUT NATCH NO GUARANTEE. MAIN ENGINE WORKING GREAT; SOME PROBLEMS WITH GENERATOR WHICH MAY HAVE TO WAIT TILL HONG KONG. MIGHT RUN DOWN LOCAL KOHLER AND PERKINS SERVICE FIRM. ALL FOUR OF OUR CREW LIVING ON BOAT IN FISH HARBOR, KEELUNG. NOT AVAILABLE BY TELEPHONE. BOB WILL CALL ME WHEN THEY LEAVE AND I WILL CALL YOU. BOB WANTS ME TO BE IN HONG KONG WHEN BOAT GETS THERE, WHICH I WILL TRY TO DO. EVERYONE HERE FINE AND ALL SEND LOVE.

By 3 April it appeared that things were swinging pretty well into gear:

CAROL:

I HAVE BOOKED MYSELF ON PAN AM FLIGHT ONE, SCHEDULED TO LEAVE LAX ON SATURDAY 13 APRIL AND ARRIVE HONG KONG 2135 ON SUNDAY 14 APRIL.

REQUEST YOU HOLD CONFERENCE WITH HARLAN AND JIM TO GO OVER ALL HONG KONG ASSIGNMENTS AND PERFORM ALL TASKS FEASIBLE PRIOR TO ARRIVAL OF BOAT. MANY PURCHASES CAN BE MADE, SERVICE LINED UP. OF PARTICULAR IMPORTANCE RADIO LICENSE AND CALL SIGN. LINE UP SERVICE OUTFIT TO INSTALL VHF SSB AND ADF, BOARDING LADDER, SERVICE FOR KOHLER AND PERKINS AND FORD DIESEL: INSTALLATION OF BATTERY CHARGER, AND OF COURSE BUYING EQUIPMENT OR LINING UP SOURCES OF EQUIPMENT ON THOSE ITEMS THAT YOU FEEL I SHOULD MAKE DECISION.

A week later, Carol was still in Hong Kong, and I was still in Los Angeles, but things were looking up. Carol had gone into the supply situation in depth. She had spent considerable time with Frank Kasala, who owned a cousin boat to ours; she had met Anthony Wong of Harbor Marine, who had worked on Kasala's boat and was extremely helpful. As a matter of fact, I think that her parting line on our second telephone conversation was something like, "We've been here for ten days now, and we own the town!"

The ten days of living high on the hog that Carol, Harlan, and Jim had enjoyed as an adjunct to their Hong Kong Is tour expired on 10 April, and they moved to the Harbour Hotel. Carol telexed me as follows:

HAVE WRITTEN PERSONAL CHECK UCB NUMBER 1408 TO HARBOR MARINE FOR U.S. DLRS 600 AS DEPOSIT ON MATERIALS PURCHASE FOR TEAK, STEEL, AWNINGS, PLEXIGLASS. OUTBOARDS, LIFERAFT, AND INFLATABLES NOT IN STOCK IN HONG KONG. SUGGEST YOU PURCHASE AND SHIP ASAP.

I somehow made a deposit to cover the check. But what the hell are we going to do about the outboard engines, the liferaft, and the inflatables?

Unless we got bogged down in Hong Kong forever, there was no way on earth that I could acquire all that stuff now, have it crated, go through export formalities, and ship it all to

Hong Kong in time to mesh with the departure of the *Dagny Taggart*. The only way I could handle it would be to air freight it; and that would be ungodly expensive. Hmmmmm. The only item of that group that was *absolutely necessary* for safety was the liferaft. . . . I wonder if I could take that with me as hand luggage? Maybe my friends at Pan American would give me a little break if the plane wasn't too full.

I asked good old buddy Bill Druitt if he could round up an eight-person liferaft in the Southern California area for me in twenty-four hours, and as usual Bill came through with flying colors. And by God, as hand luggage it went!

I telexed Carol that I still planned to leave the following Saturday, 13 April, for Taipei.

MUNDANE MATTER. I HAVE ABOUT THREE THOUSAND CHARTS AND NAVIGATIONAL PUBLICATIONS TO TAKE WITH ME WHICH MAY FILL THE WHOLE BELLY OF A 747. WOULD BE NICE IF COULD AVOID ANOTHER FIFTEEN POUNDS OF PRINTED MATERIAL IN NAVIGATIONAL FORMS AND LOG BOOK PAGES. IS THERE ANYTHING COMPARABLE TO A SIR SPEEDY TYPE PRINTING DEAL WHERE WE COULD HAVE THESE FORMS DONE IN HONG KONG?

We were burning up the wires, but communication was essential. Carol replied:

WOULD LIKE TO SEE YOU BUT DO FEEL YOU SHOULD GO TO TAIPEI. LET US KNOW IF YOU SEE ANY REASON FOR ANY OF US THREE TO GO ALSO TO TAIPEI.

SOUTH CHINA SEA RACE HAS GUTTED ALL MARINE STOCKS IN HKG. HAVE ALREADY TRIED EVERYONE POSSIBLE. AN AVON SPORT 300 IS AVAILABLE THROUGH MANNERS AT U.S. DLRS 740. BUT THERE IS VERY LITTLE ELSE. OK WITH US TO TAKE CHANCE IF YOU WISH. CAN ALSO BUY A JAPANESE NATIONAL MICROVEN FOR U.S. DLRS 400 BEST PRICE. 30-POUND DANFORTH PROBABLY NOT AVAILABLE. NO HAM RADIOS HERE EITHER. DEALERS ARE QUOTING EARLY MAY FOR ARRIVAL OF NEW STOCKS. WE WILL PAY TOP DOLLAR BUT PERHAPS YOU ARE RIGHT THAT IT IS SAFER.

STILL TRACING MISSING SHIPMENT. HAVE ORDERED VARIOUS
ITEMS FABRICATED AT HARBOR MARINE (ANTHONY WONG)
RECO BY KASALA.

Part of my reply:

JANE: TALKED TO JANE THURSDAY MORNING LAX TIME. BOAT IS
GREAT IN SOME RESPECTS BUT SHE IS UNHAPPY IN OTHER
AREAS, ALL OF WHICH AREAS APPEAR TO BE ITEMS WE CAN CURE
IN HONG KONG AND WHICH TIE IN NICELY TO FACT THAT WE
HAVE TO BE IN A SHIPYARD ANYWAY. WILL SIMPLY DEDUCT
COST OF SURVEY-REQUIRED ITEMS FROM TOTAL CONSIDERA-
TION TO SMITH. HELPFUL IF YOU WOULD INFORM SHIPYARD WE
WILL BE DOING SOME WORK THERE.

INFLATABLES: PLEASE BUY AT ONCE THE AVON S-300. THIS IS
JUST ONE MODEL ABOVE THE MODEL WE WANTED ANYWAY AND
THE PRICE IS SLIGHTLY BETTER THAN THE LIST PRICE HERE. I
WILL BRING WITH ME GULP AN AVON EIGHT-MAN CORRECTION
EIGHT-PERSON LIFERAFT TO FILL UP THE SMALL SPACE LEFT ON
THE 747 AFTER ALL MY CHARTS ARE STOWED.

PRINTER: FORGET THE PRINTING. I'LL GO TO SIR SPEEDY HERE
AND SOMEHOW SQUEEZE INTO THE 747 WITH MY PADS.

In early April I learned that in spite of my premonition
about the danger of sending a shipment in two separate crates
and my consequent elaborate precautions/measures, what I
feared would happen had happened. When the *Trein Maersk*
reached Hong Kong, and it came time to unload the shipment
consigned to The John Galt Line Ltd., someone apparently
went down into the hold of the *Trein Maersk* and found a crate
marked The John Galt Line Ltd., and that was it. The other
crate just sat there. This triggered a Keystone Cops kind of
chase after the *Trein Maersk* as it went from port to port in the
Orient. I talked to the *Trein Maersk* people in Hong Kong,
Manila, Singapore, Kuala Lumpur. At the very last moment,
just as things were getting extremely tight all around on
timing, and the *Dagny Taggart* was about to leave Keelung on
15 April, I got word from the Maersk people that they had not
as yet been able to verify that the missing crate had been
unloaded off of the *Trein Maersk,* but they *could* verify that the
Trein Maersk was due in Keelung on 18 April 1974.

In Keelung! Should we tell the crew on the *Dagny Taggart* to stay right where they were and await the arrival of the *Trein Maersk,* which might have our gear on board? I gave this possibility serious consideration, but finally decided against it on grounds that, as a friend of mine used to say, we might be fighting over an empty barrel. We had no assurance that the missing crate *really* was still on the *Trein Maersk,* and, in addition, I was nervous about trying to get anything in and out of Taiwan after our recent experience of waiting for weeks and weeks and weeks to clear through Taiwan customs. Finally, while the missing crate contained some important items, nothing in it was a life-or-death matter such as the generator or autopilot on the first shipment. For those items I had had no choice but to sweat it out.

In the meantime Carol was doing everything she could to trace the shipment; I telexed her on Monday 15 April:

WOULD SURE FEEL MORE COMFORTABLE IF HAD FAVORABLE WORD ON TREIN MAERSK LOST SHIPMENT CAUSE WE CAN'T ALL SIT THERE INDEFINITELY WAITING FOR MAERSK TO COME THROUGH. APPRECIATE TELEX ON PRESENT STATUS SO I CAN TAKE APPROPRIATE ACTION WHATEVER THAT MEANS.

NO WORD ON DEPARTURE OF DAGNY TAGGART FROM TAIWAN AS OF MONDAY MORNING 15 APRIL HERE. AM CABLING SMITH AND JANE FOR INFO AND WILL RELAY TO YOU.

Carol found and purchased an Avon S-400, a seven-foot Taiwan inflatable with engine mount and oars, and a 5-horsepower Seagull outboard.

TREIN MAERSK NOW IN JAKARTA WITH OUR CRATE ABOARD. WILL UNLOAD KOBE JAPAN AND TRANSHIP HKG. AM AWAITING ETA OF SHIPMENT AND IT SHOULD WORK OUT OK.

Meanwhile, I had had a phone call from son Bob in Keelung saying that he was confident the boat would leave 17 April, although the crew were being pressured by Smith to delay so another boat could sail with the *Dagny Taggart* to Hong Kong. I urged Bob to be firm; we had already invested incredible time and money, and we had to get going. It appeared that the friction between Smith and our crewmember Randy had eased, and Bob was pleased with the boat overall—only a few minor problems. The *Dagny Taggart* had been in a dirty environment for several weeks, however, and the hull had accumulated a covering of scum; we were warned not to be disappointed in her poor superficial appearance.

I relayed all this to Carol in Hong Kong, adding:

I WOULD THINK YOU WOULD BE SAFE IN ARRANGING FOR HAUL OUT AND SURVEYS ON TUESDAY 23 APRIL 1974.

WONDERFULLY RELIEVED TO KNOW THAT TREIN MAERSK FI- NALLY LOCATED. AM CURRENTLY STILL WORKING TRYING TO RUN DOWN SMITH OR JANE OR BOB OR OTHER CONTACT IN TAIPEI KEELUNG AREA AND TRY TO ARRANGE TO GET MISSING BOX TRANSFERRED FROM TREIN MAERSK TO DAGNY TAGGART.

OUR KEELUNG GROUP MORALE IN GOOD SHAPE: AND I READ YOUR GROUP THE SAME. HOPE SO. SEE YOU THURSDAY. HAVE THE LIFERAFT IN OFFICE AND WILL TAKE AS LUGGAGE. JOANNE [MY SECRETARY] SAYS I CAN PASS IT OFF THAT I ALWAYS CARRY MY OWN LIFERAFT WITH ME WHEN I FLY, DOESN'T EVERYBODY?

After having decided not to hold up the departure of the *Dagny Taggart* for the *Trein Maersk* arrival in Keelung, I still had to cover all bases and get that damn shipment to Hong Kong, particularly when I learned that Kobe, Japan, from whence the Maersk people had planned to tranship the crate back to Hong Kong, was currently expecting a dock strike! I talked directly to the Maersk people in Taipei, who, to Maersk Line's credit, were already aware of the situation. I told them that it was essential that the crate be delivered within the next few days to Hong Kong; and I therefore expected them to air freight it. They indicated that they would do this.

On Wednesday morning 17 April at the LAX Pan Am Clipper Club, after Bloody Marys with secretary Joanne and daughter Susan, I finally broke away on Pan Am's Flight number 1 for a glorious reunion with wife, family, and crew in Hong Kong—with my liferaft packed neatly under my arm.

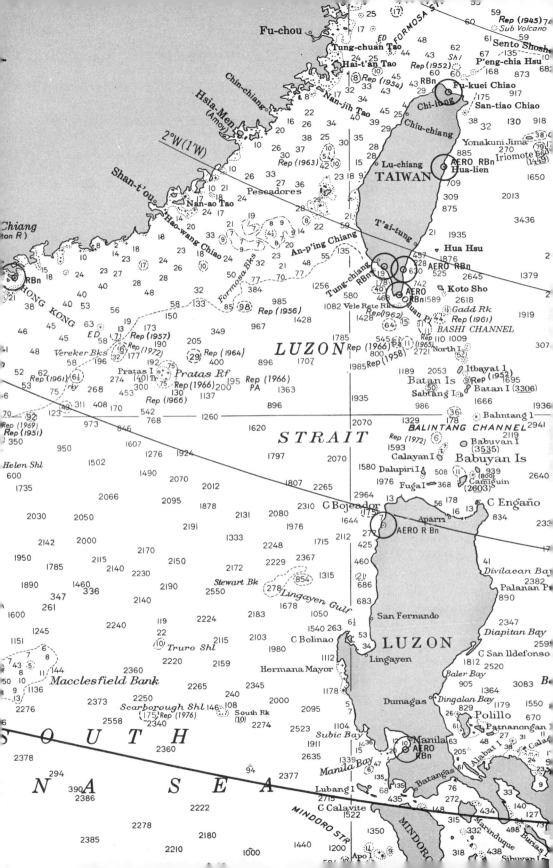

GRAND REUNION

I had the shaky feeling that I was leaving for Hong Kong too soon; this proved to be true. I also had the shaky feeling that I was getting there too late; this also proved to be true. It was foolhardy to try to squeeze any such venture into as tight a time frame as I was attempting to do.

Carol met me at the Hong Kong airport late on Thursday 18 April 1974; and we rushed to a grand reunion at the not-so-grand Harbour Hotel. I had kidded her that she should get room 901, as that had been the number of our room at the Nani Loa in Hilo a few years before on the first night of our glorious honeymoon; and by God, there it was—room 901 at the Harbour Hotel in Hong Kong! She had done it!

The next morning we met Harlan and Jim for breakfast at the New World Restaurant in beautiful downtown Hong Kong. The two of them looked as if they had been living in a Chinese whorehouse—battered and beaten around the face, tired around the eyes.

It turned out that the reason they looked as if they had been living in a Chinese whorehouse was that they had been living in a Chinese whorehouse—with man-eating mosquitoes.

After their ten days covered by the Hong Kong Is tour, Harlan and Jim, like Carol, had also sought lower-cost quarters. A fellow they had met during their ten days of high-on-the-hogging-it had recommended what Harlan and Jim thought was a boarding house—and in a sense it *was* a boarding house, except that some of the boarders took in boarders. Or something.

It worked out to be fairly satisfactory except for a lot of giggling in the hours between midnight and 0300 hours—and except for the mosquitoes, which accounted for the appearance of Harlan's and Jim's faces.

Later in the morning we met Anthony Wong, owner and manager of Harbor Marine, and reviewed with him all the things that he was going to do with and to the *Dagny Taggart*.

Still later we visited the Yacht Boutique, Hong Kong's *only* yacht marine hardware. The trio showed me Bird Alley (actually Tung Man Street, but since the shops on the lower half of the street stocked and sold all sorts of birds in lovely bamboo cages, everyone called it Bird Alley). The upper half of the steep, narrow, one-block-long Bird Alley is lined with booths, each catering to some one functional part of maintaining, sailing, or powering a boat. One stall features wire and fittings; another, anchor chain and line; another, paint and marine finishes. The principal customers were local operators of junks and sampans. Without the facilities of Bird Alley, neither we nor any other yachtsmen outfitting in Hong Kong for a long voyage could possibly get by.

I was also introduced to Bob Gaff and Estelle May of Coopers & Lybrand's Hong Kong office, both of whom had been of tremendous help to us and on whom we were to continue to impose for help of various types. Carol also introduced me to Elliott Browne, ship surveyor, whom she had lined up for the necessary survey for insurance purposes.

And finally I was shown the venerable Royal Hong Kong Yacht Club, which was to be our home-away-from-home for God only knew how long. Like many clubs, the RHKYC operates on a system of chits: books of coupons are purchased for cash, and the coupons are used to purchase drinks, food, or what have you. The price of a large glass of draft beer came out to about ten cents/U.S. and regular drinks about two-bits/U.S.

The next day we checked the RHKYC again for Ahman, the man in charge of boat storage and repair, whom Carol had commissioned to procure or to have made certain items of equipment. Carol also had had some items delivered to the club under Ahman's care. And sure enough, there was one of our crates of freight, just as I had seen it in the dockside warehouse at Los Angeles Harbor (but without its friend the second box, which was still lost) and there was our Avon inflatable dinghy in two boxes, and our Seagull outboard engine.

At long last, I could see gear and equipment commencing to accumulate at our mobilization port. Progress!

Then started the inexorable, exhausting, frustrating, prodigal shopping spree that was to rule our lives for the next (little did we know then how long it would be) four weeks. Bird Alley, Cat Alley, Bag Alley, Yacht Boutique, Manners, New Horizons, ad infinitum!

On the afternoon of that same first Saturday, the four of us made a dry-dock reconnaissance trip to Tsing Yi Island, traveling by ferry—first a large ferry powered by throbbing diesel engines and carrying hundreds of passengers, and then a small ferry, known in Hong Kong as a *walla walla*, powered by a throbbing oarsman and almost swamping with four passengers—to the David Cheng Boat Yard, which Carol had picked out for our necessary slipping (the British term for dry-docking). Carol had been told that Cheng's place was the best for us and that Cheng did good work, but to be very careful that all services to be performed, and the cost thereof, were completely understood ahead of time.

Cheng's place looked just like any other good Chinese ship yard: as if it had been hit successively by a typhoon, an earthquake, and an atomic bomb, with no recovery period between takes. At first Carol was the only one who was worried about what she would do if she had to go to the bathroom; after a while, the men worried too. Even the ship yard dogs (closely related to junkyard dogs) looked worried. But no other port, and all that. Arrangements were made for slipping on Monday 22 April. Surely the *Dagny Taggart* would be in Hong Kong by *then!*

FIREARMS

Carol and I were in complete agreement that we would carry firearms on board and that we would use them if necessary if anyone tried to get funny with us.

I am not a hunter; nor do I engage in any other form of firearm use. But I had had my fill of shooting, cleaning, breaking down, and reassembling rifles, sidearms, and anti-aircraft artillery in World War II.

We ended up buying a Marlin 30-30 rifle and a Mossberg 20-gauge pump-action shotgun.

We knew that we could not ship these firearms into Taiwan. Not only would they have been confiscated, but we might have ended up with an indefinite stay in a Taiwan jail, which is about 80 points lower on the accommodations scale than a Tijuana jail.

We hadn't anticipated any difficulty in shipping our firearms into Hong Kong. We went merrily along on this assumption until Carol was working her way through customs with our first sea freight shipment (the one that didn't get away). As Carol wended her way through the customs formalities it became obvious that we were in the process of committing a no-no. She wisely played dumb at the time, or dangerously played dumb at the time; but as soon as the crate arrived at the Royal Hong Kong Yacht Club where it was to live temporarily, Carol had the crate opened, took out the two guns and the ammo, called a taxi, and took same to the Hong Kong Police Armory. The guardians of the Police Armory (located naturally on Arsenal Street) were friendly and understanding and appreciative. In fact while they had custody of the weapons they carefully kept them in a controlled dry atmosphere and oiled them daily.

In order to meet local formal regulations it was necessary to write a letter to the arms licensing officer explaining the need for firearms being processed through the port of Hong Kong. Carol's letter to the arms licensing officer concluded as follows:

> The above listed items are presently in the keeping of the Hong Kong Police Armory. The firearms will not be used in Hong Kong, but will be shipped out of Hong Kong on the S/V *Dagny Taggart*, where they will be used in the event of emergency at sea, for signalling, and for protection from dangerous fish or animals.

THE ROYAL HONG KONG YACHT CLUB

Around Southern California you sometimes hear people say that the Newport Harbor Yacht Club is the New York Yacht Club of the West Coast. And you hear the same thing in the San Francisco area about the St. Francis Yacht Club. I think around New York you might hear that the New York Yacht Club is the Royal Hong Kong Yacht Club of the eastern United States. All the great adjectives designating age and dignity can be applied to the RHKYC: venerable, hoary, classic, steeped in history. Through Smith we were put in touch with Frank Kasala, secretary of the RHKYC. We first contacted Frank in February 1974, and through correspondence we made arrangements to put our boat on a mooring in the RHKYC Yacht Basin and to use the club as our mailing address in Hong Kong. We had no way of knowing at that time how extensive our use of the club facilities would be, and it was through Frank that we learned about the South China Sea Race, which later proved to be another of the many threads in our tapestry of adventure. Frank informed us in early March that all the facilities, especially the moorings at the club, would be overbooked until the start of the race on 7 April.

One day during our last week in Hong Kong, as our efforts to get underway reached a fever pitch, I needed to see Frank Kasala. He wasn't in his regular office, but someone on his staff told me that he was around the club someplace, as the saying goes. I looked for him in the bar and inquired of some of the patrons if they had seen him there.

Sometime later, when I finally found him, I mentioned that I had been looking for him before. Frank replied, "Yes, Taylor, I know that you were looking for me; your presence in the bar wearing a hat was reported to me as a violation of the club's rules. We are very strict here you know."

Sure enough, as I thought back on it, I *had* worn my hat in the bar! But, by the Queen's health, I was just passing through. And the bar is not formal; in fact, it is halfway open to the Hong Kong weather overlooking Hong Kong Harbour.

But gentlemen must live by gentlemen's rules.

WAITING FOR OUR SHIP TO COME IN

Carol had also arranged for our spiritual life during our stay in Hong Kong, and the very beautiful St. John's Cathedral of the Anglican Church was our Sunday morning home. Except for the skin color of the majority of the congregation, one could have been in Coventry, Devizes, Suffolk, or Newport Beach. Everything was just like home—the service, the architecture, the grounds, the atmosphere, and a great priest, the Reverend Dean Rex Howe.

St. John's followed the practice of serving a simple but adequate breakfast to the entire congregation in a hall adjoining the main church building immediately after the early morning prayer service. These occasions were most helpful to us, not only spiritually and emotionally to find ourselves welcomed and wanted, but also practically, since we were able to meet or to arrange to meet many of the merchants or service people and others whom we needed to contact about various aspects of our outfitting and cruising.

Everyone knows the stories that have been told about putting together the children's swing set, the bicycle, or the electric Wham-O outfit bought from Sears Roebuck—the one with easy assembly instructions that even a child understands. And so it was with our Avon dinghy that Sunday afternoon, when Carol and Harlan and Jim and I decided to uncrate and inflate the Avon dinghy.

Just as in all the swing-set stories we did not sit down and read the veddy Briddish instruction manual carefully enough; we were all too anxious. I think we inflated (and deflated) the thing four times before we learned everything that had to be done before the final inflation could take place. And all we had was a manual pump. And Hong Kong was hot and humid. But we did it, by God, and had the crowning glory of uncrating the Seagull outboard engine, mounting it on the Avon, pulling the starting cord, and roaring off into the crowded harbor. You would have thought that *this* was the boat in which we were to cross the Pacific. The Avon dinghy, incidentally, wasn't dinky: 18 feet long, 4½ feet wide, it could carry four or five people comfortably and as many as seven or eight uncomfortably.

But where the hell were Smith and Jane and Bob and Chuck, the mythical Randy, and the *Dagny Taggart?* On Saturday 20 April we had been able to get a call through to Smith's number-one man in Kaohsiung. He was most surprised that Smith hadn't yet reached Hong Kong, for he said the boat had left Keelung on Tuesday 16 April and surely should be in Hong Kong by now. Not very comforting.

Monday 22 April arrived—the day we were scheduled to

Dagny Taggart in the yacht basin of the Royal Hong Kong Yacht
Club. Bob Hancock is up the mast.

take the boat to David Cheng's ship yard. But no boat, no ship yard. I did some paper organizing and purchased some hardware items at the Victory Hardware. The Victory may not have been the *best* in Hong Kong, but it was good; and more important, one of the salesmen there had lived in San Francisco for three years and had perfect English and American-style thinking.

An hour or so past noon, Carol and I took one of our many long daily walks from the Harbour Hotel to the Royal Hong Kong Yacht Club. This trek involved climbing up and down several pedestrian walkways that had wisely been constructed to cut down the carnage of the local walking population by the local driving population. Even so, the walkways were frequently bypassed by those wanting to cross the street where no overpass was provided—particularly, occidentally enough, by young Chinese school-boys.

Before checking the mail or having a beer or whatever, we stopped by to check with Ahman on the status of our flags, flag pole, boat hooks.

"Your boat is here!" he cried. "I think your boat is here! Have you seen it?"

"Hell, no, we haven't seen it! Where is it?"

"Over in the yacht basin! Go quickly!" And we did!

Everything always seems to be torn up in Hong Kong; in fact, come to think of it, everything always seems to be torn up everyplace in the Far East. And the Royal Hong Kong Yacht Club was no exception. They were putting in, or perhaps taking out, a parking lot, or a new boat storage yard, or some combination thereof. There were large open areas of dirt, criss-crossed by ditches in seemingly no logical or understandable pattern. All of this stood between where Carol and I were when we received the news of the boat's arrival and the alleged location of the alleged boat. We tore around the harbor side of the club, up and over the veranda, along a long semi-indoor corridor, down some wooden steps, and then out across the construction area. Light rain was falling; in fact, come to think of it, a light rain always seems to be falling when anything crucial is going on almost anyplace in the Far East.

We came to a ditch that Carol couldn't jump. Showing utter disregard for her, I leapt across the ditch and let her go the long way. For this I was rewarded with deeper and wetter mud.

Finally we came to the seawall overlooking the RHKYC Yacht Basin, and there she was—the *Dagny Taggart* was moored just about fifty feet from the seawall.

Jesus! What a mess!

The neat small tires with sewn canvas covers that had been specified for fenders in the purchase contract turned out to be huge uncovered tractor tires that had blackened the entire white hull of the *Dagny Taggart* beyond recognition. The deck looked as if an army of Russian tanks, all leaking axle grease, had been the deck cargo. The gear on deck was in complete disarray, and it appeared as if someone, or something, had rammed into the starboard quarter, smashing teak, breaking chainplates, and snapping stays.

Unable to rouse anyone on board, not having any means of transportation to get to the boat in any event, and not about to swim across the fifty feet of polluted water between us and the boat, we took the next most logical step and walked back to the Royal Hong Kong Yacht Club bar.

And there, sitting in a booth, were our beloved Jane and Bob, together with Chuck and Randy—not entirely recognizable as our beloveds; we had run right past them on our sprint to the boat.

As good as they looked to us, they still looked terrible: unbathed, unwashed, unkempt—as if they had *already* crossed the Pacific, rather than just getting started.

"When did you get here?" We began. "When did you leave Keelung? Where is Smith? How was your trip? What took you so long?"

Jane, wisely, told us to sit down and have a beer and they would take it from the top.

JANE'S FIGHTING SHIP

The magic moment had come at 1210 hours on Thursday 18 April 1974. Jane wrote in her diary:

> Woke early at 0600 hours; up by 0730; must be in anticipation of leaving . . .

Customs came about 1130; and also newspapermen came. Finished customs at noon, and we left amid firecrackers and flashbulbs. Was exciting, and cannot believe we are going at last. Cleared the breakwater at 1215 hours. We swung compass on Keelung Light and the Island of Chi Wing Tao. Compass needed only very slight adjustment. We all had a glass of the wine which Smith had brought along.

(Obviously, our information that the boat had left Keelung on Tuesday 16 April had been incorrect. With so many false starts it was easy to understand how Smith's office could have had the wrong info.)

That evening the *Dagny Taggart* was stopped by a Taiwan Navy Patrol boat. The Taiwanese wanted to inspect our boat's papers, which they did, and everything was in order.

The next day the crew put the new boat under sail for the first time. The log entry says:

Fantastic!

Navigation was primarily by John Smith's RDF. All gear was being tested now under real conditions.

The log of the *Dagny Taggart,* en route Keelung to Hong Kong, 21 April 1974, recorded favorable wind and sea conditions, several maneuvers to avoid fishing boats, and a large amount of water in the bilge. Inspection revealed water coming in through the gland at the main propeller shaft; and there was a hole in the diaphragm of the manual bilge pump. Rain squalls followed, of course.

The log continues:

At 1215 hours, spotted a Chinese boat, not fishing, but headed directly toward us. As boat drew closer we could see it was a steel diesel-powered junk about 70 feet long bearing down on us rapidly. We attempted to get away but did not have enough speed. As the boat drew closer, we could see a large number of Chinese men on the boat wielding knives, machetes, and spears; gesturing us to move toward the Chinese mainland coast. As the junk drew closer, the men on board started to throw objects at the *Dagny Taggart.* We first thought that the objects were hand grenades or bombs of some nature.

We were able to outmaneuver the junk by turning inside of its turning circle; but after several escapes this way another smaller diesel-powered junk, working in coordination with the larger vessel, blocked us from this maneuver. Smith indicated to the rest of the crew that he saw no course but to surrender to one or the other of the two vessels. The larger junk seemed to contain all males as crew, perhaps 40 or 50 of them, who were wielding weapons and shouting in a hysterically hateful manner, all of which was very frightening. The other smaller vessel appeared to contain families, children, and dogs, and was not nearly as hostile appearing.

Smith chose to surrender the *Dagny Taggart* to the smaller of the two vessels, a steel Chinese junk about 50 feet in length.

As the smaller junk approached on the starboard quarter of the *Dagny Taggart* for boarding purposes, the bow of the junk crashed into her hull.

Up until that point the *Dagny Taggart* had not been flying a flag. Jane thought that conceivably a show of the British flag might in some way discourage the Chinese from capturing the boat. She went below to get the Red Duster and appeared on deck just as the junk crashed into the hull. Jane displayed the Red Duster prominently. At that precise moment, just as in the old John Wayne movies, looming out of the haze there appeared a large freighter, the *Malaysian Princess*, very close to all three vessels.

Either because of the British flag, or due to the arrival of the freighter, or for some other reason, the two Chinese junks came about and headed away from the *Dagny Taggart*.

A cursory survey of damages indicated two cracked and bent chainplates on the starboard mizzen shroud and a split teak rail and capping on the starboard quarter. As far as could be ascertained there was no actual hull damage nor any further structural damage.

The course of the freighter indicated that it was heading for Hong Kong. The *Dagny Taggart* followed behind in its wake as close as possible for as long as possible. The wind came up again in the late afternoon and evening, gusting to 30 knots. As darkness fell, still another Chinese junk was observed bearing down on the *Dagny Taggart*. This time, with good wind as well as the engine, our boat had a little more speed. With the advantage of heavy seas, poor visibility, and approaching darkness, the *Dagny Taggart* was able to avoid another confrontation. Throughout the coming night, no lights were displayed, not even navigational lights, and the watches were doubled.

Following are entries in the ship's log and in Jane's diary for Monday 22 April, the day after the ramming episode.

> Winds gusting to 35 knots; seas 15 feet. On a run with wind on starboard quarter. Doubled up all watches, making four-hour watches instead of two-hour. Boat handling well; ran dark all night after having to run from fourth junk. Sighted a number of freighters and fishing boats so must be on a good course for Hong Kong.

> Not even two hours sleep; up at 0300 hours 'til dawn. Didn't feel RDF bearings had been good, but sighted Wang Lan Light at 0545.

> Main engine running very warm. Checked fresh water. Low. Refilled. Engine still overheating. Discovered starboard battery had fallen over against engine, damaging battery, bending oil filter, and blocking hose carrying incoming seawater to the heat exchanger.

> Headed into Hong Kong Harbor. Docked at Royal Hong Kong Yacht Club at 1200—four days noon to noon. Had shandy and lunch at Club with Frank Kasala and Smith. T and C not to be found at hotel, but arrived at 1400 hours. Hong Kong looks just wonderful.

THE LOST BOX

Monday 22 April was truly a big day! We telexed my secretary Joanne in Los Angeles:

DAGNY TAGGART AND ALL CREW MEMBERS ARRIVED SAFE AND SOUND IN HONG KONG.

And Joanne and Bill Druitt telexed back the same day, Los Angeles time:

MISSING BOX SHIPPED CATHAY PACIFIC FLIGHT NO CX TWON
WAYBILL 160-19230-4. LEAVING TAIPEI 23 APRIL 1350 HOURS
LOCAL TIME WILL ARRIVE HONG KONG 1515 HOURS SAME DAY.
GOOD LUCK.

After month upon month of frustration in getting the boat,
the people, and the equipment all in Hong Kong at the same
time, we had finally made it!
Well, almost.

FIRST SLIPPING

After we had heard the story of the voyage from Keelung to
Hong Kong, it seemed only logical to proceed with our best
laid plans of mice and men to get the boat into dry dock so we
could check its condition for purchase, qualify for our insurance coverage, and fill the slipping requirement in connection
with British registration.

We finished our beers and a quick lunch at the RHKYC and
grabbed a ride on the local ship-to-shore water taxi for our first
closeup of the *Dagny Taggart*. She was beautiful/terrible; lovely/
filthy; everywhere there was something missing, something
dirty, something unfinished; something that needed doing. I
was sure we'd *never* get out of Hong Kong!

Well, for *sure* we'd never get out of Hong Kong if we didn't
get moving to the boatyard for our slipping.

In preparation for the trip I had looked at many different
forms of prepared ship's logs, ranging from official U.S. Navy
logs to standard merchant marine log forms, and including a
dozen or more commercially available yacht logs in nautical
bookstores and marine hardwares.

Although I picked up a lot of good ideas, I never found a
form that met all my requirements:

—Appropriate places to enter complete technical data (taff-
    rail log reading, course, wind, sea, temperature every
    hour, etc.)

—Separate and cumulative running time on main engine and generator engine, with periodic check and recording of all fluid levels.

—Entries for periodic checking of bilges, battery water and condition, potable water supply, fuel supply.

—Space for narrative log entries by each watch without limitation by page size or number of pages.

I ended up designing my own log forms and having them printed. I solved the unlimited narrative log entry matter by having one page for each day's technical log with all specific entries on a standard 8½-by-11-inch page and separate pages for the narrative log entries. It worked quite well. I would follow the same system next time.

Our first log entry in my super-duper specially designed log book was on Tuesday 22 April 1974:

1630: Underway in Hong Kong Harbor, from Royal Hong Kong Yacht Basin to David Cheng Boat Yard on Tsing Yi Island for slipping of boat. Current time on main engine 2.5 hours; cumulative time 90 hours.

Before leaving for David Cheng's Boat Yard, Bob gave me my first lesson on the start-up procedure on the *Dagny Taggart.* Smith was off doing something, so I assumed the role of skipper. The *Dagny T* was battered and beat, but she was at home in the water. She handled like a dream; she was the largest boat that I had handled for a good many years—and I guess the largest sailboat I had ever handled. Her response to the rudder and propeller was excellent for any boat—almost astonishing for a boat of her heavy displacement and relatively light power. Probably that oversized prop did it—the same thing that robbed us of one or two knots of speed while under sail.

One of my several assignments during the Big War had been serving on eighty-three-foot U.S. Coast Guard cutters, operating off the East Coast of the United States. From time to time we had occasion to put in to New York Harbor. Being at the con of an eighty-three-foot boat in the traffic jungle of New York Harbor during wartime traffic was like trying to dodge hailstones in a hailstorm. No one seemed to give a damn for any rules of the road or for any other boat, ship, or person. Horrifying. I figured I'd never see anything like it again.

Not so.

A mere thirty or so years later I found myself at the con of a fifty-foot sailboat in Hong Kong Harbour. Ever present, coming from all directions, at fixed high rates of speeds, were the Hong Kong ferries—the big kind with throbbing diesel engines. In the four weeks we were there, most of the time on or near the water, I think I only once saw a Hong Kong ferry change its course or speed to avoid another vessel underway.

And the tugs with tows! They also came at you pretty fast and of course would never change course for a mere sailboat.

And the junks! Everywhere! There are no docks in Hong Kong Harbour in the conventional sense. Virtually all unloading and loading of cargo vessels is done by junks. The ships lie at anchor in a random pattern throughout the harbor, each with a fleet of up to forty or sixty junks surrounding the large vessel—each junk in a stage of loading, unloading, securing, unsecuring, coming, going. Steering one's way through this army of junks as they ply between ship and shore is like broken field running against the Chicago Bears. What's that over there? Hey, that's the wreck of the Queen Elizabeth I, which lies where she sank back in 1965. Remember? They used her as a setting in the James Bond movie *You Only Live Twice*.

Carol had double-double checked with Frank Kasala as to the clearance under the bridge between Tsing Yi Island and Kowloon, under which we had to pass to get to the David Cheng Boat Yard on Tsing Yi. Frank had assured Carol that the clearance, although tight, was adequate at any stage of the tide. As we approached the bridge, I asked Bob to take a station as far forward on the bowsprit as he could, and set Jane about midship as an audio relay station. Bob was to sight in on the clearance between the top of our mast and the bottom of the bridge as we approached it and was to warn me if he wasn't satisfied that we would pass under safely. As we neared the bridge, I was glad that I had set up an observation and communication network, for the closer we got, the scarier the situation became. And the current, which was considerable, was naturally adverse, carrying us toward the bridge faster than I wanted to go.

A hundred yards:

"How does it look, Bob?"

"You're okay!"

Fifty yards:

"You're okay!"

At twenty yards I heard Bob holler:

"We're not gonna make it! We're not gonna make it!"

Gulp.

I backed her down. Hard. But not hard enough. We could look up and see the bottom of the bridge with all sorts of complicated understructure reaching down to grab our mast and rigging. The bottom of the bridge now looked to be no more than fifty feet from our deck. And the top of our mast was seventy-three feet above the waterline! There was no way.

As we held our breath, and anything else we could get our hands on, we somehow slipped under that monster of a bridge with no damage.

And then I discovered—as is so often the case on boats and in real life—that the whole flap had been an error in communication. Bob was trying to reassure me "We *are* gonna make it!" But Jane and I heard him as shouting a warning. As the books say, a system of positive hand signals is a valuable tool in a situation such as this.

From the boat we couldn't raise anyone at the David Cheng Boat Yard. There was no place at the yard to tie up; so we dropped anchor, rowed the Avon ashore, and finally found Mr. Cheng. We made final arrangements for entering the dry dock, but it was too late to enter that afternoon. We asked Harlan and Jim to stay on the boat while the rest of us took the ferries back to the Hong Kong side to allow our dauntless quartet from Keelung to clean up after their harrowing voyage, and for the rest of us to pack our gear to get ready to move aboard for our Great Adventure.

THIS AIN'T NO CHRIS CRAFT!

For the next few days after the great reunion with Jane and Bob and the *Dagny Taggart,* I was going in several directions at once. The boat was so beautiful! But it had so many things wrong with it! At first I seriously considered telling Smith he could take his boat and shove it—back to Taiwan or wherever. I certainly wasn't accepting it in its present condition, and it seemed fairly clear that he had no intention of bringing the boat up to our standards. With the help of the crew, mainly Jane and Bob, I compiled a list of items that needed correcting or replacing: about *thirty* major items!

The list was impressively and depressingly long. And although much of the bad appearance of the boat was merely cosmetic, several items were basically wrong.

This put us—me—in a difficult spot. While I felt that I had a legal right not to accept the boat unless or until Smith put it in good condition, I knew that if I turned the boat down, I would have a hell of a time getting back my money paid to date. Smith himself had warned me not to structure the deal the way I had—why hadn't I listened! And Jane and Bob knew—in fact Smith had confirmed—that Smith intended to return to Taiwan almost immediately.

All we had going *for* us—and it was a lot—was that we felt Smith wanted/needed the final payment pretty badly.

Smith checked in with us Monday evening, and we arranged to have breakfast the next morning to review the status of all deficiencies and to decide what to do about each. After a thorough discussion of the pros and cons, Carol and Jane and I decided that Jane should be present at the meeting.

Jane and I met with Smith at seven the next morning, Tuesday 23 April, in the Harbour Hotel coffee shop. Smith acknowledged in his soft, confidential voice that the boat wasn't in perfect condition; that some of the equipment was poor; that it was dirty; that it was in far from showroom condition. He proceeded to attempt to justify the deficiencies. As we hit each item on our three-page checklist, either Smith explained it away or agreed to replace or fix, or we adjusted the sale price downward. Who knows how well we made out? I wrote in my diary: "Worked out a fairly good settlement."

Smith's two strong arguments were (1) that we were getting probably the best shaken-down new boat ever delivered, the boat having proved itself in a very rough four-hundred-mile sail from Keelung to Hong Kong; and (2) that we would have to realize and accept the fact that we were not buying a spanking new Chris Craft off the showroom floor, but a special bargain, partially customized boat, on which my crew had been living for three months in a filthy harbor in preparation for the delivery trip, which we all knew was necessary from the beginning.

I think if I could have walked away from the deal anywhere near whole at that time, I would have done so. But in the pocket into which I had neatly maneuvered myself, I didn't feel I had that choice. I had to make the best of a bad situation—and I did just that.

SURVEYING

At the time it seemed as if we were in that boatyard about twenty-four hours short of forever. But according to the boat's log it was only from Monday afternoon to Wednesday noon. We were surveyed for insurance and purchase purposes by Elliott Browne of Wood & Browne. We passed that survey subject only to completing the asbestos wrapping on part of the exhaust manifold and replacing the through-hull fitting that had let go in Keelung Harbor.

For British registration purposes the boat was surveyed by A. C. Cheung of the Hong Kong Vessel Registration Bureau. This registration survey gave us a lingering problem. We had understood, somehow, that it would *not* be necessary to *frame* the boat for the government survey. Framing the boat consists literally of building a light wooden frame around the boat, with all the framing lumber properly in line with the main lines of the boat in such a way that the boat is in a sense expanded to become a six-sided oblong box. These sides and the angles between them are then measured to ascertain whether the boat is properly true or squared off.

Carol and I had some tight scheduling on the day the boat was to leave the David Cheng Boat Yard on Wednesday 24 April. Since a pilot from Anthony Wong's Harbor Marine was to take the boat from Cheng's to Wong's, we sent trusty Jane to settle with Cheng and to see that we got to Harbor Marine okay.

Jane found that the boat after all *had* been framed: Cheng insisted that the framing was necessary for the government

Looking aft toward the pilot house as **Dagny Taggart** *lies in Harbor Marine Boatyard, Hong Kong. Note the double plexiglass for storm protection over the pilot house windows.*

survey. And he would not release the boat without receiving full pay for all the yard work, consisting of the haul-out itself, surface repair to the rudder (which was damaged, probably in the pirate affair), replacement of the through-hull, and the controversial framing, which was the major charge. Poor Jane had a tough one on her hands . . . again. She couldn't reach Carol or me for help. She knew we *had* to meet our schedule. The pilot from Anthony Wong's was impatient to get going. Although Jane felt that she and we were being framed along with the *Dagny Taggart,* she had no choice. She paid Cheng in full and got out.

At 1430 hours on the same day, the *Dagny Taggart* arrived at Harbor Marine Ltd., in the Shaukiwan District of Victoria Island, as the log says, ". . . for extensive work."

And on that same day we took title to the *Dagny Taggart* in the splendiferous name of The John Galt Line Limited, having completed the necessary legal mumbo-jumbo formalities of corporate formation while waiting for the Robert E. Lee to arrive.

The juxtaposition of the Chinese and English cultures in Hong Kong is delightful and sometimes thrilling. That evening Carol and Jane and Bob and I walked a few blocks from the Harbour Hotel, bought some fish and chips at a street stand, and munched same as we sat in a municipal stadium watching two Chinese teams play English football.

The next morning we stopped payment on the check to David Cheng, because Jane felt she had been forced to sign under duress. Later we received a little start from Frank Kasala when we told him about the incident. Kasala predicted that when Cheng learned of the stopped check, he would black-ball the *Dagny Taggart* with the other boatyards and service and supply businesses in the Hong Kong area. We took up this matter with Anthony Wong, who assured us that he would not consider black-balling us, and that he did not think it was a serious problem. In fact, some time later Wong told us that he felt we had been misinformed about Cheng, that Cheng was a close friend of Wong's, and a good man to do business with.

HONG KONG TRANSPORT

Hong Kong has possibly the finest public transportation system of any major city in the world today. If you assume any remote degree of accuracy in this statement, you are confronted with an anomaly; this is because the Hong Kong transportation system is not really a *system* at all. There obviously is no master plan; there are no subways; no monorails. And much of the system, probably most, is pure unbridled, unregulated, free enterprise! Possibly therein lies the secret? The final anomaly, and possibly the reason that the system is so good, is that it consists of many different transportation modes, all covering many of the same routes—the delightful, albeit slow, double-decker trolleys; lumbering double-decker buses; hordes of ferries connecting almost any point on the water to any other point on the water; plentiful taxis (and inexpensive when compared with most cities). The final touch that completes the picture is the light buses (van-size vehicles seating up to twelve people). There are numerous routes, expresses and locals; the fare for the light buses is three or four times the cost of the trolleys and large buses but far below the cost of a taxi. The versatility of the light buses seems to add just the right touch to the Hong Kong transportation picture; they fill in all the gaps and make for a superb system that serves the public well in spite of the fact that they use primarily surface streets in poor traffic conditions.

PEP TALK

We had had dozens of crew meetings before—in Marina del Rey, in Hong Kong—but never before with *the* crew; previously there had always been some noncrew present and some real crew absent.

So, late Wednesday afternoon, on board the *Dagny Taggart*

tied up at Harbor Marine Boatyard in Hong Kong, we held our first *official* crew meeting. I wanted to consolidate the crew, to let them know how much I appreciated the work they had done so far and the strains—physical, emotional, and financial—that each had undergone. I also felt it was time to make a statement of my philosophy of the voyage, the crew, and the all-important crew relationship and to outline in broad principle the handling of many details of mechanical and physical items that still faced us before we could get out of Hong Kong.

"I promise that we will have plenty of time at this meeting to discuss all items, and to make decisions. I would appreciate being able to have my say, and then we will be open for discussion and comments, preferably one person at a time.

"My idea of our purpose here is two-fold: first, to get this boat and ourselves back to Marina del Rey as safely and as economically as possible; and second, to have all the fun that is reasonably possible in doing this."

Suddenly Jane seemed to want to make a point; this surprised me after my plea to let me have my say first, and I attempted to put her down.

"Goddammit T, the head is overflowing! You didn't set the valves properly when you used it a few minutes ago!"

And sure enough, Hong Kong Harbor was pouring into the *Dagny Taggart* by way of our Wilcox Crittendon head!

After receiving a much-needed lesson in how to use the forward head, I proceeded to outline the principles governing responsibility for and control of the boat:

"First, it is essential that one specific person be in charge of the boat, or any one operation, at all times. There can be no question who that person is. In the overall operation, I am that person. Others will be assigned to be in charge during particular time frames, in regard to particular duties, and in connection with specific functions.

"I feel strongly that a vessel cannot be run on democratic principles. Someone must have the authority to make decisions. I realize that you all expect this of me; I intend to live up to and to honor this obligation and duty. However, this does *not* mean that we will not have input from all crewmembers. We fully intend to have input, at regular crew meetings and at any other time.

"Probably the most important element to the success of this

forthcoming voyage," I continued, "is our being able to maintain satisfactory personal relationships with each other. If a piece of machinery or equipment goes bad, one way or another it can be repaired, replaced, or bypassed, and the voyage can continue on a positive basis. But if a person or a relationship goes bad there are no valves to turn, no parts to replace; it can ruin the whole trip.

"Okay, so far I haven't gotten into specifics, just philosophy and purpose. This would be a good time to pause for questions."

About the only comment I can recall at this stage was from Harlan: "I agree with most of what you said, Taylor, but you have to realize that we are not a paid crew here. You can't expect us to serve you as a paid crew would; we expect to have some fun, to see things and places, to read and relax."

"Sure, Harlan, I believe we all expect that. But don't you feel that the safety of the vessel and the objective of the trip, to get the boat back to the States, comes first?"

"Yes, but not to the extent that we all have to act as if we were paid crewmembers."

This exchange was not hostile at all—but it was not too satisfactory either. It was unclear just how much of my philosophy was being accepted by Harlan.

I proceeded to delve into some of the specific principles of day-to-day operations. In port we would always have an Officer of the Day, a duty that would go from 0800 hours on one day to 0800 hours on the next day. The Officer of the Day was to keep track of everything that was going on, both on and off the boat—where everyone is, who is on and off the boat and why. The OD would be responsible for order and discipline on board and would be responsible for the condition of the vessel, to see that workmen and crew picked up after each job, and that those who were responsible for particular duties performed them. Naturally the OD must never leave the boat without being relieved.

At sea, we would always have an Officer of the Deck, with the same basic responsibilities of the OD in port, only more so. The Officer of the Deck would be responsible for everything: navigation, comfort of the crew, condition of the boat, navigation lights, log, radio, reporting, sails, engines, the whole bit.

In general terms, we intended to have a one-watch-on and

three-watches-off routine. That way the cook and cook-helper for the day could have a full day off without watches. We would start with two people on watch at all times at sea. I would stand my own watches at sea, and probably also in port.

"For those who have never stood regular watches on a long sea voyage before, I should lay a little sealore on you in the matter of the point of honor in always relieving your watch on time. This should be considered somewhat in the nature of a sacred obligation. And it's not always easy, depending on the degrees of wetness, coldness, tiredness, sickness, or what have you, that might be involved.

"On the other side of the coin, it is against the tradition of the sea to think that you are doing your watch relief a favor by not waking him or her when relief time approaches. To the contrary, such a practice can creep in and upset the routine of the whole crew and is, in fact, a serious disfavor to everyone, including your relief watch. Including me."

The inspirational part over, we spent the next hour or so on specific assignments of responsibility: navigation and charts, engines and bilges, stowage and supplies, electric and electronic equipment. I explained that I had purposely left myself without a specific field of responsibility so that I would be able to manage the whole operation and pitch in where help was needed most. This seemed to be understood and supported by all.

I didn't feel as good about the crew as I wanted to—as good about their individual competence or their spirit. But I didn't feel bad, either; and how could I even *expect* to feel good about their competence when all were green for what we were setting out to do?

LIFE IN A HONG KONG SHIP YARD

The first week that the *Dagny Taggart* was at Harbor Marine was exceedingly frustrating for all of us. We were most pleased with Anthony Wong and his crew of workmen; nevertheless, the progress on the boat went exceedingly slowly, or so it seemed to us. I felt that Carol had ordered many items that we did not really need and that waiting for the fabrication of these items was using up valuable time. On the other hand, some of the mechanical work and added safety features were absolutely necessary. And, beyond any question, we had to use this time to procure and install or store a great number of additional supplies, equipment, and provisions, so we couldn't say that the time was wasted.

Carol's and my daily routine was generally to work on the boat in the mornings and to spend the afternoons in an agonizing search for necessary equipment and supplies. It seemed as if the more we looked for necessary items, the less we found; but at the same time, our list of necessary items seemed to grow every day. As we started doing actual outfitting work on the boat, each of us kept running into items or tools that we felt we would need to make the voyage, to make it successful, to make it comfortable, or what-have-you. In the meantime, I was running out of time, money, patience, all those good things that one needs for a trip of this nature.

On Friday 26 April 1974 I sent a telex to my boss, explaining that our estimated departure date from Hong Kong was now between May 10 and 15 (the latter date being the absolute limit because of the impending typhoon season). If necessary, I added, I could come back to Los Angeles until then and return to Hong Kong for the first leg of the voyage.

I felt a good spirit developing in the crew during this time. Toward the end of each workday, which sometimes was far into the evening, I would pick up a few liters of ice-cold San Miguel beer at our local friendly hole-in-the-wall general store and bring it on board to form the nucleus of a crew meeting to review our various projects.

On one typical day of this period, Carol and I went to the Hong Kong Police Arsenal to apply for a permit to get our firearms out of the arsenal and onto the boat on the day that we were scheduled to depart; we went to buy towels at a shop specializing in towels; we checked Far East Yacht Specialties, the Yacht Boutique, to see whether some ordered fittings had arrived. Carol spotted some deck chairs in the shop next door which we bought; I checked with Frank Kasala at the club about getting RHKYC visitors' cards for all our crew, and about getting the crate of our equipment from the club down to Harbor Marine. I checked with Ahman in regard to varnish, teak finish, and acquisition of fenders.

Back on the boat, I finished making up and posting in-port watch lists for the remainder of time we would be in Hong Kong.

Chuck continued his pursuit of some 12-watt light bulbs that would fit the electric fittings that had been installed in the *Dagny Taggart's* staterooms. The base of these 12-volt fittings was the same size as for a 110-volt bulb; nowhere in Hong Kong were matching bulbs to be found.

Carol was working on getting the Kohler service contact in Hong Kong to check out a difficulty Bob had reported in the Kohler generator. Jim was trying to reach someone who could install our two radio antennas and get our radio sets in operation. We acquired 300 feet of three-eighths-inch German galvanized anchor chain in Bird Alley and had it delivered to Harbor Marine.

We gave up on finding a spare diaphragm for our Taiwan-imitation Edson bilge pump and sent a message back to Bill Druitt asking if he could find one and airmail it to us.

And so it continued: auxiliary compass, fire extinguishers, stowage, tapedeck installation, on and on. One of Carol's log entries as officer of the day reported:

> Both Lehman and Perkins radiators needed topping up. Perkins was started some 10 or 15 times for 110-volt current as needed. While Jane and Harlan happened to be watching the Perkins exhaust, the engine quit. Perkins was very hot. Our supposition is that something has entered the unscreened Perkins' seawater intake, and clogged the line or the pump, or both.

> Relieved by Harlan until 2230 hours. While I was gone, Jim was hoisted up mainmast in bosun's chair. An eyesplice parted. Fortunately Jim was already on the way down, and had reached the lower spreaders. No harm done to Jim, thank God!

As an area of prime responsibility, Bob had been assigned the ship's plumbing system. The concept of plumbing is used here in the broadest sense—not just the heads, basins, and sinks, but the entire hydraulic system of the boat: two heads, through-hulls for an additional head, two showers, two basins, one double sink, cold fresh-water system, hot fresh-water system, cold salt-water system for galley, salt-water intakes and outlets for each diesel engine, fresh-water cooling system for each engine, two electric bilge pumps, one manual bilge pump, two fresh-water tanks, two fuel tanks, and of course, hundreds of feet of hoses, multiple valves, crossovers, connections, inlets, outlets.

Assigning Bob this duty proved to be one of the few things that I did right and one of the blessings of the voyage. Bob understood the importance of marine hydraulic systems long before Taiwan, but the experience of watching the final months of construction, and literally living with the subject during those last weeks in Keelung Harbor, had brought home to him dramatically the life-and-death role of a boat's plumbing system.

In view of the above, it was certainly understandable that Bob was very concerned about getting a spare diaphragm for the manual bilge pump—our first line of defense in the event of a serious leak in the hydraulic system or in the hull itself. We figured that it would be nip-and-tuck as to whether the new diaphragm would arrive from the States prior to our departure. Therefore, when I picked up a package at the yacht club that looked as if it might be the diaphragm—and sure enough it was, and only four days after our telex to Bill Druitt—it was understandable that when I climbed on board the *Dagny Taggart* with my load of mail, I sang out in a loud, clear voice: "Hey Bob! Your new diaphragm is here!"

Needless to say, we had a good running gag with this for the rest of the trip.

THE DREADED TYPHOON

In the Atlantic, Caribbean, and Eastern Pacific they are known as hurricanes; in the Indian Ocean they are called cyclones; in the Australian area they are known as willy-willies; in most of the South Pacific and the Western Pacific they are known as typhoons.

To the meteorologist, the hurricane or typhoon is defined as a tropical cyclone with winds of 65 knots or more. And a tropical cyclone is simply a storm that originates over the tropical oceans, with a closed-wind circulation in a counterclockwise mode in the Northern Hemisphere and clockwise in the Southern Hemisphere. Just like the water going out of the bathtub.

Fortunately, very special conditions must be present before a typhoon can form. First, the sea surface temperature must be at least 79° Fahrenheit; at this temperature the surface air is able to hold enough moisture, and to rise high enough, to establish the deep vertical air currents that give the typhoon its tremendous energy. The second requirement is an assist from the earth's rotation itself, which sets up the counterclockwise rotation (in the Northern Hemisphere) of the horizontal winds that spiral inward to feed the vertical air currents. Within about 6 degrees on either side of the equator, this force from the earth's rotation, called the Coriolis force, is too small to sustain hurricane development. The third necessary condition is a situation in which the regular wind direction and speed change very little between the surface of the sea and a height of about 50,000 feet. This condition allows the energy released by condensation to remain near the center of the storm to power the strong winds aloft, and also allows the hurricane/typhoon to keep a nearly circular shape, which prevents its energy from being dissipated.

There are only a few areas, all in the tropics, in which these three conditions may occur at the same time. Although the source regions for hurricanes/typhoons are geographically quite limited, once the hurricane/typhoon is formed, it can travel great distances, as residents of Long Island or Japan or New England will readily attest. With minor variations, however, the basic path of the hurricane/typhoon is from south to north in the Northern Hemisphere. Therefore, since the typhoon is formed only at 6° latitude or higher, and since it generally goes away from the equator, the closer one is to the equator, the safer.

On Wednesday 8 May I visited the Royal Hong Kong Observatory to gather general weather data for our planned leg from Hong Kong to Guam and to arrange to pick up the very latest forecast a few days later, just before we were to sail.

I was royally treated by Mr. Hans Van Meurs at the observatory. The local forecast at that time was fine, as the British say, to Friday, at which time there was a possibility of rain, but no storm. Mr. Van Meurs suggested that we check weather forecasts from passing ships whenever we encountered one. He felt that our leg to Guam would be relatively safe as far as typhoons were concerned, at least until we got quite close to Guam. He felt we should expect one storm between Luzon Strait and Guam itself. He predicted, however, that this would be only a tropical storm, not a typhoon. Inasmuch as a tropical storm is defined as a tropical cyclone with winds between 35 and 64 knots (below 35 knots the phenomenon is called a tropical depression), Mr. Van Meurs' information that we should expect one did not comfort me. Mr. Van Meurs pointed out the danger signals of an impending tropical storm or typhoon—extensive cirrus clouds combined with a dropping barometer and long swells. Upon reading these danger signals, in the part of the world in which we would be, his advice was to head southeast. He stressed that we would be safe from typhoons below a latitude of about 12° or 14°.

Both Mr. Van Meurs and Mr. Robert Lau, who joined us, assured me that we would be safe through Luzon Strait.

As far as sailing conditions were concerned, this was the time of year in which the southwest monsoon takes over from the northeast monsoon in the South China Sea. Basically we should have moderate winds and good sailing with the wind southeasterly between the Philippines and Guam, changing to easterly as we approached Guam. The temperature should be in the range of 28° to 50° Celsius, hot and generally cloudy.

Inasmuch as our main concern would be just west of Guam, we should make radio contact with Guam as soon as possible in order to start picking up weather forecasts from the weather service there.

Having ridden out hurricanes in the Caribbean and a typhoon off Okinawa, all with winds in excess of 100 knots, I didn't need anybody's warning to have great respect for this fearful phenomenon of nature. A typhoon had hit Guam a few years before our expected arrival, knocking out wind speed indicators at 145 knots and also wiping out virtually all ships and shipping in the area.

In a larger vessel the safest (I use the word loosely) place in a typhoon would be riding out at sea. In a fifty-foot sailboat the odds of the boat maintaining its ability to float in a severe typhoon get relatively marginal, and the odds of getting through a severe typhoon with no major damage are practically obscure.

It is difficult to realize or appreciate the awesome force, hostile to the nth degree, at the height of a typhoon. The shrieking, pushing, pulling, permeating wind seems to take charge as if it were a living thing. If you are inside a boat or inside any kind of structure, you are in constant fear that the structure will be overturned, blown away, or torn apart by the velocity of the wind. And the wind is not air, it is half air and half water.

In a typhoon there is actually no line of demarcation between the air and the surface of the sea; and therein lies its devastating danger. A person in the finest life jacket in the world would have absolutely no chance of survival if tossed into the sea. There's nothing in which to swim. There is a layer from perhaps three to twelve feet deep that is nothing but churning water and foam—with not enough air to be breatheable, and not enough water to be swimmable. This area of foam or transition environment is one of the worst killers of the typhoon. As the typhoon gets more severe, the size that a boat must be to stay afloat obviously gets larger and larger.

The singular conclusion is that the only way to win against a typhoon is not to enter the ring at all—to be someplace else at the time. And this was our intent, the main factor behind our drive in Hong Kong to perform that grand old navy maneuver of getting the hell out of there.

With the help of Mr. Van Meurs and Mr. Lau I reviewed in detail the elaborate and beautiful records on typhoons maintained by the Royal Observatory. They were plotted as to time of year, duration, area covered, wind force—every imaginable facet was covered. In that part of the world, the typhoon season lasts from May through November, with the most active period from June through October. There had been no typhoons in the Guam area prior to June over the past twenty-five or thirty years. And there never had been any typhoons south of latitude 10° N.

The Royal Hong Kong Observatory is on the Kowloon side of Hong Kong. On my walk from the observatory back to take the ferry to Victoria Island, I passed the stately Peninsula Hotel, which one might describe as the Waldorf Astoria of the Far East. Sure enough, the automatic door openers were still there: two brightly scrubbed young Chinese boys in sparkling white uniforms, standing at attention twenty-four hours a day by the massive swinging front doors. Even though I was pretty scroungy, I had to walk into the place. I had not been there in several years. What a difference! Not in the hotel, but in me. Before, I was neatly attired (well, attired anyway) in a business suit and tie, carrying my Wall Street black leather briefcase. This time I was wearing battered tennies, dirty shorts, an old navy shirt, and my white canvas plantation hat. Nevertheless, I took time out to sit in the lovely lobby and sip a San Miguel, contemplating the difference between the two worlds that I found myself in from time to time and wondering which one of them was real.

There was no question in my mind—in spite of the disappointments, hardships, and frustrations we were currently encountering—no question which world had the most appeal for me.

HONG KONG MORNING BREAKFAST WATCH

Our deal with the crew was that each person was responsible for getting himself or herself to Hong Kong and for all personal expenses. Carol and I would provide food and lodging on the boat. None of us had anticipated the length of time the crew had to subsist onshore before finally moving aboard the boat in Hong Kong. Everyone was pretty good about this—in fact, very good. I don't remember anybody (except Jane and Bob on their special recon mission) putting the bite on me for any onshore living costs. I'm sure they all realized that the delay was hurting Carol and me pretty badly, without also adding the crew's individual living costs to our burden. I appreciated this.

Once we moved aboard the boat, I felt obligated to have decent meals available for anybody who wanted them, three times a day, under all circumstances.

In order to conserve both dwindling money and dwindling time, I worked up a morning scrounge routine in the Shaukiwan area. My object was to get the crew up and fed prior to 0730 hours, which was when the Anthony Wong workers would swarm over the boat. I would arise about 0600 hours, meet my personal needs, and be on the street between 0630 and 0700 hours, when the stores and local teahouses started to open. The *pièce de résistance* each day was the fresh fruit, primarily pineapple, which I bought from a store run by an extremely old Chinese gentleman assisted by two of his descendants. The boy must have been about nine and the girl perhaps thirteen at the very most.

The girl was a little doll. Although neither of us spoke the other's language, we had, literally, a tearful farewell on the day I made it clear that this would be my last visit. The old man taught me the right way to peel pineapple. The outside is cut off very thinly without wasting any of the fruit, and then the little eyes are cut out in such a way that you end up with a beautiful hunk of dripping, sweet pineapple with a spiral indentation running around the fruit a dozen or so times. I became quite proud of my artistic accomplishment. Other fruits were not uncommon—bananas, various citrus fruits, even Sunkist oranges from California!

Next I would head for a little restaurant/bakery that featured freshly baked round rolls, about half the size of a U.S. hamburger bun, into which was inserted half a fried egg and a thin piece of ham. I would get one or two of these rolls per person.

Then I would top off this simple meal by stopping at a restaurant, except it really wasn't a restaurant at all; it was merely a part of an alley that had been partitioned off—an eating section, a dishwashing section, and a cooking section. I would present the lady in charge with our big thermos jug, which she would first wash out with ceremony and boiling water and then fill with delicious hot tea brewed over a little two-burner propane stove.

All of the above, which would run me around US$2.00 a day total, more than satisfied our hard-working crew of eight for breakfast—they were, in fact, extremely happy with it.

Certainly I never had any complaints from the cook of the day. We would vary this routine from time to time, usually with oatmeal, which to my surprise turned out to be one of the favorites of the crew.

ANTHONY WONG AND FEI POHL

Living on board the *Dagny Taggart* at Harbor Marine was a little like living in a recreational van being remodeled in a junkyard on the South Side of Chicago. We were tied up alongside a large boat about one hundred feet in length, with decks at least four feet higher than the decks of the *Dagny T.* The big boat had no name; it was just The Big Boat to us. To get on board *our* boat, one had to climb up a very precarious gangway which at high tide was at a very steep angle, onto the extreme point of the bow of The Big Boat, walk along its deck for fifty feet or so, then crawl or jump about four feet down to our deck. After several days the sporadic *thump* of another 160-pound body hitting our deck became reasonably ignorable. Going to and from the *Dagny Taggart* also meant walking past a disarray of piles of material, past little shacks (some containing other piles of material, some containing chickens, and some containing humans), and then past Anthony Wong's air-conditioned office, through a gate in the fence, and then *whamo!* right on to Wan Chai Boulevard, probably the busiest street in what might be the busiest city in the world: buses, taxis, light buses, roaring traffic twenty-four hours a day.

Just leaving the boat to make a telephone call and returning was probably more adventure than most people ever get, or want, in their entire lifetime.

And yet, with all this, the place was somehow utterly delightful, primarily because of the people who worked there, in particular Anthony Wong, the owner-manager, and Fei Pohl, his foreman.

We would frequently meet with Anthony and Fei in the late afternoon or early evening to assess progress and to monitor what remained to be done. When we required a construction job such as the bow pulpit or the accommodation ladder or the awning over the aft cockpit or the boom crutch, we would start by sketching something on the back of an envelope, or perhaps work from a picture out of a catalog.

The next morning, there would appear a full-size mockup of the installation in pot metal, plywood, or any handy and appropriate material. We would try this mockup on for size, angle, location, and the like, making whatever changes we saw fit. And lo and behold, twenty-four hours later there would appear the finished product in stainless steel or teak, ready to be installed.

Both Anthony and Fei gave us the absolute ultimate in cooperation, in spirit and in deed.

Anthony had three children in the States, all doctors or married to doctors; he was very proud of being a Christian; and he surely practiced the Christian ethic. He was an honest and sincere businessman. We felt he had our real interest at heart and that he knocked himself out to do a good job within our time parameters.

Fei Pohl was almost a junior Anthony. Fei didn't have Anthony's fluent English—but language was no more than a minor barrier in dealing with him. The thing we loved most about Fei was his can-do attitude. The word no was almost missing from his vocabulary. Also to his credit, he was a working foreman—there seemed to be nothing Fei would ask his men to do that he couldn't do himself.

The crazy juxtaposition of the good and the bad in Anthony's yard, as well as in Hong Kong itself, was epitomized in Randy's log entry of 3 May:

> Weather improved. Cloudy but no precipitation. Harbor water is now a beautiful combination of blue, green, and brown sewage.

CAROL'S SACRED BULKHEAD

We were constantly looking for places to mount things: clocks, chronometers, radios, fans, microwave oven, bulletin boards. The logical place for all of these mountings was in the pilot house, which served as the inside steering station, the radio room, the family room, the galley, and the dining room. However, all but the aft side of the pilot house was taken up by counters and windows; and the aft side was halfway taken up with entries and exits. The only true bulkhead left was the port half of the aft side, which was a beautifully finished teak bulkhead, perhaps five feet by four feet in size. Hardly a day went by in which someone didn't propose that some vital instrument or piece of equipment had to be mounted on this bulkhead; otherwise there would be no conceivable place on the boat to mount said particular instrument or equipment. And just as often, Carol would insist that this bulkhead be kept aesthetically pure for the mounting of framed pictures at a later date when the boat was to be the Hancock family home.

On Sunday 5 May, Jane and Carol and I goofed off after church and took the special cog railroad, known locally as the tram, to Victoria Peak, where one sits and has tea in the restaurant at the top, relishes the cool weather at an altitude of several thousand feet, and mainly enjoys the spectacular view—which was not being shown on this particular day because of fog.

When we returned to the boat it looked as if there had been a local garage sale, featuring old shoes. It appeared that there were more shoes strewn around the cabin sole in the pilot house than could possibly be needed for the people on board. We picked up all the shoes and put them somewhere. Later that evening at our crew meeting, those who had been inconvenienced by having their shoes removed from the pilot house complained about invasion of personal property rights, or disregard for the belongings of others. Jane and Carol and I defended ourselves. Carol was especially adamant that the pilot house was a place for the entire crew, and to leave one's personal property, particularly shoes, strewn about was a disfavor to the entire balance of the crew.

The next day I went ashore to pick up some shackles at Far East Yacht Specialties, and our deck chairs at the furniture place next door, where allegedly some new brass hinges were being installed to replace the ones that had rusted away in a couple of days. I also had to stop by Coopers & Lybrand's office to sign some documents and pick up some mail. I had been with Carol part of the time ashore, but I got back to the boat before she did. When I walked into the pilot house I was completely and utterly aghast; on the Carol Hancock sacred bulkhead were mounted the chronometer, the ship's clock, the VHF radio and microphone, and a bookshelf! I could just hear Carol's screams as she saw her sacred spot so defaced.

I guess I had a small suspicion from the beginning, and when I examined the bulkhead closely I could see that a great many hours of loving work had gone into suspending all the above paraphernalia on some strong nylon thread that exactly matched the color of the teak and therefore was invisible at a distance greater than about six inches.

I couldn't help but join in the fun as we all lay in wait for Carol to return. True to form, she screamed at least as loudly as we all had expected. And then, to her great credit, she accepted the whole thing as a good practical joke with some kind of message probably loosely entwined.

THE LAST LAP

Later that same Sunday I closeted myself with myself and reviewed just where we were and how we could get to some other place from here. In reviewing all the work that we had on our various worklists, two truths stood out. First, to wind up the many things that we had going would take at least all of the following week; and second, we were simply going to have to let some things go by the boards. I also decided that it was essential to set a fixed and firm schedule and adhere to it if we intended to get away before the drop-dead date of Wednesday 15 May.

I arranged all of the remaining acquisitions, installations, and servicing into the following four categories: (1) essential—highest priority, necessary for sailing or for safety; (2) high priority—very important; leaving without a category 2 item would be highly inconvenient; (3) medium priority—important, but if necessary we would be willing to leave without completion; and (4) low priority; we were willing to sacrifice if the item could not be finished by Saturday morning 11 May.

We gave Anthony Wong a copy of the above with all remaining ship yard items duly placed in one of the above four categories. I then worked out and typed up a daily schedule for our remaining time in Hong Kong. We wanted all ship yard work completed by May 10, giving us May 11 for cleaning up and May 12 for sea trials. On Monday the thirteenth we would finish provisioning, make any changes that appeared necessary after the sea trials, and have a farewell-to-Hong-Kong crew dinner at RHKYC. Tuesday would be devoted to final preparations for departure: last-minute stores, immigration, banking, sail plan, paying all bills, getting the arms from the armory. In the evening we would have a reception on the *Dagny Taggart,* including blessing of the boat and crew by Dean Rex Howe of St. John's Cathedral.

Wednesday 15 May 1974 at 0600 hours we would depart Hong Kong for Apra Harbor, Guam.

Apparently our strategy was working, or some strategy was helping us. Harlan's log of the next day read:

Crew up at 0730, for a change. Much activity among the workmen; many jobs finished.

And Jane wrote:

Up at 0730 so workmen can get on board at 0800 . . . Wong really poured on the manpower today. Must have been fifteen workmen on board, and another fifteen on shore working directly for the boat—you never know, we may make our deadline yet, with all things finished.

Our various checklists started to shrink to a semimanageable size. Our Anthony Wong checklist for Friday 10 May was down to only fourteen essentials that had to get done in order for us to leave. On that day Mr. Ho from the Hong Kong Marine Department inspected the carving of the ship's name on the bows and on the transom; and by filling in some more forms back in the office of the Marine Department, we officially became a registered British ship, with all the rights and responsibilities pertinent thereto! This in turn enabled us to get our radio license from the Port Authority and to be assigned the call letters ZEKL—*zulu echo kilo lima*—which we were to say over and over and over again for many months.

On Saturday 11 May Anthony Wong informed us that he was not going to be able to finish all his work on that day, but that he would bring his crew back on Sunday to finish up. This was a sad blow; not only were we eager to leave Hong Kong, but in spite of the fine spirit and good workmanship of Anthony Wong and Fei Pohl and their people, we were getting mighty tired of having the boat constantly swarming with ship yard workers. In spite of being behind schedule, the ship yard carried out its big cleanup on Saturday. We of the crew took virtually everything that wasn't screwed or glued down off the *Dagny Taggart* and piled it all over the decks of The Big Boat to which we were tied.

Carol had explained to Fei Pohl that she wanted the inside of the bilges hosed down and wanted to have water squirted up beneath the floorboards on the inside of the hull as far up as possible to wash down all the sawdust, scraps, and crap that kept rolling or falling into the bilges and jamming up the pumps and hoses.

Something got lost in the translation, for when we later went down to see how the hosing down party was doing, we discovered to our horror that the workers were simply stand- ing in the middle of each cabin shooting the water all over the inside of the boat. This did give us a pretty good cleaning job, but it certainly disrupted our lives for a while. In fact, that night we ended up sleeping on the decks of The Big Boat.

SSB, VHF, ADF, RDF

How much does a marine radio cost?

How much does an automobile cost?

When planning for the trip, I had asked a good friend of mine who is an expert in the marine radio field for rec- ommendations in the way of marine radios. Norm's reply was a seemingly uncooperative, laconic, "You get what you pay for."

In retrospect, this was probably about as good advice as I could have asked for. Our budget didn't allow much for radio equipment. And we didn't get much.

We had two transceivers (instruments that are able to transmit and to receive). One was an SSB (single sideband) designed for long-distance transmitting and receiving with crystals for KMI in Oakland and KQM in Honolulu. This set also contained three AM channels, two for ship-to-ship work and the international distress frequency, 2182 kHz.

Our second transceiver was a VHF (very high frequency) designed for short-range work; a VHF is generally limited to transmission and receipt on a line-of-sight basis.

We also had several straight receivers on board: the ADF (automatic direction finder), a small portable RDF (radio direction finder) and a Zenith TransOceanic all-band receiver—all the great sailing books state that this is a must for worldwide cruising. It *is* pretty much a standard, and for us it was quite good.

Our radio equipment had been purchased in the States and shipped to Hong Kong (by way of Kuala Lumpur and Taipei). It seemed to be in good shape, but none of us in the crew felt capable of making the installation, even though I had originally purchased the equipment with the thought that I would install it myself. It was not easy to find a company or person in Hong Kong who was both willing and able to install our radio equipment. Finally we decided on and persuaded the Marconi International people to take on the job, and a Mr. Wan from Marconi began the installation on Thursday 9 May in preparation for testing the equipment at sea at our sea trials planned for the following Sunday.

If nothing else, we picked a company with a name that inspired confidence.

MY KINGDOM FOR A SKIPPER

From the beginning I had been supremely confident that from one of the various sources available to me I could find a qualified skipper-type person either to make the entire trip with us or to pick up the balance of the voyage after I had finished the first leg as skipper. One source was my old boating friends, primarily in Newport Beach, and I had a vast new well of potential skippers in the Wind 'n Sea Club. Malcolm ran a very tight organization; those who had qualified to be skippers, as they were designated by the club, were practically in the category of Master Mariner as far as operating a sailboat is concerned. At one time in our planning the problem had been that we had a *surplus* of qualified people who were interested in being a skipper for all or part of the trip—Malcolm himself, Ed Perry, Bruce Leavitt, John LaMontagne. Furthermore, I thought that if we didn't get such a person we could find one as we went from port to port across the Pacific; perhaps someone in the armed services, or recently retired, or just a qualified guy who happened to be out there and would welcome a free ride back to the States.

And finally, in my optimistic little heart, I felt that if all else failed there would be one or more persons in our crew who, after all the planning and preparation followed by three or four weeks at sea, would emerge as competent to take over as skipper upon my departure.

On 12 April I had written to a business contact in Guam, explaining our situation and saying that if he happened to know someone there who was a qualified mariner with experience in sailing the Pacific and with good celestial and piloting navigation experience, we could give him a free ride to Los Angeles.

One of our best hopes was my long-time friend John LaMontagne. John had sailed all his life and had been skipper of an LST in the Pacific both during World War II and during the Korean War. He had all the qualifications, besides being a great guy. I had one of those good feelings that John would be unable to say no, since he loves to sail and since he knew that both Carol and I had complete confidence in him.

However, on 10 May we received the following telex from Joanne:

TAYLOR, JOHN LA MONTAGNE JUST CALLED IN RESPONSE TO THE LETTER FROM CAROL REQUESTING THAT HE JOIN YOU FOR THE VOYAGE.

HE MOST SINCERELY REGRETS THAT HE WILL NOT BE ABLE TO MAKE THE TRIP AS HIS LIVELIHOOD DEMANDS THAT HE STAY IN CALIFORNIA. AN AIR MAIL LETTER FROM JOHN IS IN THE MAIL. BOTH JOHN AND I ARE WORKING ON OPTIONS TO FIND A SUITABLE SKIPPER - DO NOT BECOME DISCOURAGED.

SAIL POWER

Our tentative schedule of activities for the Great Day of our sea trials (Sunday 12 May) was prepared and posted the night before, beginning with breakfast at 0700.

Morning: Check compass deviation; adjust as necessary; calibrate compass and gather sufficient information to prepare deviation chart. Rig roller-furling genoa, mizzen staysail, storm foresail, and storm trysail. Raise and lower each of the other four sails that are permanently bent on. Test and sail with all sail combinations.

Noon: Anchor, testing all anchor gear, winches, lead line, depth sounder. Cold beer and sandwiches. Rest. Clean bottom of hull (each person assigned to one-eighth of the underwater hull). Check all through-hull fittings. Calibrate ADF and RDF. Test all radios. Check chronometer and set all accurate watches to match chronometer. Practice sun sights if horizon available.

Afternoon: Complete all items left over from morning. Practice drills: person overboard; fire; abandon ship; damage control; loss of steering; repel attackers. Sail as much as possible, timing reaching mooring V-2 at RHKYC yacht anchorage at 1900 hours.

In the real world, by noon on Sunday, Anthony's workers had finished up all they could do. The ship's crew and the yard workers spent the next three or four hours in a final cleanup. In setting the digital chronometer, the digital dials fell completely apart, and Jim had a jigsaw puzzle on his hands. He finally got them back together again at about 1340. At 1500 hours we topped off our water tanks and prepared to get underway. Last minutes being what they are, it was not until 1655 that we departed good old Harbor Marine, and not without a flourish.

While living on the *Morgan* we had found that it made much more sense for Carol rather than me to take the helm as we went in and out of moorings and slips and anchorages. First and foremost, she is very mechanically oriented and is a good helmsman/pilot. Second, with Carol at the helm, I found myself free to fend off, pick up navigational aids, signal other boats, use the radio, and apply my skills much more effectively than if I were tied down to the helm. This practice was far more than just a sop from a sailing husband to a nonsailing wife; however, it did have a very good effect on our sharing the boat and the sport of sailing together, rather than our sailing and cruising being just a one-person show for my benefit.

I could sense that at this great moment of leaving what seemed to have become our permanent dock at Anthony Wong's place, Carol expected to be at the helm.

Since Carol had handled only one other good-size boat before in her life and had to learn a whole new set of controls and instrumentation, and since getting out to Hong Kong Harbor from Anthony Wong's involved backing down and turning around in a tight basin surrounded by moored junks on almost all sides, I had at least some hesitation about putting Carol on the helm. On the other hand, if this were to be our lifestyle from now on, and since she had her heart set on it, I weighed the various factors and decided that it was a damn-the-torpedoes situation.

We double-, triple-, and quadruple-checked all systems— water flowing through the engine satisfactorily, water temp and oil pressure okay, engine responding to throttle controls, transmission responding to gear controls, lines singled-up, everybody on board, lines cast off, Red Duster at the stern. Carol backed down slowly and carefully. It was a tough situation, since she had to get enough way on the boat so that the rudder would be effective in reverse to swing the stern hard to port to allow her to turn her bow sharply to starboard to get out of the ridiculously small turning basin that the moored junks had boxed us into. We almost made it; or, applying the my-glass-is-half-*full* theory, *we made it* with only the slightest of mishaps. As we backed down toward a large junk you would have thought that the female proprietor thereof was watching a T-2 tanker drift down on her boat/home. We couldn't understand her words, but there was no doubt about her meaning. We were going slowly enough to fend off satisfactorily, with our arms and legs, except for the fact that the only place we had been able to figure out to mount our SSB antenna, which was about fifteen feet in length, was over the stern, raked aft, so that the upper tip was perhaps seven or eight feet astern of our boat; thus the antenna hit the moored junk before our arms and legs could reach out to fend us off. However, only very minor damage was done to the stainless steel support mechanism of the fiberglass antenna; and we were off on our great shakedown cruise.

Once we finally broke through the hundreds of junks that nearly blocked the exit from Anthony's yard, we really lucked out. Even though it was now after 1700 hours, we were in the Northern Hemisphere, where the days are long in May even at Hong Kong's latitude, and the sun was still fairly high in the sky. And it was a bee-yoo-tiful day! Warm but comfortable; light winds, just right to try out everything in a pleasant atmosphere.

We cruised to an area known as Junk Bay, which is several miles across, giving us good room to maneuver. While we certainly didn't cover our entire ambitious agenda for the day, we did marvelously well considering the time we had. The boat sailed beautifully. Everything worked—it was amazing. I don't know of one item that failed. It was heady stuff.

NEXT TO LAST DAY

Most of what I had to do on the next to the last day found me on shore running down the last-minute pieces of equipment; Carol was likewise on shore most of the day involved primarily with clearance from the various Hong Kong authorities.

While we were out of Anthony Wong's ship yard, we were not yet out of his ken. There were still several things to do on the boat, including some paint touchup. I had to go by Harbor Marine and happened to be there just when Anthony wanted to send two of his painters to the boat. He asked me if I would be kind enough to take them with me since I was going back that way. Standing across the street from the shore side of Harbor Marine, waiting for a light bus to come by in the busy traffic and driving sun, I learned a valuable lesson. I was standing there in the sun, impatient, frustrated, hot, when one of the painters—old and venerable—walked over from where he was standing, tapped me on the arm, and pointed to where he was standing. The spot was only four feet away, but it was in the shade of a building. Without having to use language, the ancient Chinaman suggested to me that I should get the hell out of that sun over to where I would be cooler, calmer, and more collected.

When I returned to the *Dagny Taggart* I was overwhelmed as I stepped on board; everywhere there were cartons, bags, casks, bottles, cans, containers of various descriptions.

Jane's food had arrived.

According to the wild tales that were told, a Chinese junk about twice as big as the *Dagny Taggart,* piled high with our provision order from Dairy Lane, was suddenly seen bearing down on our boat at 1130 hours in such a fashion that Jane and others on board were sure it was going to hit.

However, as the story goes, a perfect landing was made.

With the provisions dumped on our deck, we found ourselves a foot lower in the water and a few thousand dollars lower at the bank. I certainly thought that Jane was pulling my leg when she told me that what I saw on deck was only a quarter of what had been put there at noon. But when she showed me where everything had been stored below decks, I believed her.

I'm not sure to this day if I have ever expressed my thanks adequately to Jane for the job she did in organizing the storage space and handling all of stowage on the boat. And now I know that she deserves even more credit; for having read her diary in the preparation of this book, I am keenly aware that she hated the job.

Monday evening we finally did something on schedule. With the boat securely moored in the basin, and with security provided by the club, we felt that it was safe for all of us to leave the boat and go ashore at the same time. Everybody into those ancient but glorious hot-water showers at the yacht club. Ecstasy. Then up to the terrace for a couple of drinks (with our hats off) enjoying a relaxed and wonderful view of the beautiful lights of Hong Kong Harbor; and finally up further to the dining room, air-conditioned yet, where we had the promised crew dinner hosted by Carol and me. Carol and Harlan had done a lot of work to find eight white dacron sailing jackets. After a great deal of hunting, I had found a place (well not exactly a place; a guy on a sidewalk) where I could have stencils cut. We gave each person in the crew a jacket with the boat's name in Chinese and in English stenciled on the back, and the wearer's name on the front. It worked out well. Each person liked the jacket; we made a good picture in the various ports when we all donned our jackets and went ashore together—albeit a rare occurrence.

That night Jane wrote in her diary:

We are all getting excited about leaving—only thirty hours to go! I feel happy and glad to be a part of this venture, even though at times it has been unbearably frustrating. In bed at 0030. We have such a busy day tomorrow—last full day.

LAST FULL DAY

As skipper it was up to me to get the official port clearance from the Hong Kong Marine Department. I ran into a slight problem here since the port clearance must be issued on the day of departure. We fudged just a little by listing the departure as being midnight on 14 May, even though I knew in my little black heart that we did not intend to leave until 0600 on the fifteenth. Also in my capacity as skipper, I cleared the departure of all eight of us from Hong Kong, and had each person's passport duly stamped.

I made my final and all-important call at the Royal Hong Kong Observatory in Kowloon to get the all-important, up-to-date long-range and short-range weather forecasts. Mr. Van Meurs was again there, this time accompanied by a young Chinese meteorologist named Martin Yeng. After I had again received the royal treatment, I once more found myself walking past the Peninsula Hotel and felt the need for a decision as well as for a cold beer.

I sat down with my beer on the balcony level of the lovely lobby and considered what had started to creep into my mind as a real possibility. I guess this creeping idea first hit me when I read Joanne's latest telex, which said that Bruce Leavitt would be available to pick up the trip at Ponape.

Could I possibly consider making the first leg all the way from Hong Kong to Ponape?

The big advantage would be that we would duck down to the south just as soon as we got through the Balintang Channel, which is the route we had chosen between the Philippines and Taiwan. By ducking down to the south, a few days' travel would take us farther and farther away from the typhoon danger; and by going all the way to Ponape we would do away with the problem of not having a skipper to take over in Guam. The big disadvantage would be making such an ungodly long leg on the *Dagny Taggart's* maiden voyage; we might be straining our supply of fuel and water. We would surely be straining our personal endurance and the endurance of our interpersonal relationships. And I would be staying away from my work longer than planned—longer than I thought fair.

I found it intriguing that I chose the lobby of the Peninsula Hotel to make this important decision. I don't think I fully realized what the reason was at that time; I'm far from sure that I realize it now. I think, however, that it may have been because I found this to be a secret place of my own, well insulated from the day-to-day vicissitudes, frustrations, and pressures that I found increasingly closing in on me in my role as skipper/owner of the *Dagny Taggart,* trying to whip her into shape for this 8,000-mile voyage.

After sitting there for some time, it became more and more apparent to me that the two big factors in favor of going straight to Ponape—getting out of the typhoon area and providing for competent skippers all the way to Honolulu—outweighed all other considerations. The mouthful that I had bitten off in this particular passage of my life was sailing this beautiful yacht safely from Hong Kong across the Pacific to Marina del Rey.

Either I was going to give it up as a bad deal, or I was going to do it right.

Doing it right meant getting out of the typhoon season; and doing it right meant getting a good skipper.

Ponape here we come.

Having made the big decision, I had a lot of work to do to implement it.

I was able to pass the word to all the crew and find out from each of them if they would like to have their family or anybody else notified of the change in plans. I then called trusty Joanne, who, God bless her, took care of notifying not only the families of the crew, but also the various banks, harbormasters, port authorities, and Coast Guard stations up and down the Pacific Island network, of our change in plans.

All this we were able to get in before our first big Social Event—the farewell party and the benediction ceremony for the *Dagny Taggart*.

We found in working up our guest list for the party that a large number of people had been most kind and helpful during what turned out to be our extended stay in Hong Kong: Anthony Bill of the Bank of Canton, Anthony Wong, Val and Frank Kasala, Bob Gaff and his fiancée together with Estelle May from Coopers & Lybrand, and many of the supply and service firm people who had given us assistance above and beyond, and Dean and Mrs. Rex Howe. In addition, each of the eight crewmembers had developed a personal relationship with one or more persons during our long stay, and we had welcomed the crewmembers to invite such friends.

Late in the afternoon I was startled by a message to phone Dean Howe's office. My heart sank; I was sure he wasn't going to be able to make it. What a disappointment!

Oh ye of little faith! Not only was *he* going to make it, but he was so enthusiastic about the event that he had apparently transmitted his enthusiasm to his whole family. The dean's secretary wanted to know if it would be all right if the dean brought his two teenage daughters along. . . .

The party couldn't have been nicer. We served a simple chilled white wine and cold beer, and the yacht club staff did a beautiful job on the hors d'oeuvres. Lots of reminiscing over our trials and tribs with each of our guests, all of whom were in a real sense a part of our trip.

The good dean had a marvelous sense of timing as well as a little of the dramatic in his repertoire. He chose the moment perfect for his blessing ceremony: just as the sun was setting over the hills surrounding Hong Kong Harbor. The picture:

Dean Howe, a handsome man in the first place, in a rich beige turtleneck sweater, standing amidship on the *Dagny Taggart* with his temporary flock of thirty or forty people spread out on and over the pilot house and aft cockpit. He spoke of the long voyages of the Bible, of Christ's adventures on the water, of the love and faith of those in Hong Kong that the voyage would be successful—all this in the lovely twilight, as the splashing lights of Hong Kong Harbor, which has been called the most beautiful in the world, twinkled into life. At the very least, it rated as a Precious Moment.

FREDDY THE RAT

Probably because we first heard about the rat at about the same time we heard about the pirate-ramming episode, we didn't pay too much attention. But it soon became apparent that living with a Taiwan rat in Hong Kong Harbor, or I suppose anyplace else, was a real bitch.

Nobody seems to know exactly how the rat picked up the name Freddy, particularly since the rat was female—and come to think of it, how did anybody know the rat was female in the first place?

But it sure as hell was a rat! She would let us see her body, flitting here or there from time to time, just to taunt us. And of course she left her distinctive calling cards in every nook and cranny of the boat, as well as on the dinette table, and *every morning*, without fail, in my *shoes!* She really had it in for me; I guess she knew I was the skipper!

And it wasn't just the filth of her droppings that bothered us; we knew that some of our electrical problems were caused by the rat's gnawing through the insulation on the wiring. And at the rate she was eating the labels off the canned goods, we would have no idea what our cans contained after a couple of months at sea.

The added problem was that she was a great sampler! She wouldn't content herself to sit down and eat a box of RyKrisp—no—she had to sample every box of RyKrisp on the boat!

We didn't want to resort to poison because of the awful possibility that the rat would crawl up into some inaccessible place to die and rot away for weeks or months, or what have you. But they breed one smart rat in Taiwan, that's for sure! We must have tried a dozen or more different types of traps. Each one guaranteed to be that panacea of all mankind—the perfect rat trap. Not only did she not get caught, but almost invariably she figured out a way to get the bait, either without springing the trap at all, or by springing it and then taking out the bait.

Finally, in complete desperation two days before we were scheduled to leave, we got some D-Con, a very efficient rat poison that is excellent around the house and farm since it drives an animal outside looking for water.

We didn't have too much hope that Freddy could be driven out into the open on a boat; we just hoped that she would die, and that death would occur in an accessible place.

Next to me, I think Bob was bothered the most by the rat being on board, probably because she presented such a serious threat to the watertight integrity of the boat and its operation. Therefore it was symbolic or significant or coincidental or something that it was Bob who discovered Freddy dying in the bilges beneath the floor boards of the after cabin on the day before we were scheduled to leave Hong Kong. Bob bravely called for his dear old daddy to dispose of the rat!

Not wanting to get bubonic plague from the teeth of a mad rodent, I used the bacon tongs to grasp Freddy firmly around the midriff, and with a little ceremony I dropped her softly into the waters of the Yacht Basin of the Royal Hong Kong Yacht Club. I swear her soft brown eyes looked at me reproachfully as she sank below the water.

Harlan's log entry was simple and direct:

Fred the Rat (RATUS ratus) died today.

IV

The Voyage

The Great Day dawned, as great days always do, bright and early. We didn't make our early ETD of 0600, but by that time I was on my way ashore to send a telex to Joanne. With a change in our next port distance of some 1,500 miles I didn't want to take any chance of a communication misunderstanding.

Following are excerpts from our last telex-imposition on Estelle May:

JOANNE DAVIS FROM TAYLOR HANCOCK:

CONFIRMING TELEPHONE CONVERSATION, FOLLOWING IS OUR PRESENT ITINERARY: DEPART HONG KONG WEDNESDAY MORNING 15 MAY 1974 WITH FIRST SCHEDULED STOP - PONAPE - IN CAROLINE ISLANDS. APPROXIMATELY 3,000 MILES AT A CONSERVATIVE 100 MILES PER DAY SHOULD GET US TO PONAPE BY 15 JUNE 1974, ALTHOUGH IT COULD BE LONGER OR SHORTER. AS AN OFFICIAL SAIL PLAN I WOULD SAY 20 JUNE 1974.

PLEASE GIVE NOTICE OF NEW SAIL PLAN TO HARBORMASTER IN PONAPE, AND ANYONE ELSE THAT BRUCE SUGGESTS BE NOTIFIED.

WE WILL HANDLE CHANGE OF SAIL PLAN WITH HONG KONG PORT AUTHORITIES.

PLEASE NOTIFY EACH FAMILY CONTACT FOR ALL EIGHT OF THE
CREW ON YOUR LIST PER CHANGE OF PLANS, TELLING THEM
THAT THE REASON FOR THE CHANGE IS THAT WE HAD AN
OPPORTUNITY TO HAVE AN EXCELLENT SKIPPER TAKE MY PLACE
TO TAKE THE BOAT FROM PONAPE TO HONOLULU, BUT NO
REPLACEMENT FROM GUAM TO PONAPE. THEREFORE, I HAVE
DECIDED TO TAKE THE BOAT ON TO PONAPE, BYPASSING GUAM,
WHICH MEANS ONLY ABOUT SIX DAYS MORE OR LESS ADDI-
TIONAL TIME.

I asked her to follow up on our letters to Trust Territory
officials, telling them of our change in plans and requesting
clearance to enter Ponape and Majuro; to see if she could get
our mail forwarded from Guam; and to see what I should do
about my now-obsolete return plane ticket.

CONFIRM WITH BRUCE THAT WE ARE DELIGHTED THAT HE AND
BETTY CAN MAKE THE TRIP, AND CREW LOOKING FORWARD TO
SEEING THEM IN PONAPE. I WILL DO MY BEST TO SEND REVISED
ETA'S IF CAN MAKE ANY CONTACT VIA RADIO AND IN ANY
EVENT WILL TELEPHONE AS SOON AS ARRIVE IN PONAPE. ALSO,
CONFIRM THAT IF FOR SOME UNLIKELY REASON BRUCE CAN'T
MAKE IT, EITHER OF THE OTHER PEOPLE HE MENTIONED
SOUNDS FINE TO ME, OR ANYONE ELSE THAT BRUCE WOULD
ELECT.

THANKS AGAIN JOANNE FOR YOUR ASSISTANCE AND SUPPORT.
THE HOLY BLESSING WENT BEAUTIFULLY LAST NIGHT. GOOD
CROWD AND FOND FAREWELLS. THE WHOLE BIT. LOVE AND
KISSES. OH, ANOTHER THOUGHT: MONEY AND COMMUNICA-
TIONS; WORKING EITHER THROUGH SECURITY PACIFIC OR MOR-
GAN GUARANTY, PLEASE DO WHATEVER IS NECESSARY TO
ENABLE US TO HAVE FUNDS AVAILABLE IN PONAPE, INCLUDING
IF NECESSARY OPENING AN ACCOUNT AND DEPOSITING FUNDS.
ALSO PLEASE FIND OUT IF THERE IS A TELEX ON PONAPE AND
LEAVE WORD WITH US AT HARBORMASTER'S OFFICE ABOUT
SAME.

THANKS AGAIN.

Meantime, the *Dagny Taggart* crew had completed all preparations for sea, and at 1045 hours, within minutes of my

return, we left the Yacht Basin of the Royal Hong Kong Yacht Club, underway for the Shaukiwan fuel dock.

After filling up our diesel fuel tanks, topping off our water tanks, and filling all our emergency jerrycans with water, diesel, kerosene, and lubricating oil, respectively, we headed out to sea—or as Harlan wrote in the sail plan that we filed with the Hong Kong Port Authorities:

> From Hong Kong we will sail southeast across the China Sea, through the Balintang channel, and down the East Coast of Luzon Island in the Philippines. From Luzon Island we will strike out boldly across the Pacific to Ponape.

On our shakedown cruise we had made only a very cursory check of our compass deviation. And, although said cursory check indicated we had very little if any deviation, we took an hour or so as we were leaving Hong Kong Harbor, powering on various courses to swing ship using whatever was available by way of navigational aids on which to take bearings. We couldn't believe how free of deviation the compass was! We ran a rather crude deviation table, but in view of the fact that the maximum deviation was less than 2°, and over most of the compass rose it was less than 1°, and in view of the fact that as a practical matter one cannot steer a fifty-foot sailboat nor take a bearing within more than 1 or 2 degrees, we virtually ignored the deviation.

This last ritual of preparation for the voyage completed, we settled down to navigate the long and beautiful channel out of Hong Kong and into the South China Sea.

Clunk!

The clunk was immediately followed by the stopping of the engine. Good god! What have we hit? It sure didn't feel like a rock. It could have been a log. But why did the engine stop? Something must have hit the propeller.

Bob's mind was racing down the same path as mine. Only his was quicker. Within seconds he was over the side, reporting that we had gone over one of the ubiquitous straw mats that serve as mattress, pillow, blanket, partition, and who knows what else for the Chinese living in their junks. Bob soon had the mat free of the propeller, and we all breathed a sigh of relief.

I tossed Bob some goggles and fins and donned my own in order to inspect the underwater part of the hull for any damage from the incident. All appeared to be fine. Bob and I crawled back on board, and once again we struck out boldly across the Pacific!

At Bob's suggestion we made a thorough inspection of the inside of the hull, particularly at the stern gland where the drive shaft goes through the hull, and at the rudder post where the rudder control goes through. To our dismay, Bob discovered a pretty hefty leak at the rudder post. Tightening all the bolts holding the rudder post against the hull cut the flow down somewhat, but there was still a substantial leak. While I chewed away at the rudder post leak, Bob busied himself inspecting the rest of the interior of the hull. He discovered a leak in the starboard diesel fuel tank, right at the point where the fuel enters the tank.

Bob and I worked on our respective leaks for about an hour. We were both working under tough physical conditions—in a small, poorly ventilated area, needing both hands to work on the job and a third hand to hold a light. The heat was about 120° F and the humidity about 95 percent. It was not comfortable.

After about an hour I went on deck to breathe a little air and called Bob up for consultation: "What do you think, ol' buddy?"

"Gee Dad, if we're gonna try to stretch 300 gallons to go 3,000 miles, it's hard to see how we can do it with a leak in the fuel tank."

He was right, of course; the only thing was that the fuel tank leak might be just because the tanks were overly full. If the fuel leak had been our only problem, I think I'd have gone ahead, but I was more concerned about that damned rudder post. We could take care of the leak with our pumps without any problem, but I couldn't tell for sure whether it was leaking because of the poor sealing job, or whether there was a structural defect back there.

"I guess that does it," I said. "Let's see if we can catch the gang at Anthony's before they all go home."

With my barking orders like Captain Bligh, at 1445 hours we swung the boat around and headed at flank speed back to Hong Kong. We made it back to Harbor Marine at 1630 hours; however, the dreaded junk area around Harbor Marine had closed in, and we could neither get through the junks, nor arouse anybody's attention at the ship yard, which was several hundred yards away. Oh, frustration.

Finally, by that universal language of signs and gestures, we enticed a Chinese youngster on a small sampan to come alongside. Randy and I leapt into the sampan, leaving Carol at the helm cruising the crowded junks to wait for us, hopefully to get one of Anthony's people to come to our rescue, either making a path for us or piloting us in.

The dock (and I use the word loosely) where Randy and I landed was nearly a mile from Anthony's office. We finally made it over fences and through backyards to Wan Chai Boulevard and ran the rest of the way to Harbor Marine, where we burst into Anthony Wong's air-conditioned office.

Anthony Wong has a very expressive face. His face immediately became *very expressive*. He took off his large horn-rimmed glasses and stared up from behind his desk in complete disbelief. He told us later that he honestly thought he was seeing a ghost.

Because of our short time fuse—by this time it was about 1730 hours—I was extremely businesslike and brief with Anthony, telling him essentially what our two problems were and asking him if he could get us into the yard, get them fixed, and get us on our way.

Several weeks before (or was it years?) when our second replacement chainplate had not arrived from Taiwan, we had taken the bull by the horns and asked Anthony if his people could fabricate a new one. Yes they could; they could do anything. Anthony had the necessary stainless steel stock; but the only method the ship yard had to cut it was by a hand hacksaw. For four days one of Anthony's workers, a guy about five feet in all dimensions, stood at a huge vice, hacksawing that quarter-inch stainless steel plate by hand for ten or twelve hours per day. What a speciman of a circus strong man he was! We nicknamed him The Boxer.

It turned out the The Boxer was also Anthony's pilot. The

Boxer and Fei Pohl and Anthony really swung into action. Within minutes they had the *Dagny Taggart* tied up alongside one of their rickety floating docks; swarms of workmen descended on the boat.

We felt right at home again!

After a quick analytical investigation by Fei Pohl and Anthony, down came the electric cords to the boat, together with electric equipment to back out the lag bolts that held the rudder post to the transom. Out came the old lag bolts, which were about a quarter inch in diameter and two and one-half inches long. New holes were drilled; new white sealant was placed between the rudder post and the transom; and new stainless steel bolts (the biggest bolts I ever saw—they must have been three-quarters of an inch in diameter) were inserted. We were assured by Fei Pohl that there was no structural defect in either the rudder post or the transom.

Meanwhile, Bob, working with Fei Pohl and one of the other workmen, satisfied himself that the diesel fuel leak either had been sealed or was not a serious problem.

And once more it was . . . do you know the way to Ponape?

THE SOUTH CHINA SEA

Sitting on a rugged rock off the coast of mainland China is Wang Lan Light, marking the entrance to one of a series of major channels that lead to Hong Kong from the South China Sea. Conversely, when leaving Hong Kong, Wang Lan Light marks the entrance to the South China Sea. We passed this famous landmark at 2110 hours on Wednesday 15 May 1974.

To Chinese fishermen a light is a light is a light. None of that fancy stuff of red on one side; green on the other; a stern light; and a bow light. Why have anything more than just one light up there someplace? As we entered the South China Sea, and for many miles to come, there were bobbing lights in all directions; the ones we worried about the most were those in front of us. There was no way to tell whether a fishing boat was crossing our bow, bearing down on us, at anchor, adrift, or underway.

And our quartet from Taiwan was still a little jumpy, since

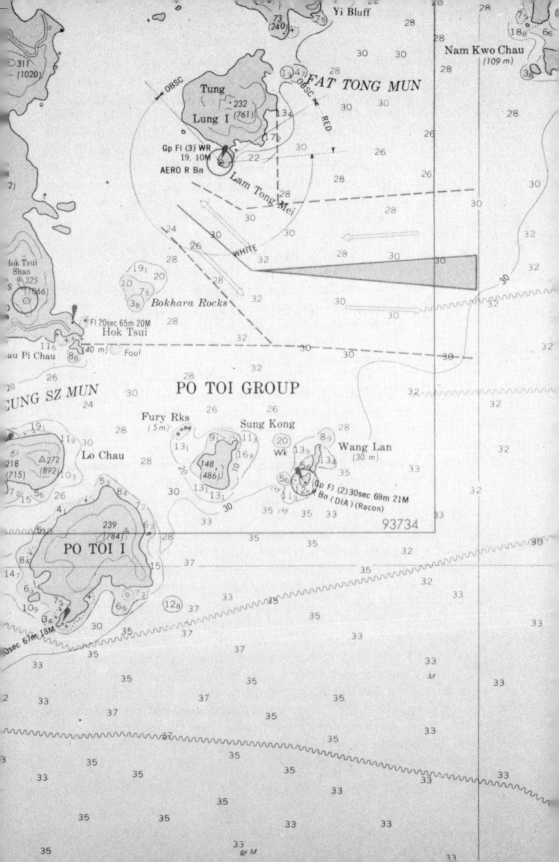

there was no way we could tell if a bobbing white light ahead was on a small, innocuous fishing boat or on a seventy-foot diesel-powered steel junk. Come to think of it, we were all a little jumpy on the same subject.

Around midnight we lost the protection of various bodies of land and islands and encountered the full swell of the South China Sea coming in from the east. The wind was also coming in from the east, building a fair chop on top of the large, rolling swells. The boat seemed to be taking it well, but not the crew! I couldn't believe it! For the first time in fifteen years I was seasick!

Damn! What a lousy time to get sick!

Among other things, the way the numbers came up, I was cook for this first day at sea. Luckily, everyone else on board was also sick, and no one wanted to eat. I suppose I would have made it somehow, but I'm glad I wasn't tested.

We hadn't realized that the jack staff from which the Red Duster was flown off the stern might interfere with the sheets that control the mizzen boom, which extends beyond the transom. That first morning, the sheets caught the jack staff and broke it off into the wake of the boat. By that time, we had winds of 25 to 30 knots, which made it impractical to attempt to come about to pick up the jack staff. That day we also made our first and last water temperature readings for some time to come. The thermometer we were trailing behind the boat once every hour broke in the process of being hauled in for a reading.

On the noon-to-1600 watch that afternoon, since we were beating almost dead into the wind, Bob (who had the con) decided to take down the mainsail, which was merely flapping in the wind. While the sail was being lowered, it jammed; we were unable either to pull it up or to pull it down.

Jim volunteered to go up the mast in a bosun's chair—a very brave thing to do in that sea and wind condition—particularly since he had nearly been killed going up the mizzen in a bosun's chair a week or so before in the stillness of Hong Kong harbor. Jim did the job successfully and reported that the mast track, on which the sail slides up and down on the after edge of the mast, was seriously pulled away from the mast itself.

That meant we would not be able to use the mainsail until we could get the track repaired.

There is only one navigational danger on the route from Wang Lan Light to the Balintang Channel—a little outcrop of rock called Pratis Island. I was fighting my seasickness and doing my best to be sharp in our navigation to be sure we didn't pile up on Pratis Island.

The weather had moderated considerably; the boat was riding comfortably; and most, if not all, of the crew were beginning to get their sea legs and their stomachs back in place again. I think only Carol and Bob still had a touch of seasickness. From past experience at sea with each of them, I knew that it would take them three or four days to conquer their queasiness.

We were making lousy progress even though we were using the engine and the forestaysail, mizzen, and main engine.

Bob was prowling the bilges looking for leaks. Unfortunately, he found what he was looking for. A combination of the uneasy stomach, the roll of the boat, and the smell of diesel fuel was too much for him—I took over.

To my horror I found that not only were we leaking diesel, but we were losing fresh water. Our sounding of water tanks indicated that they were down 55 gallons in the last 36 hours!

We had two diesel fuel tanks and two fresh-water tanks, one of each on each side, each with four openings: one opening to take on a new supply of fuel (or water); one opening for the purpose of sounding or measuring; one opening as a vent to the outside to allow air to come in as the fuel (or water) left the tank; and of course the opening for the fuel (or water) to get out of the tank.

Bob and I analyzed the situation and came to the tentative conclusion that the leaks seemed to be coming from the *tops* of the tanks. While this conclusion didn't make us exactly ecstatic, it was a lot better than finding out that the leaks were from the *bottoms* of the tanks.

The space between the top of the tanks and the top of the engine room compartment where the tanks were located was only two inches. And about the only way to gain any access to that two inches of space was by lying on the cabin sole of the pilot house, with the engine hatch open, more or less standing on your head while you worked with the oily bilge splashing below.

We studied the matter of the fuel and water leaks for a long time—not good. We then agonized over the matter of the sail track that was pulled loose from the mast. The track was pulled out in three different places. It was obvious that since it had pulled out once under winds of 30 to 35 knots, we could count on it to pull out again under similar or greater stress.

In order to fix the track, we would have to send someone up there in a bosun's chair and either replace the old screws with bigger ones or drill new holes and put in additional larger screws in the crucial places. We had the equipment to do the job on the sail track—not a perfect job, but one we thought would hold us until the next port. The difficulty was that it was physically impossible to do that type of work except in the calmest of waters. And we couldn't strike out boldly across the Pacific without the use of our mainsail, especially when we couldn't depend on our fuel supply—not to mention our water supply.

About this time things went from bad to worse. Since we didn't have use of the main, we tried to run up the big genoa even though we knew there was a problem in the roller reefing. Without the roller reefing, and because of the heavy bolt wire in the luff of the genoa, the only way we could fly the thing was without the luff attached to anything. This we tried with an initial modicum of success.

Two very serious drawbacks developed. First, getting that baby down in any kind of wind was a real killer—particularly with the heavy wire in the luff. When that thing hit you, it could maim you, or worse, knock you overboard.

The other problem was that the fitting in the mast through which the genoa halyard was run was not constructed to take the heavy and extremely dynamic force that was exerted by the now free-flying jib. Consequently, the wire halyard for the fitting was damaging the mast.

We were faced with a real dilemma. There was nothing in any of our equipment failures that we didn't have the tools and the talent to repair on board. The difficulty was that any one of these jobs would take a long time; all four of them put together would take longer still. We desperately needed a port of refuge unless we could anticipate a long period of flat calm.

Meantime, here we were up at the higher latitudes, subject to the typhoon season, which was too close for comfort. I sat up on the bow pulpit for a while to clear my lungs of the smell of diesel fuel and to try to clear my head for another important decision. I then cloistered myself with my sailing directions and my charts to see what I could conjure up.

In planning the voyage, way back when, I had laid out at least two alternate destinations for each of our intended ports of call. I had seriously considered Manila as our first port of call but had rejected the idea when I found that the distance between Manila and Los Angeles is almost the same as the distance between Hong Kong and Los Angeles.

Unfortunately, I had not brought along any detailed charts of Manila or the Philippines—merely large-area small-scale charts suitable for cruising past the Philippines, but not suitable for cruising into the islands.

I suppose we *could* go back to Hong Kong . . . back to Hong Kong! Think what *that* would do to the crew's morale—what it would do to *my* morale! For one thing, we would really be caught behind the eight ball as far as the typhoon season was concerned. How could I afford to send everybody home, maintain the boat in Hong Kong, and come back for it later?— all of which would probably be the logical thing to do!

I poured over the charts and sailing directions some more, trying to find a port of refuge, someplace on Luzon Island. Unfortunately, what I learned was exactly what I didn't want to find out: there are no decent ports in that area of the Philippines. The place is full of bad currents, navigational dangers, and local pirates.

More and more, a little voice was whispering to me: Manila, Manila, Manila.

But if we went to Manila we wouldn't be much closer to Marina del Rey than if we had stayed in Hong Kong—maybe a little, but not much. However there *were* some big positives in going to Manila for repairs. Psychologically we would have a good passage under our belts, and we would all have a lot more confidence. The Philippines are beautiful, and the people friendly—what better port for our travel-happy crew to start with as cruising tourists? Manila is a major seaport and should have good repair facilities; my company had an office there so we knew we could get helpful and friendly advice and recommendations; we knew that there was a Manila Yacht

Club. And most convincing, we would be heading almost directly south, getting nearer that part of the eastern Pacific where we would be free from typhoons.

Captain Bligh into action again!

At midnight on 17 May I gave the order to change course to 150° magnetic and head down the east coast of Luzon Island toward Manila, where we could make our repairs and get on with our journey.

PERSON OVERBOARD

One of the greatest risks in long-distance racing or cruising is the ever-present possibility that someone will fall overboard under conditions that make it impossible, or nearly so, to effect a rescue. This is the case especially at night, when the person in the water can't be seen; or in a storm; or worse yet in a storm at night. Naturally those who haven't fallen off the boat will take all corrective action within their power, but depending on the severity of the adverse conditions, the chances of recovery may be very small indeed. The odds are that the odds will be against it.

On the *Dagny Taggart* we planned, and took, all the standard precautions, and a few extras, attempting to decrease the horrifying danger of leaving one of our shipmates out there someplace in the cruel sea.

We insisted that everyone adhere to a set of strict rules to protect all of us from a person-overboard experience.

Everyone on deck at night or during rough weather was required to wear a safety harness, which in turn was attached by a tether to a secure line or fitting on the boat. The tether and harness had to be strong enough to hold the person to the boat so he or she could be pulled back on board in case the dreaded thing happened. We had sturdy safety rails along both sides and at the stern, and a bow pulpit with good Anthony Wong-built rails on each side. Around the aft cockpit, where we spent most of our time on deck, the stanchions for the safety rails were in effect about six and a half feet tall, forming the support for a fixed awning. Between these tall stanchions we ran extra horizontal dacron lines, the result being that the aft steering station was practically a cage—a nice cage, but still a cage. In order to give us a reasonable amount of freedom to work on deck while wearing a safety harness, Harlan had done a superb job of running two half-inch dacron lines the entire length of the boat, one on each side, as safety lines to which we could attach the ring at the end of the harness tether. The ring would slide along the safety line, eliminating to a great extent the need to refasten oneself every ten feet.

We had the conventional lifering (actually a horseshoe buoy) ready to toss over at any time. To the buoy was attached a strobe light that would automatically activate itself upon hitting the water.

Following a frustrating experience in the South China Sea when Jim went over the side to retrieve something that had been lost overboard, and then had a devil of a time getting back on board, we kept a coil of about one hundred feet of light polypropylene line tied loosely to the aft cockpit super-structure, ready to toss over to anyone in the water in the event of a mishap. This line would float.

It was our good fortune never to have to use this line in an actual save-a-life situation. We did get a good feel for its use, however, by employing it many many times during swim calls when the boat, although seemingly dead in the water, might have slight headway on. I became convinced that having that line ready to throw over the side was one of our best safety practices. In fact, many long-distance cruising sailors have written that they are willing to sacrifice a small amount of speed by trailing such a line at all times; a very smart idea. We'll do that next time I think.

And then there was our *pièce de résistance*. In addition to the conventional man-overboard pole with a red and yellow code flag on top plus a separate strobe light designed to float on the surface, our man-overboard pole was a super-duper special model that had a strobe light built in at the *top* of the pole. This light was designed to go on automatically when the pole hit the water. The fact that the strobe light was several feet above the water instead of floating at the surface would give those on board a tremendous advantage in finding and keeping an eye on it in a stormy sea—certainly well worth the extra price. One small problem: the light somehow got broken before we left Hong Kong. We never were able to get the thing to work. . . .

CRUISING THE COAST OF LUZON

Once we made the agonizing decision to put into Manila and put behind us the horrible disappointment of an even further delay of our trip, all of us settled down to a life at sea. We performed our respective duties and proceeded with the business of driving a vessel through the water toward a given destination.

During those first few days in the South China Sea I had been so busy, first being seasick, then being a plumber, then a rigger, then a decision-maker, that I had done very little about navigation of the vessel—in the sense of knowing for sure right where we were.

Fortunately Jim, with help from Harlan and Jane, had been taking whatever sights we could get, primarily sun sights, and I had been checking them out. By constantly paying attention to our DR position, and by judicious use of the sights we had obtained, I felt reasonably comfortable about our position.

Except for Pratis Island, which by the grace of God we had managed to avoid, there had been no navigational dangers on our trip so far. True, there was always the chance that we might collide with one of the thousands of fishing boats in the area, or with a larger ship, or with one of the whales we had sighted. But the danger of hitting these movable objects was not related to whether we knew exactly where we happened to be on the face of the earth at the moment.

We sighted many vessels, primarily fishing boats or ships. Large trawlers from Japan, Korea, and Taiwan were setting out giant nets, which we were careful to avoid. If we couldn't avoid their nets we would stop our propeller while we slid over them.

We took our first showers, salt-water of course. We began having appetites again, and while we didn't serve gourmet

LUZON

C Bojeador
Aparri
AERO R Bn
San Fernando
C Bolinao
Lingayen
Lingayen Gulf
Subic Bay
Manila
AERO R Bn
Manila Bay
Batangas
Lubang I
C Calavite
MINDORO
Apo I
Semirara I
Busuanga
Culion I
Cuyo Is
Cuyo I
Dumaran I
P Princesa
Cagayan Is
Cavili I
Tubbataha Rfs
SULU SEA
gayan Sulu

Divilacan Bay
Palanan Pt
Diapitan Bay
C San Ildefonso
Baler Bay
Dumagas
Dingalan Bay
Polillo
Patnanongan I
Alabat I
Calaguia Is
San Miguel Bay
Catanduanes
Lagonoy Gulf
Benham Bank
Rep (1968)
Rep (1954)
C Engaño
C Espiritu Santo
Garnay Bay
Borongan
Calicoan I
Suluan
Dinagat I
Siargao I
Cauit
Lianga Bay
Bangai Pt
Boston

SAN BERNARDINO STR
MINDORO STR

Marinduque
Burias
Sibuyan I
Masbate
Capiz
PANAY
Iloilo
Guimaras
NEGROS
CEBU
BOHOL
Dumaguete
Siquijor
Camiguin I
SAMAR
LEYTE
Biliran I

Basilan I
MORO GULF
Zamboanga
BASILAN STR
Laparan I
SULU ARCHIPELAGO
Tawitawi Gp
SIBUTU

MINDANAO
Misamis
Cagayan
Polloc Hbr
Illana B
Cotabato
Davao
Davao Gulf
Kalingmomo Pt
Lebak
Tubalan Hd
Milbuk
Makar
Tinaca Pt
Sarangani Is
Marore
Kawio Is
Nenoesa Is
C San Augustin
Pujada Bay
Palmas I
Butuan

PHILIPPINES

AERO R Bn
Fuga I
Camiguin

Rep (1962)
Rep (1970)

meals, we certainly had civilized fare. Our menu on Saturday
18 May:

> *Breakfast:* Scrambled eggs with tarragon
> Bread with margarine and jam
> Coffee, tea, or milk
>
> *Lunch:* Leftover macaroni and cheese
> with ham
> Fruit salad
> Cold drinks and cookies
>
> *Dinner:* Beef stew
> Fresh tomatoes, onions, and
> more leftover macaroni and cheese
> Pudding with fresh bananas

Jane and Carol applied Vaseline to the remainder of our egg
supply; some eggs that had not been treated yet had already
mildewed and had to be disposed of. Some of the bread was
beginning to mold. The carrots and parsnips were going
soggy. The pineapple was getting overripe, and the lettuce was
beginning to rot from the core out. But the oranges, peppers,
yams, potatoes, and coconuts were all in good shape.

During this part of our trip, except for temporary periods of
high wind and seas, the weather was generally benign.

Back at Anthony Wong's I had been extremely happy with
our purchase of five beautiful blue inflated fenders—the nicest
fenders both in looks and function that I had ever worked with
in all my years at sea. When we set out from Hong Kong I
checked, double-checked, triple-checked that those fenders
were securely tied down, each to a single lifeline stanchion; but
lo and behold, during one of those high-wind and high-seas
sessions, a sudden squall of short duration but high intensity,
one of my precious Anthony Wong blue fenders somehow
worked loose and was lost overboard. No joy in Mudville, and
all that.

On Sunday 19 May I had the 2000-midnight watch. We were
passing through intermittent squalls, with heavy rain, thunder,
and lightning. The swells, which had been from the southeast,
had shifted around and were from the east and had increased,

but not enough to make us uncomfortable. We were flying all the sails we could get up, which at that point consisted of our only two working headsails and the mizzensail. Our main motive power was coming from the Ford Lehman. Suddenly, as I stood at the wheel in the aft cockpit, I was engulfed with a warm feeling up to my navel!

At first I didn't realize that it was actually seawater that was giving me this warm feeling. I had not been over the side since Bob and I had inspected the hull after encountering the straw mat just out Hong Kong Harbor a few days before; I was not aware of how warm the water was here in the South China Sea, at latitude 19° north. No particular harm was done by the freak large wave that had swept over our stern, but we did observe a fair amount of seawater leaking through the deck into the after cabin.

Our DR position showed us that we were too far away to pick up any lights on the coast of Luzon; yet one gets awfully anxious approaching a new shore. Here is Jane's log entry for the 0400-0800 watch on the morning of 20 May:

> Enroute as before in South China Sea. Sighted yellow light off port beam at approximately 0430. Seemed above horizon, and disappeared after 15 seconds. Appeared again for another few seconds. At 0500 the clouds dispersed a little, and we discovered our light to be the moon rising—it's just a sliver.

And the next morning, Jim wrote in the log:

> 0820: passed boat [that] appeared to be a Taiwanese fishing junk, with marker buoys laid across our track at intervals of 100 yards; changed course to 070° magnetic to flank the line of buoys, with our propeller in neutral. Resumed course, 160° magnetic at 0845. Calm water. Sunny, hot day, barometer rising. Ocean getting calmer. No wind. Observed two boats about three miles off port bow. Appeared to be commercial fishing boats. 1045: passed close to black marker buoy with flag; put gears in neutral, and eased on by.

And that afternoon, Jane's log:

> Turned off engine, and spent a fun 20 minutes swimming.

Swim call—South China Sea.

Water warm, but exhilarating. Kept good watch for sharks—
had rifle ready. Returned to our course toward Manila at 160°
magnetic. Sighted freighter on horizon. Freighter changed
course so that we crossed his bow. It was a Red Chinese ship
called: GUARGMING. Sighted a number of other vessels,
including what appeared to be a large U.S. Navy vessel which
the WW II skipper-expert was unable to identify, but which
contained the large number of 36 on its bow. Attempted to
contact No. 36 by radio and blinker light to no avail.

That evening on the 2000-midnight watch, I was awakened
by Carol, who was on watch, calling to me, "My God! We're
surrounded!"

I dashed up on deck, and sure enough, we *were* surrounded.
I could see fifty or maybe a hundred lights around us in all
directions. "Where the hell did all of those lights come from?
How come you didn't call me earlier?"

Carol said she didn't know. They just suddenly appeared. I
got out my trusty binoculars and carefully studied the many
lights. They were navigational lights, properly placed. The
vessels were not large, except there seemed to be a long
underbody . . .

"Jesus Christ! We're in the middle of a fleet of submarines! I
sure as hell hope they're ours. And that *they* know we're *theirs.*"

As if on signal the subs' blinker lights all started flashing. I
grabbed our own blinker light and started trying to get a
message through to the nearest sub: We are a British sailing
yacht, heading for Manila, not too sure of our latitude. Can
you give us a navigational fix? For a long time I thought that I
was getting through, but I finally admitted to myself, forlornly,
that we were being ignored. Apparently we were in the midst
of a naval maneuver in which there was both radio silence and
no inclination to deal with what I am sure appeared to them to
be simply local fisher-folk.

LETTERS OF CREDIT AND ALL THAT

These few words have nothing to do with the matter of
raising the money in the first place—that's another story—only

how to spend it. Seemingly the latter subject shouldn't be any problem, but it actually is.

I suppose the simplest and neatest way to handle finances on a long voyage is to carry cash, but this has too many drawbacks. The primary and obvious one is the lack of security and the attendant risk of losing all of said cash—and consequently being up the proverbial creek without a paddle.

Many people use travelers' checks, which certainly have a lot going for them, depending on where you plan to be. If you lose your travelers' checks, you may have a little difficulty getting replacements on Yap or Kwajelein. Also, on board a boat you always run the risk of losing not only the checks, but also the record of the checks.

Many people go the letter-of-credit route. This is a nice, sophisticated/metropolitan way to go. It works in population centers, but not in out-of-the way places.

Some world cruisers attempt to forecast where they will be on or by certain dates, and have mail containing checks or other forms of negotiable instruments forwarded to them in care of General Delivery, yacht clubs, or what have you. With the present unreliability of the world mail system, as well as the unexpected detours and delays in world cruising, this likewise does not seem too satisfactory.

The system we employed was pretty conventional, and it worked extremely well. We had the advantage, of course, of being recognized members of the business community associated with a recognized corporation and having (God knows why!) good personal credit. The simple method we used was to set up an account in the name of the corporation owning the boat with a recognized Hong Kong bank (this could have been any recognized bank, of course). We attempted to have word sent ahead of time from our primary bank to a bank at the next port of call; then we simply opened a bank account at the next port of call with a check on our Hong Kong bank and paid all local bills with checks drawn on the local bank.

It helps to have a friendly banker! Our friendly bankers Dick Tunnicluff and Pat Hoover of the Security Pacific National Bank in Los Angeles set up our original arrangements with Anthony Bill, chief credit officer of the Bank of

Canton in Hong Kong. After we established this original solid relationship with Anthony Bill at the Bank of Canton, everything else seemed to flow quite smoothly from that point on.

FIRST LANDFALL

We had been able to get some pretty good sun shots as we neared the Manila area, and we were reasonably confident of our position. On the midnight to 0400 watch on Tuesday 21 May I picked up a good radio beacon signal at 130° true, broadcasting signal RS; but I couldn't identify it. I thought it might be Rosario or Langely Point Aero Beacon near Cavite, Manila Bay. I picked up Subic Bay Beacon at 0305, but it was too weak to get a good bearing.

At 0700 we changed course to head more easterly, hoping to pick up the coast of Luzon, and at 0915 came that beautiful call: *"Land off the port bow!"*

We spent the whole day searching for landmarks or some sign of culture or civilization. We also tried to raise someone, anyone, on our two radios, transmitting on the two international frequencies 2182 on AM, and channel 16 on VHF. No response.

That afternoon we did spot something we could recognize: a large school of tuna.

Nighttime found us fairly close to shore, close enough to see many lights near what apparently was a fishing village. But none of the lights showed up on our charts, nor could we find any of the characteristics of the lights listed in our sailing directions. We were of course severely hampered by not having detailed charts of the Luzon coast. Had we had proper charts we would have had no problem identifying where we were.

We thought we'd seen everything when we cruised through the Chinese fishing fleets along the coast of China—no conventional navigational lights, only a single white light visible from all directions. But by comparison with the Filipinos, the Chinese were law-abiding mariners. We found that the vessels of the Philippine fishing fleet simply *didn't carry any lights at all!*

Besides being a little jumpy because of our Red Chinese pirate incident, we had also heard stories that the Philippine Islands were rife with pirates.

About 2000 hours the same evening that we had first sighted land, while Jane and Harlan were on watch, a Philippine powerboat seemed to be heading straight toward the *Dagny Taggart*. As the noise of the engine came closer and closer, suddenly we could hear the voices of those aboard, speaking in a language that we could not understand, sounding as if they were right on top of us. Jane was at the helm. Harlan had gone forward. Carol and I were in the sack in our cabin, with the hatch open immediately adjacent to the after cockpit steering station. We heard Harlan holler, "They're boarding us! They're boarding us!"

Carol said to me, "Get the rifle; I'll get the shotgun."

Well, hell, maybe we *were* being boarded. I guess that's what we had the rifle for. So I grabbed the rifle and put some shells in my pocket; I hated to load the thing and take the chance of an accidental firing. All this took only seconds, but by the time I was on deck it was reasonably apparent that we *were not* being boarded. I think what happened was that the poor fishermen, in the dark, hadn't seen our boat until they were right upon us, and one of the passengers was hollering to the pilot to make a sharp turn or else they would have made a sudden stop against the hull of the *Dagny Taggart*.

On the afternoon of the twenty-first we still had not picked up any positive navigational aids, nor had we identified any feature on shore.

By this time we had some good RDF bearings on the aerial beacon that I had picked up early that morning on a couple of Manila commercial radio stations. We had made several decent running fixes on these RDF bearings, which checked out reasonably well with our sun lines. Everything indicated that we were zeroing in on the entrance to Manila Bay. However, I had an uneasy feeling. I was not absolutely certain of the identification of that aerial beacon; we had no way of knowing just where the Manila commercial stations might have their broadcasting towers; and directional bearings on commercial radio stations are generally not very reliable, particularly since much high terrain, like mountains, lay between us and the

apparent direction of the towers. I studied our charts, such as they were, and recognized that if we were very much off from where we thought we were, especially if we were to the south of our plotted position, we could be sailing down toward Mindanao into some very dangerous waters with many reefs and small islands that doubtless would be unlighted.

In addition, as I scanned the coastline to the north with the binoculars, land that we had already passed, I spotted what seemed to be an island with the same general shape as Corregidor.

Faced with all this navigational uncertainty and the possibility, even though remote, of cruising into a dangerous area at night, we came about (over the moaning and groaning of the crew) and went back north to check out what I thought might be Corregidor and hopefully to pick up an identifiable navigational light.

Fortunately, the horizon cleared in the west while the sun was still high enough to give us some good sun shots and enabled us to plot a good line of position. Then we caught a good shot of Venus and one of the major stars at twilight. We were quite satisfied that we had a decent navigational fix based on the intersection of these three lines of position.

Harlan and I had taken sights simultaneously and had checked each other's work. In each case our respective lines of position were almost within yards one of the other.

We plotted this navigational fix on our large-area small-scale chart of the Philippine Islands, and it was reasonably close to our DR position. Feeling pretty good about all this, I decided we would head for the nearest major navigational light shown on the chart, which I figured to be Capone's Point about 33 miles to the south. At midnight we changed our course to 200° magnetic, which we calculated would take us past Capone's Point at a safe distance, but close enough to see the light. Not having picked up the light by 0400, we boldly changed course to 140° magnetic in order to come closer to shore to spot the light. And sure enough, at 0442 my log entry was as follows:

> Sighted Capone's Light with monocular bearing 110° magnetic; right on! Good running fix on Capone's Point at 0600. Changed our course to 130° heading for entrance point to Manila Bay.

Great feeling!

The next log entry, by Bob, wasn't so great, however:

Automatic pilot not working!

Yuk!

At sea, the whole world—everything that seems important, everything that matters—seems to be right there with you on your little vessel. One might think that on a long voyage a lot of time would be spent picking up news broadcasts to find out what is going on in the world capitals, or back home, or whatever. We didn't find that to be the case. Even though we had some good long-distance radio receivers on board, very seldom did any of us take the time to fiddle with the shortwave to pick up the Armed Service Radio, or the BBC, or radio Tokyo. Therefore, when we saw airplanes strafing and bombing an offshore island as we approached the entrance to Manila Bay, we had no way of telling whether the U.S. or Philippine Air Force was engaged in strafing/bombing practice, or whether we had landed in the middle of a Philippine revolution, or whether World War III had started without us.

As we came closer, it became clear that the island was uninhabited and that the bombing was practice. Real, but practice. I have seen my share of bombing runs, practice and otherwise, but no one else on board had ever seen such a sight in the flesh. The incident held everyone's attention for the next hour or so as we roared along at our speed of five knots toward the entrance to Manila Bay.

Shortly after noon, the wind picked up considerably; we raised our three operable sails and picked up speed. At 1445 hours we rounded Luzon Point, heading on a port tack at full speed toward the entrance to Manila Bay; and at 1600 hours, heading almost directly east, we entered the bay, taking Corregidor Island to starboard.

The crew, certainly including the skipper, felt a surge of emotion, a contact with history, as we sailed past the rock that had been the scene of historic resistance by U.S. troops against the Japanese in World War II.

The Japanese are probably the most tourist-oriented people in the world. There is today, in Manila, a thriving tourist business based on hauling visitors from Manila to Corregidor Island and back; 90 percent of these tourists are Japanese.

We certainly could say something for the entrance to Manila: it is doubtless the most obscure entrance to any major port in the world today! Almost no sign of life or civilization of any kind. Once inside the bay, one can see some buildings and an oil refinery on the port side. But it is still a long way to Manila—approximately forty miles. The bay is about thirty miles wide. Unless it is a clear day, which is rare in the Manila area, you can sail for miles and miles without sighting the shore. This we did. As we feared, by the time we reached the entrance to Manila Harbor it was pitch black. Not even a moon, dammit.

We had no choice but to stand off to size up the situation and to try to raise somebody by radio. In the meantime we turned off the engine to save fuel and sailed back and forth outside Manila Harbor awaiting the light of day.

I'LL TAKE MANILA

On the morning of 23 May, in the cold light of dawn, we were absolutely horror-stricken. As the light began to dispel the darkness we couldn't tell at first what it was we were seeing all around us, and what seemed to be all over Manila Bay. Whatever it was there were hundreds of them, perhaps thousands. As the light increased slightly we could see that we had been cruising for some time, perhaps all night, in and among swarms of small, unlighted Philippine fishing boats. How we ever missed running one down, I'll never know. Or maybe we did. With our steering station aft, our bow nine or ten feet high, and our vision impaired by sails, plus the fact that it was pitch black and squalling—boy! Obviously the fishermen were just good at keeping out of our way.

We approached the harbor entrance under power, flying the yellow international flag for quarantine. We spotted and contacted the pilot boat, which directed us to stand by at the harbor breakwater entrance until a public health doctor, a customs official, and an immigration official boarded us. All the Philippine officials were courteous, cooperative, and efficient. They were not very experienced, however, in handling the entry into Philippine waters of a boat as small as ours. The immigration official referred several times to having spotted our yellow handkerchief, meaning our quarantine flag, which was somewhat smaller than the flags to which he was accustomed.

As I thought about it, I realized that this was the first time I had made a real entry into an international port as skipper of my own boat. Although the officials laughed at our flag, they basically treated us as they would any other vessel entering the port, referring to me as captain, asking permission to come aboard and permission to leave. I even think I got a salute or two.

When we inquired about our inability to raise anyone by radio as we approached Manila, either on the conventional channels or on the international distress frequencies, they answered, "Oh, but yesterday was a national holiday!"

One never should be so presumptuous in the Philippines as to be in distress on a national holiday!

We were directed to the Manila Yacht Club anchorage, where we tied up to a fore-and-aft mooring buoy in the early afternoon. I went ashore to line up our necessary repair operations. I also had to go to the customs officials to get clearance for our entry.

When I had posted the daily duty assignments for the day before we expected to enter Manila Bay, I had also posted a notice to the effect that the *Dagny Taggart* might well be boarded by all or some of the following: military authorities, port authorities, immigration, customs, yacht club personnel, and friends. Accordingly, I asked that all hands turn to for a general cleanup and put the boat in top condition for port. I allocated responsibilities to each crewmember.

In the afternoon of that same day, we held a crew meeting during which I explained that running this vessel and feeding the crew was costing me around US$150 per day and that the delays so far had run me about US$20,000 over my estimates. Further expenses had been or would be incurred in flying our new skipper and his wife to Ponape and repairing or replacing damaged or lost equipment.

Because of the delays to date, I deemed it essential that we get south to around 10° latitude right away. This was going to mean more fuel, and slower going, and possibly obtaining a professional skipper before we got to Ponape. I felt the boat was in very poor shape. The painted surfaces were dirty; the teak was cracking; we had many leaks. Although Jane's original stowage plan was quite good, most of us were not following it, and stowage of the items that needed to be used frequently was not satisfactory.

"I would like to generate a new spirit, a spirit of Manila, if you will. We have now made our first landfall. Let's make this a new era. We have a new watch schedule which I think will prove to be superior. I want the Officer of the Deck to be on the prowl at all times, checking, looking, tightening, adjusting, looking after his or her flock. We now have three people completely off watch daily. I have taken myself off all watches except the navigation watch, in order to be a better supervisor or captain, and also to get some standardization into our navigation. I hope this helps us."

I couldn't believe it when I put together, with the crew's help, our worklist for Manila. It was just as though we were back at Anthony Wong's again! And our worklist for ourselves, the crew, was even more impressive, bigger than when we left Hong Kong!

My first step on shore was to identify myself and establish a relationship with the Manila Yacht Club. We were readily accepted as a visiting yacht from the California Yacht Club, with all privileges of the Manila Club extended to us. The privileges included a mooring, dining room and bar facilities, and (oh glory!) the shower facilities. In addition, and not common among yacht clubs, the Manila Yacht Club had its own repair facilities. This was something of a mixed blessing. Since as a visiting yacht we were enjoying the hospitality of the club, we felt we were locked-in customers. If a particular service was available through the club, it was a little embarrassing to go elsewhere. It worked out pretty well, however. Felix, who was in charge of the club's repair facilities, was extremely cooperative. The club itself maintained a limited staff of people and facilities for repair work; in most cases, I would explain to Felix what I wanted, and he would contact the proper person to come down to the boat.

Unfortunately, we spent most of our time at a mooring,

Dagny Taggart *rests before her Pacific crossing—Manila Yacht Club harbor.*

rather than dockside. This certainly slowed things up considerably. It also raised problems. While it was a little more trouble
for crewmembers to get off the boat, they sure as hell found a
way; and once off the boat, they would disappear for many
hours, and in a couple of cases, for days.

We found a schism developing in Manila. Jane and Carol
and I felt as if we were bearing the lion's share of the work to
be done; that only we had a sense of purpose regarding the
mission of the voyage. The others (Harlan, Jim, Chuck, and
Randy) thought that we were expecting too much of them and
that we all should relax and have a little fun. Poor Bob was
swing man; he liked his fun as much as anybody, but he also
had a lot of respect for his old man, and had more of a sense of
the purpose of the trip. Not by a long shot, however, did the
four fellows or Bob goof off all the time we were in Manila; far
from it. We assigned each crewmember a pretty tough list of
things to get done, and with a few exceptions these things did
get done.

After getting duly checked in with the club, my next move
was to call Web Rice, who was in charge of our company's
operations in Manila. I had always known Web as a pretty
imperturbable guy; but when I reached him on the phone and
announced who and where I was, and all he said was that he
had been expecting me, I was stunned! It seems that Web had
had a dream!

When we talked this over later, I was entirely convinced that
Web was in no way pulling my leg; he actually *had* had a dream
that we and the *Dagny Taggart* would be diverted to Manila. I
wished to hell I'd had him with me when I bought those charts!

That evening Carol and Jane and I were guests in the lovely
home of Jan and Web Rice. Wonderful to be in a private home
again, eating a family meal. Most enjoyable.

Web was a tremendous help to us in cashing checks,
communicating with Los Angeles, helping us locate parts and
service people.

Some time in the early morning hours of the next day,
Friday 24 May, Carol and I were awakened by the bell-like
tones of giggling young females coming from the afterdeck
outside the hatch to our cabin. With a little listening—it wasn't
eavesdropping; there was no way to avoid it—we detected the

voices of Bob, Chuck, Randy, and Jim, our four young bucks. With a little looking, by sticking my head and shoulders up and out of our hatch, I detected four reasonably attractive, apparently very young, Filipinas.

I wasn't sure exactly how I felt about this. I guessed that it was not really appropriate for me to try to dictate morals to young men in their twenties; I had no way of knowing how long they had been there or what they had been doing, although there were some fairly easy conclusions to which to jump. Carol made it clear that she didn't give a damn about their morals, but she sure as hell resented having her sleep interrupted. Everything considered, this appeared to be a pretty logical approach. I asked the boys to take the girls ashore, which they did. Later that day, Jane, whose sleep had apparently been interrupted considerably more than Carol's and mine, expressed herself very strongly with the four bucks, to the general tune that she was not happy about their turning the boat into a whorehouse. The boys staunchly defended the status of the Filipinas; I don't think Jane was ever convinced.

Carol made the log entry for our first full day in Manila:

General workday. Ramon, contractor for leak-finding and repair, on board all day. Anuncio, splicing and rigging, worked on mainsail track, and found bearings defective in roller furling mechanism. Randy remounted VHF, and made new flagpole. Harlan installed runner for chart storage in pilot house overhead. Mizzen stays'l rip repaired. Philippine flag acquired. Necessary charts and harbor items were purchased. Taylor on company business during afternoon and evening. All eight aboard at dinner.

I was able to relieve a few of my guilt feelings about being gone from the company for so long. By a happy coincidence, some matters were taking place in our Philippine operations that called for my services as a lawyer and that related to a company personnel matter in which I was involved because I had helped set up the Philippine operation several years before.

On Saturday 25 May we moved from our offshore mooring to the Manila Yacht Club pier, tying stern-to, Mediterranean style. We had a lot of confidence in Ramon, the leak fixer, and he assured us that he was doing very well, although he was certainly amazed at the poor quality of the hoses, the fittings, and their installation.

While tied stern-to at the Manila Yacht Club pier, Bob was doing his personal laundry on the foredeck. When he finished, rather than dumping the bucket of soapy water over the side, which would have been okay, he sluiced it down the deck, which normally would also have been okay. However, Bob didn't realize that Ramon was amidships working on a leak at the port diesel fuel cap, and had the cap off. The soapy water raced along the deck to reach a scupper, but unfortunately the first place to which gravity pulled it was down the open diesel fuel cap. We were never sure how much water got in the fuel that day, but we knew it had to be a significant amount.

We had no way of knowing how much trouble that little accident was to cause us—and not in the manner that one would initially suspect.

TROUBLE RIGHT HERE IN RIVER CITY

In forming the crew initially I had violated one of my precepts. Because of the exigencies of the situation, I had signed Randy on without ever having known him. Randy and Bob had been friends at the University of Oregon. They had sailed together, although only on small boats. Through Bob, Randy heard about our planned trip and had made a strong pitch to Bob that he would like to join us. Bob felt that Randy was a good guy, that he had electronic and electrical skills. Although not much on which to judge a person, the fact that Randy was off working in Alaska at the time Bob proposed him as a crewmember at least indicated to me that Randy was not afraid of trying new things.

The first time Randy passed across my mental radar screen as an individual, it had been as an individual with a problem. That was when I learned that John Smith wouldn't allow Randy to sail with him from Keelung to Hong Kong. In the miserably short time that I had had to spend with Smith in Hong Kong, the Randy episode was too far down my list of priorities to delve into; and in any event, there was probably little to be gained by doing so.

During the outfitting and shakedown in Hong Kong, I had found Randy to be very likable. He was a dark-haired, handsome young man. The fact that he tended to be very serious was of no concern to me then. The fact that he would not perform any task or job until he fully understood the exact reason why the task had to be performed appealed to the logical side of me, although it was sometimes a pain in the butt from a practical standpoint.

If there was a necessary job that Randy *wanted* to do, he would pitch in at any hour for all hours necessary. If, on the other hand, Randy was asked to do something that wasn't particularly appealing to him, there always seemed to be some other task that was more important for the good of the boat, or for the good of the nation, or something. Several times in Hong Kong I found that Randy had refused or neglected to perform a particular task solely because he did not agree with my decision to make the move or to install the particular equipment at the place I had designated. I tried—not very successfully, I'm afraid—to work with Randy in all of these matters, to explain the basis of my decision and to make him realize that in the nature of things someone had to make the final decisions, and in this particular infrastructure *I* was that someone.

Under the arrangement that I had set up for the leg of the voyage between Hong Kong and Manila, it worked out that Randy and I stood watches together fairly frequently. When it seemed to me that he was a little too casual on watch, not taking his duties seriously enough, I attempted to explain to him the theory behind watch-standing, the reason for keeping an alert lookout at all times, telling him the importance of maintaining discipline and order on a boat at sea.

Randy was intelligent, receptive, and generally responsive in our discussions. On the other hand, late in the game, I found him one morning lying across the transom seat reading a book while he was the only one on watch. Another time when we were on watch together, I asked Randy to go forward to keep a sharp lookout; he replied that he could not because he did not have his contact lenses on. That was the first time I knew he wore contacts—which is certainly no reason for disqualifying him as a member of the crew, but a person with poor eyesight is certainly disqualified from standing watches unless he is wearing corrective lenses. It turned out that Randy didn't even own a pair of glasses; he depended entirely on his contact lenses, and when they were uncomfortable, he simply did not wear them.

Except for Jane, no crewmember was exactly an eager beaver when it came to cleanup duty or the various other tasks to which we were all assigned. Randy's name easily led (or bottomed) all the lists when it came to cook-helper and various cleaner-upper duties.

Carol and Jane had both reported to me, independently, that Randy had been rifling the stores for between-meal snacks. This was pretty serious. Although rifling stores might not seem like a heinous crime, it is absolutely essential on a boat at sea to maintain the integrity of the provisions. If any person can enter a food storage area at any time and take whatever is there, it completely louses up menu planning, ordering food at the next port, and all attempts to keep tabs on the food supply.

When we had sighted the practice bombing runs as we approached the entrance to Manila Bay—even though this had occurred during the time that we had designated for special cleaning of the boat before entering Manila—I set aside an hour for the crew to enjoy the rare sight of witnessing the strafing and bombing. However, after an hour of watching the festivities, the crew had voluntarily returned to their assigned tasks—all except Randy. If we were going to accomplish our task, I felt that it was important for everyone to pitch in, as much for the spirit of the thing as for what might be lost by one person's not doing his job. I asked, perhaps ordered, Randy to get on with his assigned tasks. I respected his just-a-minute-I've-never-seen-this-before; I-sure-find-it-interesting. But when the just-a-minute turned into another twenty minutes, I said, "Randy, it's not fair for you to stand here without doing anything while everyone else in the crew is turning to. I insist that you get with it."

Even then, it was another five minutes before Randy moseyed on down to where he was supposed to be working, and there was a noted lack of enthusiasm, a *determined* lack of enthusiasm, in his application to the job at hand.

The second day in Manila, Friday, neither Randy nor Chuck was anywhere to be found. I was told that they had felt they had the right to see some of the Philippines and had simply taken off for two days to be tourists.

On Sunday Carol and Jane really laid it on me; Carol went so far as to say that unless Randy left, she would leave. Jane didn't go that far, but she too was most unhappy. It wasn't just Randy, as Carol and Jane saw it, but his conduct was the focus of our problems. They reviewed the matter: their emphasis was Randy's lack of discipline, his negative, even surly attitude, and his unwillingness to carry out his responsibilities. They felt that all these things were pulling down the morale and performance of the rest of the crew. The others were thinking, "Why should I knock myself out if Randy isn't pulling his oar?"

I was by no means happy with Randy. On the other hand— good God—what a blow to kick somebody off the crew in the Philippines! It seemed to me that we at least owed it to Randy to give him a firm warning, with the understanding that he was on probation for the next leg and that if he did not shape up and do what was required of him he would be dumped in the next port.

I asked Randy to come into the yacht club with me, and we had our serious talk. This type of presentation is always difficult: you want to let the individual know that you are serious, that if things don't take a turn for the better you will have to disrupt the relationship. On the other hand, you don't want to be so tough that you damage the relationship for good.

Again, typical of such a confrontation, Randy made it hard on me by insisting that I tell him just exactly what the problems were. And then of course when I proceeded to tell him what the problems were, he proceeded to defend himself in each matter.

However, I did get his absolute assurance that he would do everything possible to remedy the deficiencies of which he believed I had accused him.

I relayed this back to Jane and Carol.

Jane's diary entry for Saturday had included the following:

Things are coming to a head, I believe, as far as crew togetherness is concerned, or rather crew untogetherness— don't know how it's going to turn out—may find myself going back to Los Angeles by an alternate route.

On Sunday:

> Things with the crew are not good; and we do not know how to handle it, really. I am going to see how things go until we get to Ponape—if no improvement in crew compatibility and to- getherness, I think it will be in my best interests to fly back to the U.S., and then after sorting my things out, back to England for a while. I really hope things work out all right, as I want to see this thing through, yet not at the cost of my happiness or my life.

THE AUTOPILOT

If you ask a long-distance cruising sailor who has made a series of ocean passages which single item of equipment on board he would hesitate the longest to give up, the automatic pilot would probably be close to the top of the list. The autopilot brings freedom from what has so aptly been called the Tyranny of the Helm. There are many types and variations of autopilot: one group is operated by an independent power source, usually a battery, and the other by the wind. Realizing the importance of this item, I had chosen what I deemed to be the best in the field: a Wood-Freeman electrically operated autopilot. We had had no problems with it until the last few days of our trip down the coast of Luzon.

I had a tough time finding a company or person in Manila who was willing and qualified to work on our autopilot. I finally found a company that seemed to have ability along these lines, and their two representatives, Pete and Jack, came to our boat on Monday morning. At their request, and also because I wanted to learn as much about the autopilot as I could, I worked closely with them. By two or three o'clock that afternoon, Pete and Jack thought that they had found and corrected the problem, but a short and most disappointing shakedown cruise in Manila Bay showed us that they were wrong.

We had our plans firmly set for departure from Manila at midnight that same night. I felt that everything else was pretty well in order.

Damn! Now I had to make *another* tough decision. With eight able-bodied people on a fifty-foot sailboat, we can, and will if necessary, sail without an autopilot. But with our crew morale as poor as it is already, I hate to strain it further by always having to have somebody at the helm. It's not worth a long delay, but we *will* take one more crack at it. If we can't get it fixed tomorrow, Tuesday, we'll sail without it.

On Tuesday morning, Pete and Jack, God bless them, were aboard at an early hour and went over the entire autopilot unit with a fine-tooth comb. An autopilot is a complex mechanism. A sensing compass sends messages to an electronic unit, which interprets the messages to determine which way the wheel should be turned to maintain a preset course. The electronic unit then directs a drive unit to turn the wheel, which turns the rudder in the proper direction. It is necessary to locate the sensing compass some distance from the rest of the unit so it will not be affected by the metal or the electronic mechanism, so a long, flexible shaft runs between the compass section and the electronic/drive unit section.

Early Tuesday afternoon, maybe by blind luck, we finally found the problem: an almost undetectable break in a small spiral spring within the flexible shaft which had to be in compression at the point where the shaft was joined to the electronic unit. It was tough to find, because the defect was a defect only when the shaft was coupled to the electronic unit. Anyhow, we found it; now what do we do about it? There was no Wood-Freeman representative in Manila; otherwise I'm sure our problems would have been solved long ago. Pete and Jack were good technicians, but they had no special parts for the mechanism.

Finally, Pete (I think it was) said, "Haven't you got any kind of supply of small springs on this boat?"

I brought out my supply of small springs, but none of them filled the bill.

At last, the electric lightbulb came on! I pulled out my

cheapie ballpoint pen, unscrewed it, and handed Pete the small spring that holds the ballpoint down.

And it worked! At 1530 hours we got the hell out of there!

GETTING THE HELL OUT OF MANILA

You would have thought we were an ocean liner with a thousand passengers on board, all of them with radiation poisioning, judging from the paperwork necessary to get out of Manila.

We mailed the harbormaster in Ponape a sail plan, giving a description of our vessel, its power, its equipment, and our ETA in Ponape as between 22 and 30 June. We sent copies to the harbormasters at Hong Kong and Manila, so that they could close their plans on us, and to the Philippine Coast Guard, the office of the Trust Territory, the harbormaster in Guam, and of course to trusty Joanne in Los Angeles. Before leaving, we obtained a written clearance from the commandant of the Philippine Coast Guard and from the Bureau of Customs of the Department of Finance of the Republic of the Philippines.

We checked out with all of our friends and helpers in Manila, particularly Jan and Web Rice, who had been so very helpful and friendly. Jan had a going-away gift for us, which proved to be practically invaluable: an electric toaster.

We sent a telex to Joanne, to be sent by Web Rice upon our departure. It outlined our revised sail plan and ended:

PLEASE ASK BILL DRUITT TO ORDER AND TO AIR SHIP TO PONAPE CARE OF HARBORMASTER ONE COMPLETE STANDARD SIX-FOOT FLEXIBLE SHAFT AND FITTINGS FOR MODEL 420 WOOD-FREEMAN 12-VOLT AUTOPILOT. THIS IS SHAFT THAT RUNS FROM COMPASS UNIT. WE HAVE SHAFT REPAIRED TEMPORARILY USING SPRING FROM U.S. BALLPOINT PEN BUT YOU KNOW HOW AMERICANS MAKE BALLPOINT PENS THESE DAYS.

Our original plans had been to leave Manila at midnight so we could navigate the somewhat tricky approaches to the Verde Island passage south of Corregidor during daylight hours, when we could see the various navigational dangers we would have to avoid. But with a little of the damn-the-torpedoes attitude, we decided that it was more important to get going ASAP. We had acquired excellent charts and navigational information from the Philippine Hydrographic Service; it appeared that by navigating carefully (with good charts for a refreshing change) and by keeping an alert lookout we could miss the various rocks and reefs in the Verde Island passage.

The long forty-mile run from Manila Harbor to Corregidor was relatively uneventful. We had a reasonably clear night, although with no moon; but just as we hit the Corregidor Passage all hell broke loose. One of those great tropical squalls hit us with a bang and a vengeance. Harlan was at the wheel; I was on watch with Harlan, but had ducked down to make some navigational calculations. I could feel the whole boat shudder as the squall hit—almost as if we had collided with something. In a sense, we *had* collided—with a wall of water. My first thought was selfish: Gee, I'm glad I'm not up there (although with that great awning from Anthony Wong, we had pretty good protection from the rain at the steering station). Harlan hollered something—something that we couldn't make out because of the howling of the wind and the pounding of the rain—but from the decibel level, it was a pretty sure thing he was doing more than just passing the time of day.

Sure enough, he was saying: "I'm turning around!"

This didn't seem to be the best step in the world toward getting our Mission Impossible accomplished. But since Harlan couldn't see more than about thirty inches in front of his face, he elected to head back toward Manila until the fury of the storm subsided. It lasted about thirty minutes, after which we came about and once more headed for the entrance (the exit really) of Manila Bay.

On Tuesday 28 May, about one mile west of Corregidor, at 2100 hours and well out of Manila Bay, we hung a sharp left and headed south for our next signpost: La Monja Light.

PHILIPPINE ROULETTE

While the Philippines were a territory of the United States, the U.S. Corps of Engineers and the U.S. Navy Hydrographic Office did a fantastically good job of mapping the Philippine land area and charting the waters. The Philippines consist of some seven thousand islands, with a lot of water in between, so this was no mean task. In addition, the United States installed an excellent system of navigational aids—lights, markers, buoys, and ranges.

After Philippine independence, the maps and charts had been well kept up as far as we could tell—or perhaps they were still current because there had been few physical changes.

But the navigational aids and lights were another story!

We developed a term for approaching the location of a charted Philippine light at night: Philippine roulette. There was a good chance that the light might be there; but then again . . .

Corregidor Light was flashing brightly, thank God; we watched it fade astern for several hours as we sailed in a southerly direction seeking the Verde Island passage. Our first navigational checkpoint was La Monja Light, shown on the chart as a flashing red light on a small island off the coast of Luzon, visible for eight miles. Our calculations showed that we were a lot closer to it than eight miles, but we had not picked it up yet. There was no moon; the sky was overcast; but as far as we could tell the atmosphere at the surface was reasonably clear.

I was getting nervous. Our calculations showed that we should have reached the light by now. I went forward to maintain a lookout. "Good God! Right full rudder! La Monja dead ahead, fifty yards!"

My eyes aren't really that good—I had just been able to make out part of the black of the night that was a little blacker than the rest; and sure enough, as we passed the island we could make out its silhouette—even the silhouette of the defunct alleged lighthouse! Fortunately, La Monja Island was the tip of a mountain peak, with deep water right in close to its shore.

The Philippine Island passage was like another world. A good world. The area covered by water was so big that at times we would be out of sight of land, although seldom for long. Despite the constant danger of a miscalculation in an area that was new to all of us, we found the piloting, or coastal navigation, refreshingly simple and definitive after struggling with the wonders of celestial navigation on our first leg. It was a challenge, but we took great satisfaction in picking up literally all of our navigational targets right on—whether their lights were burning or not.

On the morning watch on Wednesday 29 May a loud knocking developed in the Perkins diesel engine while we were operating it to power the generator for cooking and battery charging. We secured the engine, hoping that the knocking would go away.

The islands were lush and verdant. Most of us, certainly I, wished that we could have stopped and explored the ones that looked to be the most attractive. We saw few people or signs of life on shore, but a considerable amount of water traffic kept us on the alert and made life interesting. It consisted primarily of fishing boats, but there were also larger vessels, mostly what appeared to be interisland freighters. Because the Philippines are an island nation it is obvious that the primary means of transportation—and communication too, for that matter—was by water.

We were subjected to frequent rain squalls, some quite severe, with winds up to thirty or forty knots. But they never lasted very long. We had reasonably good winds for sailing, although in the what-else-is-new department, the winds usually were from the wrong direction. In making a long passage on a sailboat, myriad close-call decisions must be made regarding course and whether to power, to sail, or to power-sail. You may be able to go like a bomb under sail, but the closest you can come to your desired course may be 45° away from the direction in which you want to go. This means you have to consider your fuel supply, the navigational hazards you might encounter on the course that is fastest but not quite right, and the time or time pressure involved. Our most frequent decision was to opt for the most direct route, even though it meant using more of our precious fuel. Often these decisions were mighty close, mighty tough, and mighty agonizing.

On Wednesday night I sacked in early, about 2100 hours, in preparation for the 0400 navigational watch the next morning. We were power-sailing in the Sibuyan Sea, expecting to pick up Tres Reyes Light between 2130 and 2145. Shortly after dozing off I felt an increase in the speed of the Ford Lehman, and in spurts between dozes I felt and heard a succession of increases in rpm's until it sounded and felt as if we were at flank speed. At the same time the port heel of the boat was increasing more and more.

Chuck and Randy, who were on watch, had not called me. Nevertheless, with the boat vibrating at flank speed and heeling as if in an all-out ocean race, I thought I'd perhaps better meander topside to see what was up.

Unfortunately I didn't have my magic eye movie camera handy, for it was really a sight: Chuck at the wheel in yellow slicker and hat looking fully the part of the ancient mariner; Randy forward, peering through the driving rain and shouting distances back to Chuck. We had picked up Tres Reyes Light right-on at 2145 hours and had changed course to steer toward it as per our navigational plan. As we approached the light, planning to take it fairly close on our port side, then to turn to the left after passing the light, a combination of a vicious current and the ubiquitous and fierce Philippine squall had driven the *Dagny Taggart* down down down on the point guarded by Tres Reyes Light. Chuck at the con had increased the speed of the engine and changed the boat's heading more and more to starboard to try to offset what seemed to be the firm determination of the weather conditions to drive us on the rocks.

There wasn't much that I could think of to add to the steps that Chuck and Randy had already taken. I prayed that nothing would happen to the engine, for as close as we were to that lee shore, in the driving wind and onshore current we wouldn't have stood a chance of getting off it without power. And even with power it was no cinch. Finally, every blade of fiberglass straining, we pulled forward of the light and started to turn to port, home free, when *whamo*, there were *the* Three Kings: three unlighted, scraggy rocks or small islands lying

about 500 yards offshore from the lighthouse. Back to the same old exercise of fighting the wheel, wind, current, praying for no hiccup in the Lehman Ford diesel.

Finally, at about 0100 hours, we cleared the last of the Three Kings and I dived below to get in three hours' sack time before my 0400 watch.

TO GIMBAL OR NOT TO GIMBAL

I suppose if you were to read a hundred or so books by experts on outfitting a large sailboat for world cruising, you'd get roughly fifty who would be very strong for gimbaling your stove and dining table; and the other fifty would be just as strong against gimbaling.

I would be somewhere to the left of center.

It certainly is great to have your stove or table remain horizontal when your boat is well heeled over (which is what gimbaling does)—particularly on a long cruise when you may remain on the same tack for a couple of weeks at a time. On the surface of things, it would seem that all the points are in favor of gimbaling. Who wants to try to cook or keep the dishes on the table at a 30 degree angle? Worse yet, to try to pick up the mess when the dishes fall all over the cabin sole.

The two points on the other side, against gimbaling, are: (1) small point—gimbaling takes more room and makes a more complicated installation; and (2) big point—I've always felt that there was a hidden danger in gimbaling; everything goes along smoothly and all feels secure, until that fatal time when there is a lurch, someone loses his or her balance, and grabs or leans on one side of the gimbaled stove or table; and there go the two quarts of water boiling for the spaghetti all over somebody's face!

My prejudices, obviously, were against gimbaling. So we didn't. We partially handled the difficulty of cooking while heeled by having Anthony Wong manufacture what amounted to a beautiful stainless steel template that fitted over the stove, which was designed to take each of the different sizes of the Corning special cookware. And we partially solved the table problem by purchasing from Yachting Tableware of Wilmington, Delaware, a set of dinnerware and a set of insulated mugs, each piece of which had a special circle of neoprene embedded in its base in such a way that it would cling beautifully to our teak tabletop at angles of up to 25 or 30 degrees. In fact, the food would slide off the plates long before the plates would slide off the table.

FIRST SHARK

Once around the dreaded Tres Reyes, we had the wind strong on our port quarter and were able to make good time under full sail. Navigation was exhilarating! It was as if we were cadets at the academy, some academy, out practicing. On my 0400 watch on 30 May, I obtained bearings on four different tangents on four different islands, plotted them, and all four lines crossed on an *exact dot!* I felt good about our steering compass and about our lovely monocular bearing compass. We also had the luxury of being able to change our course slightly from time to time in order better to see an island or a navigational aid on which to get a fix.

The final passage through the San Bernardino Strait appeared, from the charts and the Philippine sailing directions, to be tricky. If we continued our present pace, we would find ourselves traversing the strait in darkness. Partly to avoid that, partly for a good bottom cleaning (which we did not do in Manila because of the condition of the water in the harbor), and more importantly for the purpose of letting all of us relax for a few hours and smell the roses, we pored over the charts and sailing directions for some appropriate spot where we could anchor for the night and make the San Bernardino Strait passage the next morning. We found a place called Port Barrera that looked as if it would meet our needs very nicely.

Bob's log entry on the noon to 1600 watch on that day was:

Sighted Mt. Engano (Burias Island) and Cape Agugar for port passage to Masabate Pass; changed course at 1250 hours from 110° to 125° in order to get better fix and course direction to

Bugui Point. Passed Bugui Point at 1350 hours, and into Masabate Pass. Weather clear with nice breeze. Good easy navigational fixes. On course for Port Barrera after changing course from 125° to 133°.

Entering *any* harbor with a thirty-ton boat is a delicate operation. No matter how many times a conscientious navigator has entered a harbor, he or she will be concerned about reefs or shoaling, local traffic, bottom holding conditions, tide and current, weather, possible danger from sea or shore animal or vegetable life, the friendliness of the natives, and so on ad nauseum.

Entering a *new* harbor for the first time, all the usual concerns are doubled, tripled, quadrupled, you name it.

Our timing was great; we had planned to anchor before we lost daylight. This we did; but we also had enough short Philippine twilight so that the light on Colorado Point marking the entrance to Port Barrera was plainly visible against the darkening sky.

Our charts, as well as Harlan's good heaving of the lead line, showed one small difficulty in anchoring in the shelter of Colorado Point: the water was extremely deep right up to a narrow shelf extending not more than thirty or fifty yards from shore. Fortunately, for a change, the conditions for anchoring were beautiful: we had plenty of light but not too much; the wind had died down to almost nothing; we had good charts; the anchor winch and windlass worked perfectly. So, about thirty yards from an absolutely gorgeous beach, we dropped the trusty starboard anchor, followed by 100 feet of Swedish anchor chain. I backed her down and felt the anchor dig in, just like in the book.

I left Carol at the con with the engine turning over easily while I donned mask and fins and dove over the side to check the anchor position and its bite in the bottom. Perfecto!

Surreptitiously, a local boat had appeared while we were anchoring; and Harlan was negotiating from the aft cockpit with a Filipino fisherman for the purchase of a large fish of some description. In spite of the language barrier a trade was soon struck, and we had a handsome tuna for our dinner.

All hands over the side!

Jane stayed on board to clean the fish. Commendable. Everyone else went over the side with putty knives, sandpaper, scrapers, and what-have-you. All pitched in for a short time, but then some local residents appeared on the beach. All but Chuck and Carol and me headed for the beach. Chuck didn't resist much longer, and Carol soon pooped and climbed back on board.

Where the hell is my authority with this crew? How could all my buddies desert me like this? What am I doing wrong? I thought that stopping here for breath-catching purposes would be healthful for our morale, and for my command if you will. But here I am left to clean this crummy hull by myself.

Suddenly my heart was gladdened. Obviously the guys had seen the error of their ways; they were coming back to assist me! In fact, never had I seen any of them swim so well . . . or so fast. They were almost *walking* on the water! *Running* on it!

Problem was, when they got to the boat they practically leapt from the surface of the water to the deck of the *Dagny Taggart* —which wasn't easy. After they were all on deck they passed the word to me: They had had a nice chat with the various locals on the beach, on the where-are-you-guys-from level, until one of the Filipinos commented, "You Americans are very very brave to swim ashore here. We Filipinos never swim here; these waters are the favorite hunting grounds for thousands of local sharks."

Well, the hell with the sharks. If they haven't gotten to me by now, let them fend for themselves; we've got to have a clean bottom to make Ponape with the amount of fuel we have left.

So I finished cleaning *Dagny*'s bottom.

ENTRANCE TO THE MIGHTY PACIFIC

The next morning the anchor winch and everything else worked perfectly again for a gloriously uneventful departure from Port Barrera at 0430 hours. Well, it was almost uneventful: the roller-furling jib, which we had had refurbished and repaired in Manila, unfurled itself as we were raising the

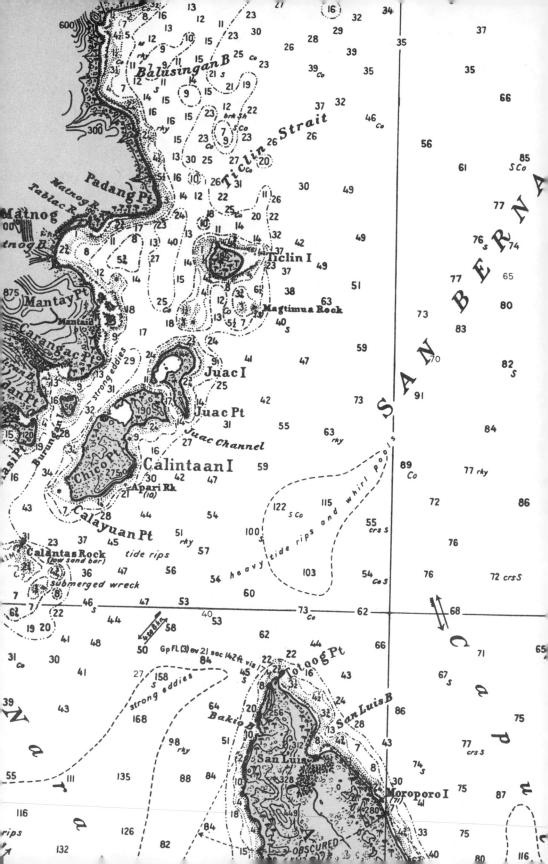

anchor. The light morning breeze caught the jib and swung us in close, dangerously close, to the beach, which had been too close for much relaxing all night anyhow.

I have a penchant for getting away from an anchorage without awakening those who are off watch and sleeping. The roller-furling jib episode almost loused up this penchant, but I think I made it without awakening Carol. Anyhow, everything looked pretty good as we pulled out of our ten-hour tropical paradise, still not having seen shark number one!

At 0730 we changed course to 115° magnetic to head for the channel between Calantas Rock and Capril Island, estimated at 1330. We passed a large workship of some sort anchored off San Miguel Island at 0735 hours and raised mizzen, main, and forestaysail at 0800. We were approaching San Bernardino Strait.

After I came off watch, I went up to the bow pulpit to take a realistic assessment of the overall situation. There was something obviously seriously wrong with the Perkins diesel engine that powered the Kohler generator. We could start it all right, but there was a vicious pounding as if a rod had been thrown.

Maybe it was just water in the diesel fuel that we took on board in Manila. Only a temporary situation that would work itself out?

According to our measurements, which weren't all that reliable, we had used about a quarter of our fuel supply, but had covered only 10 percent of the distance from Manila to Ponape. And the damn diesel fuel tanks resumed their leaky ways as the *Dagny Taggart* took the wind on her bow sailing out the San Bernardino Strait.

No doubt about it; as distasteful as it was for me to prolong the journey, we had better head for the nearest port rather than face 3,000 miles (more or less) to Ponape.

The nearest port was either Palau or Yap. A study of the sailing directions suggested to me that the repair facilities that might be available in either port were pretty limited, but that Yap had a slight edge in this department. Yap was less out of the way than Palau, and not too much out of the way on our route to Ponape.

So as we left the friendly and lovely Philippines, I announced to the crew that our next destination would be the garden Island of Yap.

Most of the crew had never heard of it.

MYSTIQUE OF THE MIZZEN STAYSAIL

Your average sail isn't all that high in the air, but ordinarily you can walk under or at least duck under your main and your mizzen. And your headsails are sort of way up there and off to one side. Your mizzen staysail, on the other hand, is *right there* —right down on the deck where you have to walk around it or through it or crawl over it. What difference this makes in my personal feeling about a mizzen staysail I can't tell you. Perhaps, being so close, it becomes a more *personal* sail; you are forced to see it, touch it, live with it. It is, as noted above, right there!

In the last helter-skelter week in Hong Kong, somebody (probably Jane, because it was her duty assignment) realized that none of us on board had really ever sailed seriously with a mizzen staysail. In fact, none of us knew exactly how to rig the damn thing. We made an emergency call on Frank Kasala, who gave us specific instructions. I made notes; we had to buy additional blocks, snatch blocks, shackles, and rope for halyards.

The first time we raised the mizzen staysail—it must have been the sea trials in Hong Kong—I remember we tore a gash in the sail getting it down, since none of us really knew what we were doing. Thanks to Harlan's sail-mending ability, we managed to get by okay until we made the next port where we had it permanently repaired.

A serious controversy developed among the crew as to whether the tack of the mizzen staysail was to be bent on the windward or leeward side of the boat—some saying one, some the other, and some saying it all depended on the point of sail. We were still arguing the point when we reached Manila. But there the problem was solved. Hanging in the bar of the Manila Yacht Club was a beautiful color photograph of a ketch not unlike ours, all sails flying—including the mizzen staysail. It was quite obvious on which side the tack of the sail was bent or affixed to the boat. Or so we thought until the next time we rigged up at sea to fly the mizzen staysail! Those of us who claimed it should be bent on the windward side had seen the picture just *that* way! And those who were leeward fans had seen the sail bent on the leeward side.

We finally figured it out, and right now I can't remember who was right and who was wrong. Probably means that I was one of the losers.

THE SECOND BATTLE OF THE PHILIPPINE SEA

Our final farewell to the land mass of the Philippine Islands was typical of our voyage through the inland passage; at 0130 hours we were unable to pick up Atalya Point Light, which should have been visible. At 0200, still unable to see Atalya Point Light, we changed course to 105° magnetic, heading for Yap Island.

That same morning, 1 June, I came on watch with a feeling of great pride and responsibility. I was disappointed, certainly, that it had taken us this long to get where we were, but happy to be at least this far along. The boat was performing well under sail and power; there seemed to be a very good spirit among the crew, and at long last we were *really* on our way. It was especially good for me to be on a vessel in the Eastern Pacific Ocean after a lapse of thirty years; actually, I should say the Philippine Sea, which is what that part of the Eastern Pacific is called.

And then, just as I was starting to take some navigational sights for reference purposes, at 0545 the main engine suddenly stopped. Dead. Cold. No apparent reason. Just like that.

When a diesel engine stops suddenly like that, it has to be a fuel problem; either lack of, or dirt, water, or air in.

First checkpoint: heaven forbid that our fuel tanks were empty! They weren't; thank God. Next checkpoint: injector pump. Plenty of fuel there. Must be air in the fuel line.

And the second Battle of the Philippine Sea was underway.

Bob and I both had been instructed on bleeding our diesel engines. Bob had bled the Perkins, but neither of us had ever bled the Ford. Out with the trusty Lehman-Ford Diesel Engine Manual. Open the first bleed nut; pump the diesel fuel hand pump until fuel with no air bubbles leaks out; close first bleed nut and open second; repeat process; third nut; fourth nut. Wipe up spilled diesel fuel and attempt to start engine. At 0630 hours, after forty-five minutes, a burned left hand, and a raw knuckle on Bob's right hand, we turned the starter key. Lo and behold ! the engine fired right up as if nothing had ever been wrong.

Again, I tried to tell myself that the problem was just the water that we inadvertently let get into the fuel tank in Manila, but I wasn't as convinced this time.

I had missed my navigational sights, but that was no problem. I had logged our position at the time of the engine failure as approximately 105 miles east of Lagispi City in the Philippines, and 625 miles northwest of Palau Island. Yet the diesel engine had taken hold so well that I abandoned any thought of diverting to Palau. We would still go with my first instinct—on to Yap.

Later that same morning we sighted our first school of tuna, one of many that we would see in the Eastern Pacific. We took the engine out of gear and ran fishing lines but had no luck, even though the tuna were literally seething in the sea around us for a distance of hundreds of yards.

Then the battle resumed; Chuck's log that afternoon:

1445 hours: engine slowed down and then stopped. While Bob and Taylor worked on engine, we had a swim party. Fuel line bled; engine running fine. Swimming party ended 1455; underway on power at 1525.

Carol's entry a few hours later:

Engine stopped again about 1800 and again bled air from fuel line. Underway again in less than 15 minutes.

By midnight, our time was pretty good:

Engine stopped again at 2400. On our way at 0008 hours.

Bob and I talked, read up, studied manuals, traced lines until we were blue in the face, attempting to find where that damned air was getting into the diesel fuel lines.

By the midnight-to-0400 watch on 2 June the engine fuel line had to be bled every two hours. Bob indicated in the log that he thought the problem might be in the primary fuel filter, that might be clogged with so much gunk that the engine pump sucked too hard against the clogged filter, either creating a vacuum, or sucking in air at some point of least resistance in the fuel line.

At least we were learning to get the air out of the line pretty fast, but it sure was a lousy way to run a railroad.

The engine stopped on me when I was on watch that morning at 0445. I cleared the line and started the engine in about five minutes. However, the log shows that stopping the engine and clearing the line interrupted my morning sight of Venus, which had gotten to be a great friend.

In order to improve all our navigational skills, confidence, and accuracy on this leg of the voyage, I inaugurated the practice of multiple shots. Two or more of us would take the same shot of the same celestial body within a short time frame. I, for instance, would take one shot timed by Jim; Jim would take one shot timed by Jane; and Jane would take one shot timed by me. Each of us would then compute each of the three shots. If there was any difference in our calculations, we would go over our navigational form sheet line by line until we discovered where the difference was, and then would review our individual calculations until we found the error and the correct answer that all of us agreed on.

After going through this exercise, and then plotting all three sights, we could have great confidence in that line of position plotted on our chart. This system was essentially self-correcting; that is, each time we went this route and found a mistake in one person's work, whether in the sight itself, the timing, the entering of the tables, or the calculations, both the person making the error and the others would be pretty good at avoiding that particular mistake the next time. Nobody's perfect, and certainly none of us was, but we got to be pretty good.

That same morning the engine stopped about 0940 hours, and Bob and Chuck and I went after Bob's theory of the clogged filters with a vengeance. We replaced completely the main filter just downstream from the fuel tanks and replaced the elements in the two Ford engine filters. The main engine was back on stream at 1220.

Bob's log entry on the 1600-to-2000 watch:

Engine running well for approximately eight hours now. Knock on wood. Passenger liner stopped dead in water in front of us as we both maneuvered to avoid collision.

And on the 2000-to-midnight watch, Carol's entry:

Engine operating well, but shaft still sounds like a cement mixer.

Oh well, you can't have everything.

THE BODY BEAUTIFUL

A few days out of Hong Kong, after we had changed course toward the emergency repair port of Manila, we found ourselves powering without wind or sails late one warm afternoon. I had the con, and things were going reasonably well, considering, although as usual I was wishing fervently for some wind in the right direction. Chuck came up to me in his very direct way. "We were talking up in the foc'sle, Taylor, and wondered if we couldn't stop for a few minutes for a swimming call?"

Swimming call! An old Navy expression, meaning of course, to stop for a swim.

Part of me said no. And a pretty *loud* no. We were in a hurry to get someplace. Stopping to dawdle along the way wouldn't help our speed record. And there was always the problem of sharks and possible other marine life.

And (although very remote) there was also the chance that a sudden squall would blow the boat away from the swimmers, or vice versa, or that someone could get hurt diving over the side or climbing back on board. The mind could conjure up probably a hundred negatives.

On the other hand, we *were* hot, tired, and sticky. Our bathing situation was awkward at the very best. Most of us loved the ocean, the sea, the water, or we wouldn't be here, and that lovely, shimmering water sure looked inviting!

Over the side we went.

And it was great!

From then on, almost without fail, if there was not enough wind for sailing in the later part of the afternoon, if the weather was warm, if the sea was calm, and if there was no compelling reason not to do so, we followed the general practice of having a swimming call. At first we went by the rule that at least two people must stay on board at all times—one at the con and one standing guard with our trusty Winchester. Later we left only one person on deck. The afternoon swim call got to be one of our best diversions at sea.

There wasn't much question about swim suits; we naturally all wore them. Then one day just out of the Philippines Jane, taking a bucket-bath shower on deck, daringly took off her swimsuit top in order to get a good rinse. Later the same day she decided to hell with swimsuits altogether, and Bob, Jim, and I followed suit, or non-suit, as Jane put it.

It took Jane, with her beautiful body, to rid the rest of us of our inhibitions. In fact, even Harlan, our elder statesman, succumbed after a while, or after a few weeks, to the convenience and freedom of swimming without a suit in the glorious, warm waters of the Eastern Pacific.

WHERE THE HELL ARE WE?

When an old friend, or a new friend for that matter, learns that we did this great thing by sailing a small boat across the Pacific, usually the question that is asked most frequently is: How the hell did you ever find your way out there? How did you know where you were?

While the subject can't exactly be tossed off lightly, the

matter of knowing where you are, and where you want to go
(in a word: navigation) is actually pretty low on any scale of
priorities on a voyage of this nature.

Since a sailboat moves so very slowly across the globe, the
general problem of finding out where you are and where you
want to go can be treated in a fairly leisurely manner unless or
until you are close to an island chain, a mass of land, or a
navigational hazard of some sort. You can't be flippant or
careless, of course, but unless you have good reason to suspect
that you are near a navigational hazard, you have time to
reflect, consult, rework—a luxury that does not exist if you are
navigating a 747, or even a Piper Cub for that matter.

Naturally the skipper or navigator must have a modicum of
training, must have the proper tools and equipment, must
have his or her head screwed on straight, and must use it
properly.

In the Coast Guard I had practiced and taught piloting and
coastal navigation extensively. I also had made numerous
ocean passages in which I had employed celestial navigation.
However, I had never been the actual navigator on a ship
making a long ocean passage. Therefore, in preparation for
this trip I had broken out my old books, bought new books,
and attended class. Still not satisfied, I had done some intensive
work to simplify the whole celestial navigation process down to
eight basic forms covering all the fundamental procedures that
one might go through to get a line of position, which is simply
a line that you can draw on a chart—and if you calculate it
correctly, your vessel is somewhere on that line. Obviously, if
you can draw two such lines on the chart, intersecting at a
respectable angle, and if both lines are reliable, your position
has to be reasonably near where these two lines intersect.

I had found that any one operation relating to any single
celestial body was relatively simple, once it was broken loose
from all the other possible operations that might be engaged in
relating to that celestial body. In fact, in my infinite wisdom, I
determined that there were basically eight, and only eight,
types of observations of celestial bodies together with calculations based thereon that would, in the normal course of events,
be used by the average sailboat navigator. I broke these eight
calculations into the following forms:

Form	Heavenly Body	Description
Dagny Taggart Form #1	Sun	Conventional sight for LOP (line of position)
Dagny Taggart Form #2	Sun	Noon sight for latitude
Dagny Taggart Form #3	Sun	Noon sight for longitude
Dagny Taggart Form #4	Moon	Conventional sight for LOP
Dagny Taggart Form #5	Planet	Conventional sight for LOP
Dagny Taggart Form #6	Star	Conventional sight for LOP
Dagny Taggart Form #7	Polaris	Sight for latitude
Dagny Taggart Form #8	Polaris	Sight for azimuth

I designed these forms on a lead-me-by-the-hand principle. In theory, anyone who has navigated in the past, or a newcomer who has taken enough of a navigation course to have a general idea of what celestial navigation is all about, can walk through these forms directed by specific and explicit signpost instructions setting forth exactly what to do at each stage of the navigational calculation.

On the *Dagny Taggart* we had a perfect arrangement for learning/teaching celestial navigation: a close-knit group of individuals proceeding on a sailboat across the Pacific. As skipper I was also the senior navigator and the only one who had ever navigated over long ocean passages. Jim had one year of Annapolis behind him and a lot of hard work in the classroom and at the end of the Venice Pier. Harlan had a superb understanding of coastal work, and two solid celestial navigation courses under his belt. Jane had about the same as Harlan. Carol had taken home study courses with me and was very dedicated to learning the ropes. Our three college guys from Oregon were all green, but sharp and eager.

My forms certainly were successful; I was able to teach Bob, his college buddies, and Carol to become excellent navigators in a short period of time. Of course we had the best of conditions—a floating classroom. And I certainly had everybody's attention; our lives depended on it.

CONTINUOUS ASSAULT BY THE SEA

Mike Macdonald put it beautifully, writing in his regular column for *Sail* magazine in September 1976:

Anything put on, in, or under the sea, will eventually sink, rust, or fail when you need it most, the skipper of a big ocean-going tug who'd had a Master's Ticket in his seabag for approximately 30 years, once told me. The tug skipper had fished salmon off the coast of Washington before the war, had been blown off the bridge of a tanker loaded with aviation gas near Saipan, and had pushed a lot of ships across the water.

His thoughts on ships and the sea weren't filtered through any romantic overburden. Boats are tools; and tools must be maintained to work well. But no matter how careful you are, eventually that tool will fail. Good seamanship is just common sense. Take care of your boat even love it if you must. But know how to fix it if it breaks, because it *will* break.

Keeping the sea out is a constant war of attrition; and it isn't the ocean that wears out. No matter what designers, builders, or poets write about boats, boats are *not* natural creatures of the ocean. The volume of air enclosed by a hull is under continuous assault by the sea. A properly handled yacht doesn't *seem* like an intruder, soaring along with the summer breeze. But the struggle is really masked by pleasant surroundings.

The stream in the sheets is the wind chafing at its restriction. The gurgle of the quarterwake is the sea rushing to heal the wound of the boat's passing. The experienced ocean racer or cruiser knows that at best he and his craft are merely tolerated passersby. The sea constantly probes for weakness in both man and boat, not out of malevolence, but for natural balance. During an ocean race or extended cruise, men test their technology, skill, and experience against the sea. Turning wind into speed, and doing it better than a competitor, is the universal appeal of sailing.

On my watch on June 3 I entered:

Chuck discovered a water leak through a hole in the starboard fresh water vent pipe. Pending devising a waterproof fitting for the vent pipe, we had Harlan use his skill with the knife to whittle a temporary wooden plug to fit the hole in the pipe through which we were losing precious fresh water.

I have no recollection of ever having removed that plug; as far as I know, it is still there, doing its job. . . .

WHERE'S THE WIND COMING FROM?

Everyone knows that if you're cooking a steak on an outdoor grill, the smoke always seems to come your way; and if you move, the smoke moves too. There must be some law of physics that accounts for this phenomenon. I guess.

The same perverseness of air movement plagued us across the Pacific. I had studied the Pilot Charts, which are fantastic publications put out by the U.S. government showing in scrupulous detail what wind directions and forces can be expected in each area of all the oceans of the world for each month of the year. Although we were sailing against the Trades, a very careful analysis had indicated (to me, anyhow) that we could expect the wind to be from a direction that would give us at least *some* assist at least *half* the time.

The way it worked out, our stale (very stale) standing answer to the question where's-the-wind-coming-from? got to be: just check the course we're trying to make—the wind is coming from *just there*.

JOANNE

I honestly think that we would not have made the voyage successfully had it not been for Joanne. I feel guilty over the amount of time that she must have taken from her work for the company, from her personal life, to be of help to me—the time on weekends, nights, and holidays she spent finding people, finding parts, taking messages, working to see that whatever we needed way out there came to pass.

She kept all our relatives and close friends duly advised of where we were and what we were doing, doling out little white lies if necessary, but always with great discretion.

On 3 June 1974 my mother wrote to Joanne, concluding with:

> Bless you for being so very good to advise the family of comings and goings. I'm wondering about little April—and how Mrs. Figge is taking the long-time care of her, when I presume she thought it would only be for a couple of weeks.
>
> I am not asking you to do anything about this—just wondering if you had news.
>
> You are really a lovely doll to keep us so informed, and me out of limbo for a while. Best of luck to you—love and happiness.

Joanne's answer to my mother was a classic in many ways, but particularly in the great geographical put-on:

> In the event they incur any more difficulties on their way from Manila to Ponape, there are many many islands between the Philippines and Ponape, where they could stop, so you don't have to worry.

Joanne also wrote on a closer-to-the-truth vein:

> To ease your mind about April—I have just talked to Mrs. Figge, and our Miss April is healthy, behaving herself very well. Taylor and Carol should count their blessings for finding such a lovely and competent young woman to take care of April. Mrs. Figge is very devoted to the children, and is certainly as loving and affectionate with April as she is with her own daughter. I made a special point of telling Taylor that with all the frustrations of the boat, one thing he didn't have to worry about was the welfare of his youngest daughter—she's in very good hands.

How blessed I have been to have had people like Joanne Davis and Mrs. Figge looking after me and after my loved ones for me in my absence!

WHERE THE HELL IS YAP?

Same song; second verse: I thought I had procured charts for every alternate port to which we might decide to divert under any and all circumstances. But I never dreamed that we might be going as far south as Yap. That's right—no charts! Again!

As it worked out I *should* have been more apprehensive than I was when we were approaching Manila without good charts. We had had a fantastic amount of luck as we milled about in Manila Bay waiting to enter Manila Harbor at daybreak. Having been burned on the approach to Manila, having had a tough time finding one of the *major* cities of the world, and now trying to find one of the world's *minor* cities in one of the world's minor ports, in one of the world's smallest island groups, surrounded by one of the world's most formidable reefs, and again having no navigational charts, *this time* I was apprehensive.

As we approached Yap in the Philippine Sea, I worked harder on my navigational homework than I had back in the South China Sea when we were approaching Manila.

As I studied the large-area, small-scale charts, the sailing directions, the literature from the Seven Seas Cruising Club, the Light Lists, the Radio Navigation Aid Lists, and anything else I could get my hands on in our fairly extensive ship's navigation library, I came up with the idea that, if I didn't have a chart of Yap, I could by-God build one.

My prime source of material for this great project was the *Sailing Directions for the Pacific Islands, Volume I, Western Groups,* known as H.O. 82, published by the government, and the appropriate Light List for the area. By using the descriptions in the sailing directions, together with the location of navigational aids given either by latitude and longitude, or by bearing and distance from a given point, I was able to construct a crude, but workable homemade chart of the area.

In order that the rest of the crew would be reasonably apprised of the various navigational points and hazards to be expected as we approached and made port at Yap, and also to give a little general background on our next port of call, I posted the following:

YAP ISLANDS INFORMATION

Radio Beacons	Yap: 317 kh. Code: YP(–·– – ·– –·):
	Guam: 385 kh. Code: GUM (– –· ··– – –):
	Palau: 371 kh. Code: ROR (·–· – – – ·–·):
Lights	Mount Matade Light; southeast slope of Mount Matade; 520′ high; flashing white; white skeleton tower 39′ high; range nine miles. Also, fixed red, flashing red and fixed white on radio tower.
Yap Islands	Four islands.
Main Settlement	Colonia, on Yap Island.
Population (1960)	6,000
Harbor	Tomil Harbor on southeast side of Yap Island, between Yap Island and Gagil-Tomil Island.
Terrain	Hilly; heavy forests of palm, bamboo, and croton trees.
Highest Point	Peak of Mount Matade, 585′.
Products	Tropical fruits, vegetables, cacao, pigs, cattle, copra (copra, always copra), trochus shells.
Navigational Hazards	All four islands are fringed by a reef extending from 600 yards to two miles from the islands. Reef contains some islets with coconut palms and sand banks. Any crew member not performing his or her respective share of shipboard responsibilities will be deposited on one of these islets. Several breaks in reef, but *only* the one leading

to Tomil Harbor is navigable. Highest point on the reef is a rock 15′ high on the reef at the south end of Yap Island.

Tidal Currents   Current at channel entrance setting westward across channel at ½ to ¾ knots (conclusion: channel entrance must run north and south!).

Landmarks   Large white dome of Weather Bureau, city of Colonia.

Entrance Buoy #1   Black can buoy with white reflector marks at edge of channel entrance on west side.

Entrance Buoy #2   Red nun buoy, with red reflector, ⅓ mile east of entrance rock, marks edge of channel on east side of entrance.

Approach   Keep beacon #4 ahead and in range with a white house, bearing 336° magnetic; thence a course of 312° through the narrow entrance.

Clear as mud; and as scary as hell!

Meanwhile, on Friday 7 June, with the wind at 20 knots, gusting to 25 knots, the *Dagny Taggart* was taking on quite a bit of water. The forward bilge was very full when on a starboard heel, slopping over the floor boards. We were able to control it with the pumps, but we were obviously taking on water from someplace, and lots of it, primarily on a heel. We knew the shaft leaked at its entry into the hull. Or the culprit could be the starboard boarding ladder support plate I discovered. In the log, Bob recommended that in Yap, the whole crew, with the help of hoses, et cetera, make a concerted effort to find those leaks.

Bob's log continues:

Diesel fuel was also prevalent in bilge; starboard fuel tank vent tube still prime suspect, but other areas must still i considered. At this point in time I'm not exactly sure what or where the leaks are!

At noon on the seventh, our dead reekoning indicated that we were approaching Yap, and Jim's log entry indicated that the current was stronger than anticipated. At 1845 we changed course to 000° to ease the motion for eating while we had dinner, and also to avoid closing Yap during darkness.

Chuck wrote at 2215 hours:

Sighted red tower lights on Yap; Bob wins the prize!

There was no question that everyone on board was glad to see those radio tower lights of Yap appear at last!

Jim wrote in the log on the 0000-to-0400 watch on Saturday 8 June:

> Shining through the darkest night
> We came upon a welcome sight
>
> A luminous spire of blinking red,
> A guardian servant, by which we were led.
>
> Oh Lofty Tower of considerable height,
> Shine on, shine on, you sweet ass light!

I knew damned well that we had sighted Yap; and I also knew damned well that something was wrong. The lights we were observing had no relationship whatsoever to the lights described in H.O. 82. The characteristics were not the same. Even the number of lights was not the same. And another thing: an hour after the original sighting, the lights had not grown any more distinct or changed in aspect in any way; after two hours, still no change. The range of the lights listed in the sailing directions was nine miles—after two hours we should have been aground on the reef surrounding the lights; but the damned things just didn't change. And another thing; what kind of navigational aid was this, with four red lights in a vertical row? Isn't that the signal for fishing at night with a large suction dredge while towing a disabled sailboat—or something? And it was difficult to make out whether the lights were fixed or flashing. They were still a long way off; that was obvious.

Somewhere along the line, from something one of us had

heard or had read, or just out of common sense, it became apparent that the difficulty was simply that rather than being a few hundred feet high, these lights were somehow a few *thousand* feet high—which was impossible on the terrain of Yap, unless there was a man-made structure of some kind. And the only possible man-made structure we could think of would have been a Loran tower.

And sure enough, Chuck wrote at 1330 hours on 8 June:

Sighted land to left and right of Sweet Ass Light which apparently is the Yap Loran tower. Winds gusting up to 30 knots with occasional drizzle.

Okay, there was Yap. Our first important navigational landfall, and we had done just great. Right on. Now, where is that lousy narrow single entrance through that lousy reef that surrounds all four of the lousy Yap Islands?

As far as I could tell, we were on the north side of the island group. The port of Colonia was on the southwest corner of the group. We had chosen to stay to the north during hours of darkness rather than risk a possible miscalculation in the dark. It appeared that we were on the wrong side of the island group and could proceed clockwise to the east and south, or counterclockwise to the west and south to make port at Colonia. Since we were already heading east, I decided to continue, keeping a sharp lookout and cutting in as close to the land as I thought safe, looking for landmarks or a friendly face.

I hadn't realized how great had been our motion on the *Dagny Taggart* for the past weeks until we rounded the northeast point of the island group and found ourselves on the southern side, protected from the large swells with which we had been living for the past weeks. Nice to be on a smooth, non-heel non-roll status again for a change; a great change. Looking for landmarks. Where is that giant weather dome?

I wasn't exactly worried. No question that this was Yap. On the other hand, where was Colonia? Or anything else recognizable? We had the giant Loran tower in sight at all times, but it was not on any of our charts, real or homemade. Well, if necessary, we could circumnavigate for a couple of days; something was bound to happen.

Wasn't it?

Good gawd! There is a Marina-del-Rey-to-Catalina hot-shot 75-horsepower outboard bouncing from wave to wave, dead ahead, coming this way. Far cry from native outrigger, or swimming-naked Polynesian maidens—this guy was coming on like gangbusters!

Wave, wave; hello, hello . . . Swish; he had gone by us!

Coming about!

Having failed to make audio contact, I quickly decided to try to get our fellow sailor's attention by visual means. We called all hands on deck in a hurry in order to come about, make appropriate sail and rigging adjustments, and try to let our friend know that we were attempting to attract his attention for a more serious reason than waving and saying hello.

And it worked.

The outboard came about, roared up alongside, slowed down, and the single occupant—a beautiful, tall, gnarled Yapese, with betel-nut-scarred teeth—inquired as to our needs.

"Where is Colonia?"

"That way!"

"Which way?"

"Follow me!"

And follow we did. I figured from my homemade charts that it would take about an hour at the outside. I didn't figure on the derring-do of our follow-the-leader pilot—nor on the oddities of the reef-trimmed coastlines of the four Yap Islands.

No less than a dozen times it appeared that our kind benefactor had reached that marvelous one single point in the reef around Yap that was penetrable by a boat of the size of the *Dagny Taggart*. The outboard would head in toward the shore, I would follow—engine racing or ready as the case might be—praying that it would not conk out just at the crucial moment of slipping through that narrow opening in the reef, with a three- to four-knot current setting down on us—but it would develop that our playful guide was just that, playful. Off he would bound again, as if seeking a break in the reef yet undiscovered. The situation was made more complicated by the fact that our friendly native guide had no way of knowing that we had a serious engine undependability problem—not that he could have done a lot about it if he *had* known.

Each time our Yapese guide made a false entry, he would

Chuck on bow lookout as Yap fishermen lead Dagny Taggart *into* Colonia.

veer off at what seemed to me to be the last possible minute, with the agility of his eighteen-foot runabout powered by a 75-horsepower outboard engine, leaving me with my thirty-ton ketch powered, if I was lucky, by an 80-horsepower diesel, to make the same sudden change of course to avoid the ever-present reef.

When our buoyant, fun-loving guide finally reached the *real entrance* through the reef, I had no way of knowing whether this was not yet another playful ploy.

Finally I picked up some of the navigational aids that H.O. 82 said we should find:

—Rock 15 feet high, located on reef east of south end of Yap Island

Yes, there was the rock!

—Entrance Buoy #1: Can buoy with white reflector
—Entrance Buoy #2: Painted red, with red reflector, one-third mile east of entrance rock.

Oh joy! At last, something familiar!
But where was the prominent weather station dome?
And what in Christ's name is that? What are those?!!

As we got a little closer, what-is-that and what-are-those turned out to be two skeletons guarding the entrance to the cave of the virgins as in the opera *Die Valkyrie*. On one side was the rusting hulk of LST 1045 left over as it developed from World War II: the crew, as local legend had it, heard about Japan's surrender and headed out to sea, regardless. On the other side was a rusting trawler/tugboat, the history of which no one seemed to know.

But it wasn't just as simple as heading midway between the two rusting wrecks marking the wrong way to go; nor was it a matter of merely following our gracious Yapese leader. He was up to 40 knots, back to zero, around and about—having a gay old time at any given moment. We couldn't possibly follow him on a point-to-point basis—he was just showing us the neighborhood!

So it was back to the charts, the Sailing Directions, the lead line, basic seamanship. All four, or some combination thereof, paid off.

Once we really found ourselves on the seaward side of Entrance Buoy #1 and Entrance Buoy #2, from a position a few hundred yards at sea, with a good compass, and assuming a good engine, it was not difficult with a little courage to find our way through that narrow gap between the breakers and into the quiet waters of Tomil Harbor.

Our available information indicated that we had plenty of water depth throughout most of Tomil Harbor; we stationed Harlan in the bow to verify all of this with the trusty lead line.

We were about to let the anchor go in a likely anchorage of about four or five fathoms when someone noticed that over there was a small sailboat tied up alongside a something-or-other . . . let's check that out! Where there's a sailboat there must be sailors! Turned out to be a twenty-eight-foot sailboat with a jib stuck aloft, tied alongside a World War II LCU (Landing Craft Utility).

We secured our anchor-handling detail, temporarily at least, and cruised by aforesaid WW II LCU:

"Ahoy! Any chance that we might tie up alongside?"

"Sure! Where are you guys from?"

"Well, right now, out of Manila, heading for Marina del Rey."

Within minutes we had made a reasonably smooth landing—although a little hairy since at the eventual tie-up spot our bow was literally only a few feet from the rocks on shore.

We had the usual friendly chit-chat as we made our mooring alongside the LCU. It developed that the person in charge of the LCU and also the local U.S. Navy installation on the Yap Island group was a fellow named Henry, who like me was WW II. The one big thing that Henry had on me was that he was the father of a local Yapese chief, named, surprisingly enough, Henry Junior.

For a long time I thought that Henry Senior and Henry Junior were kidding me about their father-son relationship, but after a while I became convinced. Certainly I would never argue the point (any point) with Henry Junior. He was about six feet tall and five feet wide. Within minutes of our tying up alongside the WW II LCU, Henry Junior was on board with

Harlan sounds with the leadline in Tomil Harbor as the Skipper searches for a safe anchorage.

friends, and with all the graciousness that you might expect from an Italian count.

And from someplace appeared a case of bee-yoo-ti-ful, ice-cold Michelob bottled beer!

But no pop-top, and no twist-top—the Real Thing.

If I hadn't seen it I would never have believed it. Henry Junior took the beer bottles, and literally, with no gimmicks, bit off the caps with his teeth!

Within ten minutes we had twenty people on board, Henry biting off the bottle caps. Somehow we found a few hors d'oeuvres, maybe a stashed away bottle of rum. Anyhow, it was a great party, with people continually coming on board.

"Hey, beautiful boat. Is it yours?" "Where are you guys from?" "How long did it take you?" "How was Manila?" "Do you know Abe Williams in Hong Kong?" "Here, have another beer."

We soon learned that many people we would want to see were not in Colonia that day. As luck wouldn't have it, the weekend that fate had picked for us to make our landfall in Yap was the weekend of *the* one big social event of the year for the Yapcse. The Big Event was the high school graduation—and the high school was on the island of Ulithi about 500 miles to the northeast of Yap! But we were assured that everyone would be back on Yap when the trusty steamer *James M. Cook*, God willing, docked in Tomil Harbor sometime Sunday evening. Then:

"Taylor, which way is Colonia—the town I mean? We'd like to walk in and look around."

"Dad, is it okay with you if I go ashore? I'd like to see downtown Yap. Where is it, by the way?"

I tried to tell my young contingent that what there was of downtown Yap was right over there a few hundred yards. But since there wasn't much of anything right over there a few hundred yards, they accused me of pulling their collective legs. I knew I couldn't convince them that there really wasn't any downtown Yap.

Fortunately for us, *all* of the important people of Yap were not attending the big social event on Ulithi. Specifically, Pat and Dal Arnold were in town; and since the arrival of the *Dagny Taggart* was the second biggest social event of the year,

Pat and Dal had wandered down to meet the new kids in town. It developed that Dal was a retired but still fairly young naval officer who had decided that the Trust Territory provided a much better environment for raising a family than in the States with its drug scene, crime, loose morals, et al.

As part of its effort to prepare the Trust Territory for self-government and self-sufficiency, the United States had been following the plan of placing a local understudy with a U.S. person in each key position in government and public works—and by 1974 most or perhaps all of the key spots were occupied by locals with U.S. persons as assistants. Frequently the assistant was far more skilled or knowledgeable in the responsibilities of the job than the title holder.

In this context, Dal was assistant director of public works in charge of all engineering and repair on Yap. And there he was, right on the *Dagny Taggart,* saying wonderful things to us such as: "Sure, I'll have my crew stop by first thing Monday morning and see if we can't find the problem in your fuel system and find and fix those leaks."

We didn't even have to go looking! Twenty minutes in Yap, and we were already talking, directly yet, to just the right person!

Not knowing when we left Manila that we were going to stop at Yap, we hadn't made any advance plans for financial transactions on Yap. Nor did we have the advantage (as we did at the *last* surprise port of Manila) of having friends and business associates to help in the crucial financial area. At the height, or one of the heights, of our Henry-biting-off-the-beer-bottle-caps party on our arrival, I asked Dal Arnold for advice in setting up banking arrangements during our contemplated short stay. Dal suggested that I check with the fellow on the other side of me. So:

"I guess we met when you came on board; I'm Taylor Hancock. Dal suggested I check with you in regard to banking facilities here on Yap."

"Yes, we did meet. I'm Wally Kluver. I'm manager of the only bank in town. How much money will you be needing?"

It was manna! Everyone had come to us instead of our having to dash all over seeking them! In fact, the party came to us, too. After a couple of hours, Henry Junior announced that he was having a big party at his place, and nothing would do but that we all come! No refusals accepted!

So after great showers, some of us at the local Seabee camp (and that's another story), and some at Pat and Dal Arnold's, it was on to the chief's house for the Big Party—or the continuation of same.

Jane wrote in her diary:

> Went up to the Seabee camp and took a shower—delicious. And more beer there. Then went out to Henry's house in Hugil for a party—about 30 people. Took shoes off at the door. Sat on mats. Drank more beer and ate lots of food. The drive out was hilarious, in a jeep, over mud roads.

It happens that Carol's mid-twenties, and first world travels, coincided with the publication of *The Ugly American,* the moral of which she took very much to heart. Thus it was that when we reached a new place, particularly an indigenous culture such as Yap, Carol was careful to inquire as to local customs, particularly regarding female dress. Having been assaulted by guards in St. Peter's for not having her bare arms covered, Carol wasn't about to risk some other transgression in Yap.

It turned out that she was wise to inquire. The male costume is called a *thu* and consists of nothing more than a twisted piece of cloth that forms a codpiece, separating the buttocks and joined to a piece of cloth encircling the waist. Women may be bare-breasted to the waist. But the big no-no in Yap is to let the female thighs be seen. Since standard attire for Jane and Carol had been a simple halter top, T-shirt, and a bikini bottom or shorts, it was well that they were told ahead of time. Both were careful to wear jeans or skirts while in Yap, and both were often invited to Yapese homes.

DICK JUSTICE OF THE GULL

At some point during our Saturday afternoon party on arrival in Yap, I heard Jane scream, "Hey, Bob, it's Dick Justice!"

And sure enough, it *was* Dick Justice—whoever he was!

Turned out that Dick Justice likewise had had a sailboat built in Taiwan, launched in Keelung, and sailed off into the wild blue yonder—which was fitting since Dick was a retired Air Force colonel. Our Keelung gang—Jane and Bob and Chuck and Randy—had known Dick while he was launching and outfitting his twenty-three-foot sloop in Keelung at the same time that our gang was working on the *Dagny Taggart*.

Dick had headed east from Taiwan, attempting to make Guam, but had been caught in the same ungodly cycle that had *almost* engulfed us. He had finally left Taiwan months later than he had planned, which resulted in serious exposure to typhoons, and even worse, exposure in the adverse-prevailing-winds department. Unfortunately for Dick, he did not have our long-range fuel capacity (although our blessing in this department was pretty well disguised much of the time!). As a result, Dick was completely at the mercy of the wind and weather. He ended up simply not being able to make decent headway to the east, and therefore gave up on making Guam, kept going in a southerly direction, and attempted to put in at Yap as a port of last resort, literally—he had no water, no food, no fuel.

When Dick finally made his landfall at Yap, he had been unable to navigate the tricky reef entrance passage to Tomil Harbor, and his sloop got badly hung up on the local friendly reef.

Dick had two teenage boys with him as crew, both of whom decided, after being hung up on the reef for a day or so, to desert the boat and swim the mile or two to shore.

The reef entrance at Yap isn't all that busy, so it was several more days before a boat finally came by and pulled Dick's sloop off of the reef and on into Colonia.

During his days on the reef Dick had tried in vain to work his boat off manually and get it over into the deep-water channel, temptingly only a few feet away. The brutal coral had worn through his tennis shoes and had cut both his feet badly. By the time we saw him on our arrival at Yap, his feet were really a mess; he could barely hobble.

We didn't hear the harrowing end to the tale until—would you believe it—on 26 June 1974, in the Ace Hardware in

Guam, I ran smack into the six-foot, two-inch frame of Dick Justice! It seems that a U.S. naval doctor was making a fortuitous tour of various medical facilities in the Trust Territory shortly after the *Dagny Taggart* had finally left Yap. One look at Dick's two feet, and the doctor went into the full Dr. Kildare on TV bit: "If you don't get proper treatment for those feet within the next few hours, you are going to lose them, sir! You have gangrene!"

A special plane was flown down from Guam; and Dick ended up at a Guam hospital with two feet.

WHAT, NO DRINKING PERMIT!?

On our first night in Yap, only Carol and I ended up on the boat, with the rest of the crew out-there-somewhere. It turned out that the party at Chief Henry Junior's had been too good to leave, or too hard to leave in present condition, and our crew had spent the night at Chief Henry's.

The next morning, being Sunday and all, and since there were a few beers still on ice, what else was there to do but tidy up the place, down the beers, and come on into town. With Henry at the helm of his trusty Land Rover, and with the *Dagny Taggart* crew hanging on the hood and running boards (yes, Virginia, there really are running boards in Yap), the local Yapese peacetime military force had stopped the entire affair and cited each member of the *Dagny Taggart* crew for drinking without a license!

Apparently there was no problem in connection with drinking in Yap—but you'd better have a license to do it!

Sure enough, the next day each of us, as time permitted, marched up to the local police department, and upon due presentation of proper identification and two United States dollar bills, each of us was issued a license to drink as much as we pleased over the next twelve months.

The *Dagny Taggart* Purple Hill Criminal Gang appeared at the scheduled hearing on Monday morning and threw themselves on the mercy of the court. The log entry for the episode reads:

Verdict at 0830 on Monday 10 June 1974: cases all dismissed. Reason: arresting officers had not warned suspects that a Drinking Permit was necessary before imbibing on Yap.

THOSE WONDERFUL SEABEES!

By coincidence we often seemed to make our first entry into a new port on a Saturday. This worked out very well. Although we seldom got much accomplished the first day by way of work on the boat, we were usually able to get a good grip on the lay of the land, finding out what services, equipment, supplies, and communication facilities were available at the particular port. Arriving on a weekend also had the advantage that the crew, typically pretty restless after a ten-day to three-week cruise to get to the new island, would have a chance to let off steam on Saturday night and Sunday, and hopefully would thereupon be ready to do whatever had to be done during the first of the next week in order to get us out of there.

Such was the case on Yap. After a certain amount of cleanup, scheduling of work plans, and bringing our ship's record and documentation up to date, on Sunday morning I persuaded myself, or Carol persuaded me, to accompany her to the Seabee camp to do our laundry, to have a good hot shower (again!), and maybe to relax for a while.

The Seabee camp was only a short walk of a mile or so from our temporary berth. It had been raining intermittently since we had arrived—in fact, I think it had been raining intermittently since Yap arrived in the Pacific. The roads were simply bulldozed out of the jungle, with a little coral mixed in with the soil—pretty sticky at best, and sometimes impossible.

I had had the privilege of working closely with the Seabees during World War II; my ship, the LST 785, had hauled Seabees from island to island from time to time in this same general part of the world. I had nothing but respect for the Seabee personnel and their mission. I wondered vaguely why they were still around after all these years, but I was certainly happy to have them there. It was not until that Sunday, 9 June, that we found out what it was all about in the Year of Our Lord 1974.

We knocked on the door of a navy-type barracks building and were welcomed by Dave, whom we had met the day before at the party on the *Dagny Taggart*. We entered upon a scene typical of Sunday afternoon at a remote military installation— one fellow reading in a corner, another couple of guys playing cards, somebody else writing a letter or report, the rest lolling about shooting the breeze and sipping on a beer or a coke. We were introduced to the ones we had not met on the afternoon or evening before: "Good to have you here." "Have a beer." "What can we do for you?" "How about taking care of your laundry?" "How about a shower?" "Would you like a sand-wich?"

It was *yes* to practically all questions. During the afternoon, and in much more detail as our days in Yap wore on, we learned something about a Seabee Civil Action Team (CAT). A CAT is a team in the full meaning of the word: twelve men, each highly trained in a different special skill, each of whom is a petty officer (like a sergeant, Virginia), plus a commissioned officer as the commanding officer. Typically, a CAT will have a master electrician, one or more master mechanics, a heavy machinery (tractor/crane) operator, a carpenter, an electronic technician, and the inevitable Doc, the pharmacist mate or paramedic.

A CAT might be likened to a Peace Corps team, but with *men, muscles*, and *machines*. My Seabee friends wouldn't like this analogy—they referred to the other group on the island as the *Peace Creeps*—but there *is* a similarity. Both outfits work with and for the indigenous population to help, train, and make life better, with the key factor being participation by the local population—unlike someone coming in from the outside, doing something, and then leaving.

Most of the island communities in the U.S. Trust Territory have one or more Seabee CATs assigned to them. The mission of the CATs is to work with local government officials to do whatever is feasible to advance the well-being of the com-munity and the population. The scope of their activities is almost limitless: roads, water systems, sanitary sewage systems, storm drains, airstrips, parks, tennis courts, harbors.

One of the primary jobs of each new Seabee team as it goes into an area is to select an understudy for each team member.

Theoretically, during their two-year tour, the Seabee team builds a whole new indigenous cadre or team, consisting of their understudies. When the team leaves after its two-year stint, a newly trained team comes in from the States; after a brief crossover period, the new team in turn sets out to find *its* understudies and to engage in whatever projects seem at that time to be most useful for the community.

After we had had a beautiful *hot* shower and sat down to talk about life, love, and adventures in the Pacific, one of our first topics of serious discussion was the availability of a good diesel mechanic or mechanics on the island and the best source of assistance in tracing down the fuel and water leaks into our bilges. In the diesel mechanic field, we were referred to Dal Arnold and his public works people. As to the leaks, as well as a host of other items on our worklist, our newly found Seabee friends assured us that they would be able to assist us (and this certainly turned out to be the case).

"Hey, we're about to show a movie. Which one of these would you like to see?"

"Hey fellas! It's whatever *you* guys want. We're just along for the ride."

But our hosts would have it no other way; I had to make the selection. As it developed there wasn't much to choose from—maybe three or four films, all of which had been seen by one or more of the fellows at one time or another. I chose the one that seemed to have been seen by the least number of people: a review of the rock music scene, with Chubby Checkers as more or less the featured artist. Just what I've always wanted. But it was great fun.

Showing a movie at a military installation has one startling similarity to watching a movie on the tube back in the States; periodically there is a beer break. In the States, of course, the break is during the commercial; at the typical small military installation, it is for the changing of reels.

During one of the reel breaks there came a knock of distress on the barracks door. It was apparently a fairly typical Sunday afternoon occurrence in the area. A Yapese family had missed a turn going around one of the mountain roads, and their car had plunged several hundred feet down an embankment. Would the Seabees help?

You're damned right they would!

Carol and I, and in fact everybody in sight, were invited to join in Operation Rescue.

Just as the pick-up truck is a status symbol in Wyoming, and the military jeep in the Philippines, the Land Rover is the status symbol in the Trust Territory. And even one step above the Land Rover is the weapons carrier, which (while certainly having the capability of carrying weapons, depending on the size of said weapons) is nothing more than an overgrown jeep. Instead of being able to crowd eight people into a jeep, you can crowd perhaps eighteen people in a weapons carrier—known as WEPS to our Seabee friends.

We climbed into the WEPS, which served as emergency rescue vehicles, and off we roared into the wild green of the jungle yonder.

After a half hour or so of cruising through valleys, over passes, through some spectacular scenery, narrowly missing squealing pigs, witnessing life in the raw as practiced by the Yapese along the roadside, we finally came upon the scene. By the time we got there word had spread around through the jungle telegraph or what have you, that there had been an accident, and that the rescue party was on its way. But as far as we could see there was nothing to rescue. It was easy to trace where a car had failed to negotiate the turn and had gone off the road, but beyond that the jungle—the vertical jungle in this case—had swallowed whatever it was that had plunged down through the greenery.

The crack Seabee team swung easily into action, as if they had done this a hundred times before. As it developed, they had.

We then discovered why the Seabees had invited everybody in sight to come along on the rescue operation. The technique was to run a cable out from a winch on one of the WEPS to the car, a Datsun, which was finally located about 150 feet down the embankment. In order to hold the vehicle with the winch in place, two more WEPS were stationed at strategic spots up and down the mountainous road, connected by winched lines, holding the anchor vehicle. After making a hookup on the chassis of the downed Datsun, all able-bodied individuals at the sight were encouraged to climb, swing, or fall down the mountainside to the spot where the Datsun was lodged between the trunks of a couple of great trees.

It was the old grunt and groan trick. At a given signal the winch operator started the winching; the two vehicles that were staked out to keep the winch truck from slipping started pulling; and those of us who were clinging for our lives to the side of the mountain started doing whatever we could to encourage the Datsun to go *up* the mountain instead of *down* the mountain, at the same time doing our damndest not to hang onto the car and add to the weight that the winch was being asked to pull *up* the mountain.

One way or another, with husky Yapese, burly Seabees, wandering sailors, and a couple of Peace Corps people who appeared from nowhere, we got that old Datsun back up to the mountain road from which it had plunged! And although the car was a lot the worse for wear, the errant driver not only managed to get the car door open, but was able to get in and gather up his family and drive on home—or wherever a Yapese under such circumstances would choose to drive.

The contrast between the last time I was in this area and the present time was made dramatic by the car incident. The last time, the Yapese were the involuntary hosts of the Japanese military, who were attacking the U.S. military. This time the Yapese were the involuntary hosts of the U.S. military, who were rescuing Japanese Datsuns!

WALLY KLUVER, BAREFOOT BANKER

After meeting Wally Kluver at our entrance-to-Yap party on Saturday, we saw him again on Sunday and then paid an official call on him at his bank on Monday. The bank on Yap was a branch of the Bank of Hawaii; Wally was manager of the branch.

There are, of course, *drive-in* banks; and I suppose all other banks, all non-drive-in banks, could be classified as *walk-in* banks. But Wally's bank was a delightful combination of both: a *drive-in/walk-in* bank! Wally and his small staff of four or five were behind glass in air-conditioned comfort. But it was not all that bad outside; so what would have amounted to the lobby outside the teller's cages was simply a roofed-over California carport-style area with tables for writing checks, each with the usual supply of deposit slips and whatever.

And Wally: there he was in Bermuda shorts, barefoot! I told him that in my work I had dealt with bankers in about twenty U.S. states and about sixty other countries, but this was a real first—a barefoot banker!

Wally was unimpressed.

We opened an account with the Bank of Hawaii, with unlimited credit extended to us by Wally Kluver!

Wally may have felt more kindly toward extending credit to me and to the *Dagny Taggart* by virtue of his experience on Yap in extending credit based on Yapese stone money. As local legend has it, shortly after Wally landed on Yap and opened the first bank on the island as a branch of the Bank of Hawaii, he received an application for a loan for the purchase of a small Japanese automobile by a Yapese whose collateral for the loan was Yapese stone money.

Wally did some research on the matter and ultimately extended to the borrower very favorable terms for the car loan, backed by Yapese stone money as collateral.

It's not difficult to conjure up a vision of the scene back in the staid board room of the Bank of Hawaii in Honolulu, when the routine matter of approving loans by outlying branches was being reviewed; and suddenly the item of "Collateral, stone money" hit the middles of those doing the reviewing.

Said legend goes on to relate that a month or two later, Smithsonian Institution representatives made an official call on Yap, investigating stone money collections. They saw the collateral stone money—which Wally had had mounted on the wall of his office since it was too big to fit in the bank's vault. The representatives offered Wally something like four times the pledged value of the stone money collateral in the event that Wally ever foreclosed—which he didn't.

And without resorting to legend, it can be told that the borrower fully repaid the automobile loan, on time, redeemed his stone money, and all lived happily, and all that.

DISMISSAL, DESERTION, MUTINY

Randy was an enigma (perhaps we all are enigmas). He could be and usually was charming, hard-working, industrious; he had certain valuable skills and intellectual understanding. The problem was (as *I* saw it of course) that he only showed those good qualities when he wanted to use his charm, his hard work, his skills, his intellect, for his own benefit. If, in any way, use of his charm, work, skill, or intellect did not coincide with what Randy wanted to do, it was like pulling the proverbial hens' teeth.

In Manila the situation with Randy had reached a crisis, and I had gone over all the bones of contention (or at least I *thought* I had) with him. I thought that we had hammered out a satisfactory working agreement.

Looking back now, I may have been remiss in not making it clear to Randy on the leg to the emergency port of Yap that I felt that he was not living up to the conditions that we had agreed upon, or at least what I had laid down, during our analysis at the Manila Yacht Club of where-do-we-go-from-here.

So what do you do? Here you had a nice, gentle lad who was likable but in my opinion was not carrying his weight, and probably bringing down the morale and efficiency of the rest of the crew. But I had lived with much worse situations than finishing the voyage with Randy; and I think I could have made it okay.

However, I had a couple of very unhappy females on my hands, as I've already mentioned, and once again Carol had given me an ultimatum; it was Randy or her. No one of the complaints against him would have been enough to have justified Carol's insistence that Randy leave, nor Jane's support. But in the overall view I felt I had no choice but to take Carol's side—not, I would like to think, because of Carol's and Jane's pressure on me, but because I felt that Carol and Jane were correct and that their position was fully justified.

Just try sometime to tell a twenty-four-year old boy on the

Island of Yap that he's being dismissed from the crew and you will be proceeding without him. To Randy's great credit, once he truly understood my message, there was no argument, there were no tears, there was no gnashing of teeth (although there was understandably a fair amount of quiet desperation). Randy went forward, off on the beach, I think, to talk to the other young fellows in the crew, including, of course, son Bob. Randy then returned, packed his gear quickly and efficiently, and left the *Dagny Taggart* forever more.

A few minutes later, Jim went and did likewise. I offered to talk the matter over with Jim to be sure that he understood our position and that we understood his position. Jim, also with no gnashing, simply said no, he felt there was nothing further to say; he did not wish to stay on board a boat on which Randy had received the treatment that we had meted out to him.

The next encounter was with Chuck.

Chuck, in his direct, open-eyed, non-blinking style, said, "I'd like to know what is going on here."

I told Chuck as best I could. He listened intently and said that he would like to have some time to think about it and decide whether he thought we were being fair and whether he would stay with us.

I figured that if *everything* went to hell, Carol and Jane and Bob and I could manage to sail the boat on to Ponape, although it wouldn't be easy.

As it developed, Randy and Jim were our only casualties, and it appears that things didn't go too badly for either of them. Inasmuch as our arrangement with Randy was to supply him transportation back to the States by way of the *Dagny Taggart,* and inasmuch as *we* had asked *him* to leave, I felt obligated to buy him a ticket home from Yap, which I did. In Jim's case, since his departure was his own decision, I left him on his own. The two of them stayed on in Yap for some time, just bumming around. Later they went up to Guam; and we saw Jim later as he too island-hopped across the Pacific. Randy, unfortunately, cut his foot rather badly on some coral while skin diving and for this reason had to go back to the States sooner than Jim.

FAREWELL TO YAP

Dal Arnold and his public works crew, after working on their off-hours in the mornings and noontimes and afternoons, told us that they felt they had done all they could to search out and remedy the sources of the air that had been getting into our fuel lines. Best of all, Dal and his people had taught us much about our own engines and fuel supply system, which gave us added confidence that we could cope with any further similar problems if, heaven forbid, they should occur.

I was far from satisfied that we were ready to mush on. But I *was* satisfied that there was nothing more that we could accomplish on Yap; so we made plans to depart Yap enroute to Ponape on Wednesday 12 June 1974.

We had been overwhelmed by the hospitality and help extended to us by the people on Yap. All we could think of to do in return (other than simple thank-you's, which we certainly utilized fully) was to show our appreciation by having a farewell party the night before we left.

Even as we tried to do something for our good friends we still found the stream running the other direction; most of the beer and all of the ice for our party were supplied by our Seabee and Coast Guard friends! We did furnish the wine, and of course the locale: the *Dagny Taggart*. I lost count of our guests somewhere; I think we had at least seventy people on board at one time!

Carol had the duty for the day, and wrote in the log:

> Invited the island for a party. Guests included Seabees, Peace Corps, Coast Guard, Bank of Hawaii, Yapese, Palauans. It was the closest that we were ever to come to being able to repay the many kindnesses and the unstinting generosity of our many friends on Yap. Even then, we were overwhelmed at the party with gifts of mints, fresh tuna, pineapple, watermelon, beer, coke, lava lava, books, and games.

At one time, sitting in the stern cockpit on that lovely June evening, just before the end of the short tropical twilight, I glanced over the transom and was horrified to observe a literal *river* of floating beer and coke cans—*hundreds*—slowly drifting to sea on the outgoing tide! Our guests were simply tossing the cans over the side as the contents were emptied. As I look back on my childhood days in California, I guess it used to be that way here, too. But having been through all the environmental impact reports in recent years, my first inclination was to dash down, get into my fins and snorkel, and splash about retrieving all those cans!

In preparation for the party, and also in preparation for leaving Yap, we had moved the *Dagny Taggart* to the main wharf in Tomil Harbor, where we could take on diesel fuel and fresh water. Taking on fuel in many places was a special problem, since the only fuel nozzles available were generally designed for loading fuel into the tanks of tramp steamers, not small sailboats. We tried funnels, flexible hoses, reducers, pumping into barrels and then siphoning into our fuel tanks, and I guess a dozen other systems. None of them worked well; some not at all. We had a good scare in Tomil Harbor, since a Trust Territory Environmental Protection Agency official was assigned to watch us, ready to give us a citation if we spilled any fuel into the harbor, no matter how small the amount—the same harbor into which we were to dump hundreds of beer cans with impunity a few hours later.

Once you get beyond or below the level of worrying about important dangers such as grounding, fire at sea, and collision, high on the secondary worry list is the possibility of somehow ending up with all your batteries dead at the same time. One can install or have available various devices to cope with this problem if it ever happens. One of the most practical is a hand cranking capability on one or more of your engines; another is a separate small gasoline-powered portable generator with a hand crank; and there are wind generators, water-powered generators, solar cells. For one reason or another we did not choose to have any of these emergency devices. We knew that we must rely on either a fool-proof system or fool-proof people. While we planned for our people to be as fool-proof as possible, we also planned for them to be human, so 100 percent fool-proofness was, of course, not to be counted on.

As the boat came out of the yard in Taiwan, it certainly did *not* have a fool-proof electrical system. I was determined that before the boat left Hong Kong it would be fail-safe in this respect. The boat came equipped with one battery; we had one additional battery installed at the yard in Taiwan and acquired two more in Hong Kong. I isolated one battery for starting the Ford main engine, one exclusively for the Perkins generator engine, and two for the rest of the boat (what would be called house current if the phrase weren't so unnautical). And in Yap, through the courtesy of the local Department of Public Works, we acquired a fifth super-heavy-duty battery, which we added to our house-circuit power source.

Working in Anthony Wong's boatyard in Hong Kong with Anthony's electrician, A. Huang, I had designed and A. Huang had installed a straight-forward system, operated by a bank of nine knife-switches, with which I could charge any one of our three banks of batteries from the generator, from the alternator of the Ford main engine, or from our LaMarche battery charger, which in turn could be energized either from shore power or from the 110-volt side of our own Kohler generator. Designing and installing this charging system would have been quite easy were it not for my absolute insistence that each battery bank be entirely independent of the other two banks, in order to prevent a short, or overuse, in one bank from dragging down the other two banks. We had blessed ourselves for having installed this elaborate separate bank system more than once, for in fighting our recurring air-in-the-fuel-problem, which meant starting and restarting one of the engines, we had from time to time run down one battery bank completely. When that would happen, we could then fire up the other engine, using another battery bank, and charge up the entire system (finally getting back to the job at hand, which had run down the battery in the first place).

It was good to know we had a fool-proof system. That is, until our seventy-people party on our last night in Yap! We found one flaw. Showing the boat to our many friends on Yap meant turning on literally every light on the boat, inside and out. And of course we had to have the stereo supplying background music, loud enough to be heard over the roar of the crowd. And the fridge was being opened frequently, which meant continuous running of its 12-volt motor . . . and on and on. And I was the goofer; in preparation for the party I had charged all three banks of batteries that afternoon, but in all the last-minute rush and planning, when I had secured the generator engine, I had neglected to disengage my three banks of charging switches. What every schoolboy knows I had overlooked: electricity can travel through a conductor in *either* direction. All three battery banks were interconnected through the generator itself, which, though not operating, still served as a perfect conductor. All five batteries in the three banks had inadvertently been connected through the generator, and the heavy discharge had run them all completely down.

Ugh!

But how lucky that we discovered our electrical Achilles heel while in port instead of in the middle of a roaring storm, or while entering a crowded harbor at night, or something.

Near the end of the farewell-to-Yap party I noticed that the lights were dim and checked to see what I had wrought. Some of the fellows from the Coast Guard Loran Station were still on board, and when they heard my moaning and groaning, they came to my rescue. They doubtless would have helped anyway, but the fact that I had been in the Coast Guard myself probably helped. They offered to bring a spare battery or a portable generator.

I said, "Golly, don't go to all that bother, just a nice long extension cord would do it, I'm sure—we can find a 110-volt outlet up on the dock someplace; and it'll wait until morning."

"Okay."

Said the commanding officer of the Loran Station, "I'll have our electrician's mate here at 0800 in the morning."

The next morning at 0800 looked like the marching scene from *The Bridge on the River Kwai!* A dozen uniformed Coast Guardsmen appeared, each carrying a box containing a yellow, 75-foot extension cord. With military precision, each man dropped his cord on the ground at locations roughly seventy-five feet apart and proceeded to unwind and plug his cord into the cord dropped by the next man up the line.

Great. Now just plug the shore power into the ship's power, set the switches in the right direction, and wait thirty minutes or so.

Klunk!

This was the first time we had had occasion to operate our LaMarche battery charger with shore power; in fact, it was the first time we had tried to use shore power plugged into our own boat's 110-volt system. Testing the 110-volt system with shore power had been one of the items I had had to forego in order to leave Hong Kong before Christmas. Mike, my friendly Coast Guard electrician's mate, had never been exposed to a yacht-size battery charger before. But we rolled up our collective sleeves, started tracing circuits, and found the defect. The LaMarche had never been connected with the boat's 110-volt system. We had used the battery charger only with our Kohler generator, to which Mr. Huang had wired the LaMarche directly. Later I was to learn that our Corning electric cooktop was similarly wired directly to the Kohler but not to the boat's regular 110-volt system. It slowly dawned on me, over the months, that the only logical explanation for some of the deficiencies in the work done by A. Huang was that the concept of a boat being tied up in a marina, with 110-volt shore power coming on board, was just not within his ken.

Our departure was delayed while the batteries were being charged, while Dal and his betel-nut-chewing mechanics gave our engines a final checkout, while our various friends, including Randy but not Jim, stopped for one final goodbye.

We finally broke away from the Yap main wharf at 1330 hours on Wednesday 12 June 1974; we threaded our way out through the harbor buoys, between the two wrecks marking the entrance to Tomil Harbor. The day was greasy, the sky overcast, the seas rough. A study of our charts prior to leaving showed that we had some 1500 miles to travel over a part of the Pacific Ocean generously sprinkled with small islands, atolls, reefs, and rocks. Our plan was to travel due east until we were well east of the longitude of the Ulithi group of islands, then to head northeast to a point slightly north of the latitude of Ponape, and then to set a course to Ponape on a diagonal that would clear us of the various reefs and islands that we might have encountered had we chosen a more direct course.

By 1700 hours our autopilot was again on the blink; and as we fought our way under sail through the mounting seas, a check of the bilges disclosed to our horror that we were *still* leaking massive amounts of diesel fuel and fresh water from our fuel and water tanks.

FIRE AT SEA

We went to work on the good old autopilot and the good old leaks. It was as if we had never made it to Yap. However, before long we were able to enter in the log:

Autopilot temporarily repaired; appears to have been a poor connection from 12-volt power source because of physical strain on wire (poor installation practice). Water and fuel leaks apparently caused by lack of proper sealing on outboard side of intakes. Plumbing and electrical workmanship of Taiwan shipyard incredibly poor.

During the first few days out of Yap we felt we were at last beginning to make some progress in conquering one of our biggest and most persistent mechanical problems—that of the leaking from our fuel and water tanks. It was impossible to make precise tests of the bilges, since there were several sources of fluid entry into them—some legit and some not— and examining the bilges as to content or chemical composition was far from an exact science. However, accepting these restrictions (as if we had any choice), as Bob and I reviewed and restudied the situation and its history, some highly significant facts finally dawned on us:

—Our leaking problems always occurred at the *beginning* of each leg. Even though we felt that we had worked on and had conquered the problem during one leg, always at the beginning of a new leg we were right back where we started.

—The one condition that was always the same at the beginning of each leg was that our water and fuel tanks were completely full—as full as we could possibly get them.

—The leaking occurred primarily, perhaps only, when we were under sail and heeling to one side or the other.

—Although access to the tanks was limited since the tanks were built into the boat, extensive and continued examination of the tanks themselves seemed to indicate that the leaks were from the top of the tanks.

During those first few days out of Yap we tested this theory by dropping all sails and proceeding under power; sure enough, even with *very* full tanks, we found ourselves losing only a minimal amount of fuel and fresh water. In order to keep from losing fuel in the bilges, we were burning it in the engine, which violated our principle of proceeding under sail as much as possible. But if we were going to lower the fuel in the tanks one way or the other, we might as well use the fuel to power the boat.

Working our theory to its conclusion, knowing (or thinking we knew) that the leaks were all from entries at the tops of the tanks, we concentrated our efforts on finding and curing those leaks. Unfortunately, the entries to the tops of the tanks were only about two inches below the bottom of the cabin sole, or floor of the pilot house. Getting at those entry holes with that two-inch space in each case was a real bitch. What we found by feel, hanging upside down for hours, flashlight in one hand, a screwdriver or other tool in the other hand, and some sort of sealant or glue or epoxy in the other hand, was that the Taiwan workers had put very good seals on each of the entries into the tanks, *but only on the side that could be seen from the engine room hatches.* The other side, the outboard side, of each entry had in effect no sealant at all!

Over a period of time, from port to port, we ended up tearing or cutting holes in the cabin sole above each of the entry points to the four fuel and water tanks so we could get at the openings and effect a good seal job.

But the final repair was long after the present leg of our journey from Yap to Ponape.

We finally lost sight of that beautiful but uncharted and unreported Loran tower at 2330 hours on the same day that we departed Yap—some forty-four miles away! And even then we lost sight only because the weather was closing in on us. We felt that we could have navigated on it all the way to Ponape if the weather had stayed clear.

On Thursday 13 June a study of the charts convinced me that we weren't all that sure of passing south of the Ulithi group of islands, nor south of Fair Island. We had an excellent navigational fix at 1100 hours on an RDF line from Yap Radio, and a sound sun line of position. Based on this fix we changed course slightly to the south, even though eventually we intended to thread our way north through the islands and reefs that appeared on the charts to be something like the Milky Way.

We tenderly raised the sails again, as we were getting good winds, although not *quite* from the right direction. The weather had worsened with the rising wind. We could use the sails along with the engine to steady the boat as well as to take advantage of saving some fuel—provided the fuel didn't all slosh out into the bilges!

And then the dreaded happened—hardly more than twenty-four hours out of Yap, the Perkins conked out, followed within the hour by the Ford main engine.

Bleed, bleed, bleed those fuel lines! Drain that filter! Tighten those nuts! We *still* weren't sure if the problem was air in the fuel, or if we were still suffering from the massive intake of water in the fuel from Bob's laundry accident in Manila.

Not to be forgotten, like a child not getting proper attention, the autopilot started acting up. With a little superficial juggling of wires and a whole chorus of loud cussing we were able to get the autopilot operating again. But the autopilot was, in the final analysis, a luxury that we had gotten by without in the past and surely could forego in the future. But bucking those prevailing winds from the east, there was no way we were going to make it almost due east to Ponape without our main engine!

Carol's log entry on the midnight-to-0400 watch on 14 June sets our mood well:

Carol and Harlan on watch. Bioluminescense noted at 0025. Sparkling dots in boat's wake, fairly widely scattered. Main engine quit at 0030. Bled lines. Started okay. Autopilot *and* main engine quit at 0045. Engine restarted at 0055. Anemometer not working. Power sailing with four working sails and main engine. Wind 12 to 15 knots. Sea choppy. Some scud; sprinkling rain. At 0300 engine off again; evidently quite a bit of air and water in fuel. Could be bad fuel from Yap. Tightened bolts on stuffing box on main shaft to cut down on water entry at that point. Bioluminescense ceases when not making way. Sprinkles increased to steady rain. Engine repaired—water drained from main fuel filters; underway and back on course at 0330.

As long as our engine was functioning we were able to make pretty good speed in the direction in which we wanted to go, but we knew that we simply could not make our goal if we had to power the entire distance to Ponape. At 0600 hours on 14 June, I calculated that we were safely past Fair Island and the Ulithi group, and could make our run somewhat northerly, through the Milky Way. Everything was fairly well in hand, except that the main engine was stopping and had to be bled and restarted every twenty minutes.

As time went on, every member of the crew became reasonably competent at bleeding the fuel lines and restarting the main engine. However, the main brunt fell on Bob and me, since, such as we were, we *were* the resident mechanics on board. Each time we went through the routine, we would tighten a nut here, a flange there, adjust the angle of a fuel line, clean a filter, replace a filter, do something, with the result that we were sure (well almost) that *this* time we had finally reached the root of the problem, and that everything would be okay from now on. So each time that the engine quit, it was not only a disappointment, but it had disproven another fine theory.

While Bob and I were working on The Problem on the evening of 14 June, and while we were drifting due to lack of both engine power and wind power, there was great excitement on deck: a large raft had been spotted off the starboard bow. When we had done our thing and restarted the engine, we altered course in order to make a dramatic rescue, or to say hello to the crew of Kon Tiki III. But the raft proved to be just and only that—a large raft made of bamboo, with no person and no other thing on it. We felt that it was big and sturdy enough to be a hazard to navigation, but there wasn't a thing we could do about it. We weren't in radio contact with anyone (we very seldom were). We could have reported it upon arrival at Ponape, but that was over a week away if we were lucky! And we knew our position at that particular time only within about ten miles.

So we went on our merry way, engine coughing, knuckles bleeding. . . .

Maybe it was the raft episode; maybe it was something else. But shortly after the raft sighting, I began to conjure up an image of the *Dagny Taggart* bucking the winds and seas toward Ponape for the next two weeks, slowly running out of engine time (we were now down to about a bleed every ten minutes), out of fuel and water, and ending up like that raft, a derelict in a part of the Pacific Ocean not regularly visited by much of anybody, or anything—except typhoons.

Much as I hated to admit it, or to do it, we simply had to put in someplace and get that damned air-in-fuel problem solved once and for all. At any cost.

But where was the nearest service station? Ulithi was the closest possible candidate. I had a fair amount of information in various publications about Ulithi, but nothing I read was encouraging. Except for the fact that it had a local high school, drawing from a school district of several thousand square miles, Ulithi had very little to offer a passing sailboat in distress. Much less than Yap. Going back to Yap hardly made sense. It was horrible from the standpoint of crew morale, and I felt that our friends on Yap had given us their all, but to no avail.

How discouraging; how unthinkable; how ridiculous. The *only* game in town was Guam. There was the Navy base, the Army base, the Air Force base, and the Dillingham base. Surely, beyond question, we could get technical advice and service in Guam to solve our heretofore unsolvable problem and get on with the show. With just a *little* luck, we could make the 350 miles or so up to Guam in three or four days, get our problem solved and repairs effected within forty-eight hours, take advantage of good long-range weather predictions, and get south again without encountering a tropical storm or typhoon.

Hopefully!

When it came to asking someone to clean up the head or the galley or the hull, or asking a crewmember to stay on board

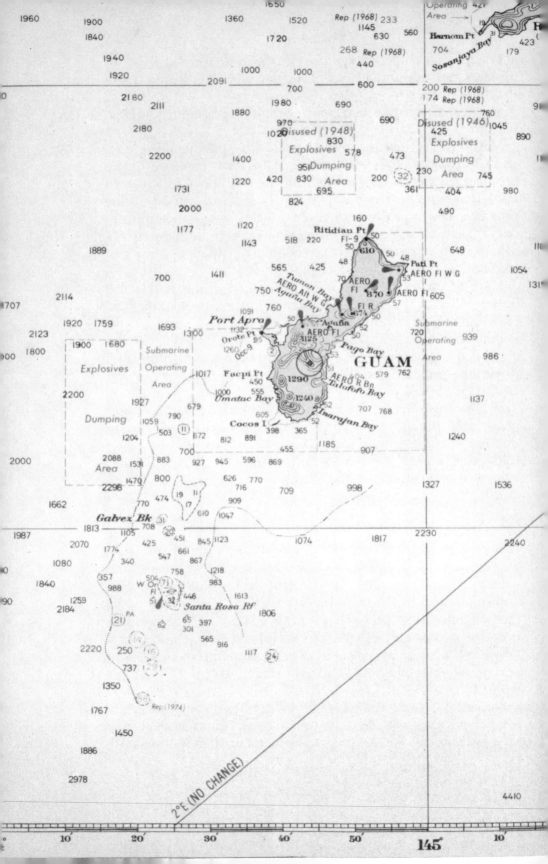

while the rest of us all went ashore for dinner, much of the time I was a miserable failure. Let someone else do it; I'm busy, I'm tired; there's something else I have to do. But when it came to making important decisions and having the crew follow my orders or decisions without question, I batted a thousand.

I said Guam; so Guam it was.

That same night at 0100 hours, we had our any-port-in-a-storm syndrome brought home loud and clear:

"Taylor! Taylor! Wake up! Wake up! The boat is on fire!"

And, by God, so it was!

For a guy who wears glasses and sleeps naked, there is always an embarrassing and sometimes disastrous delay in getting out of the sack and up where the action is, functioning like a true commanding officer. The first problem is where the hell did I leave my glasses, or from the place that I left them, where did they drift or roll to, and are they the right ones—for near-seeing or far-seeing as the case may be? And then where the hell are my pants? I can't go up there like *this.*

Between Carol and myself, within the next 120 seconds or so we got me decently attired and able to see. But even with the *right* glasses I couldn't see a thing. The smoke was so thick we could have cut it up into little cubes and sold it for souvenirs!

Grab the nearest fire extinguisher! Turn on the lights!

By the time I got topside there was no need for a fire extinguisher. Chuck, who was on watch, had turned off the main engine, and this had stopped the fire. And there were no lights anyway, because the ship's whole electrical system was completely kaput.

As we cleverly analyzed the matter the next day, or days (we had plenty of time for a complete analysis,) we determined what had happened. With repeated cranking of the Ford engine during the process of bleeding the fuel lines and starting the engine, the solenoid (which is a wonderful little device that converts electrical energy into mechanical energy, disengaging the starter motor from the diesel engine flywheel after the main engine has started) had overheated and had failed to tell the starter motor teeth to disengage from the Ford flywheel; the result was that the starter motor remained engaged to the main engine while the engine was revved up to plus or minus 1600 revolutions per minute.

At this horrifying point, the starter motor, mechanically driven by the flywheel, turned into an electric generator, humming and pumping electrical juice back into the entire electrical system, *the wrong way!*

It took only a few minutes to overload completely the capacity of all the battery cables, regular switches, knife switches, terminals, control boards, you name it. The whole system burned itself out! Some of the insulation in isolated areas of the boat smoldered for hours, maybe days. The odor of burning rubber and smoldering synthetic insulation lingered for weeks, maybe months. Even if we could somehow have rewired and saved the starter motor itself (which we couldn't), we would not have had enough battery cable (65 feet) to jury-rig even a partial electrical system.

But no matter how we cut it, it was still cheese. Devastating, devastated, charred, smoky, dirty, greasy, still smoking.

Fortunately there was no structural damage and only minimal damage to provisions and stores.

We were in real trouble.

And as never before in the history of sailing, a great calm descended over the entire Central Pacific Ocean—no wind, no swell, no waves, no clouds. Just sea and sky, all dead calm. We got a good navigational fix on the evening of 14 June when we made our prefire decision to head for Guam. Twenty-four hours later—after the fire and brimstone, when we had lots of time to work on it—we zeroed in on a near-perfect navigational fix. No question about it; we had traveled *only eighteen miles* over the past twenty-four hours. And the eighteen miles was in the *wrong* direction—we had actually been driven back by adverse currents.

The only bright spot at this point was that without anyone mentioning it, all hands seemed to be not only resigned but pleased with the fact that we had dumped Randy and Jim in Yap—the freedom from Randy's incessant negativism coupled with the greater flexibility of watch schedules, and simply having fewer people to cope with, proved to be a relief.

NO CHOICE: SAIL OR ELSE

Throughout the trip Harlan had a standard expression whenever we would get out to sea, raise the sails, and secure the engine: "Now we'll make a sailboat out of this old lady!"

Well, now we didn't have any choice. It was sink or swim. Sail or not get there at all. Wrongly or rightly I had concluded, and Bob concurred, that there was no way on God's green (or blue) earth that we could get that main engine back in operation by ourselves. Guam wasn't all that far away. And it was the *only* place. In fact, if something like this had to happen, we were lucky that it happened near a place like Guam that had fairly decent repair facilities.

To the great credit of everyone on board, there was no wailing nor gnashing of teeth nor rending of garments. A peacefulness came over us that was hard to explain. Of course it may have been that since this was our *third* emergency trip to someplace, we were all getting into a groove.

Part of the good feeling doubtless came from the fact that there wasn't anything we could do about the situation except sail the best we knew how.

And sail we did!

We had little wind, but usually enough to keep way on. The problem, as always, was that the wind was blowing from almost precisely the direction toward which we wished to travel. So we found ourselves continually pointing as high as we could.

With a heavy-displacement ketch, traveling in extremely light airs, getting caught trying to point too high is an ever-present danger. The log records repeated cases when the bow was pushed over on the other tack and we had to go through 360° to get back on course.

THE JAPANESE RETAKE GUAM!

Under a Japanese custom, doubtless dug up by the Japanese Tourist Agents' Association, it is considered good luck to have *two* wedding ceremonies—one in Japan, followed by one in another country. In recent years a combination of economic prosperity in Japan and resulting affluence of a large segment of the Japanese population, the jet-age proximity of Guam to Japan, and the very favorable climate, topography, flora and fauna of Guam all have encouraged Japanese couples to have their second wedding ceremony and honeymoon in the tropical setting of Guam.

When one of the Japanese tour groups is disgorged from a large jet and descends on a Guam resort hotel, there is frequently a notable temporary lack of service to other guests.

Our friend Chuck Griffin, living in Guam, tells the story, perhaps true, perhaps apocryphal, of a Guam businessman who was trying to get some service in a Guam hotel just as it was inundated by a Japanese tourist group. After a frustrating wait the businessman seized the banner of the tour guide, whom the Japanese tourists had been following. Waving the banner high over his head, he marched outside to an idle bus—and sure enough, the lobby was cleared as the dutiful Japanese followed their banner and boarded the bus.

A funny thing happened as we approached this latter-day Japanese Garden of Eden. For the first time in what seemed like forever, the wind was not blowing directly from the point that we were trying to reach. Wonder of wonders, the wind was blowing precisely *toward* the point we were trying to reach, and blowing pretty hard. Good. We can take lots of wind when it is blowing us toward where we want to go.

But there is a funny thing about a sailboat; it has difficulty maintaining course if the wind is *exactly* over its stern; it is much more comfortable and certainly safer to take the wind slightly to one side or the other of dead astern.

So there we were, no engine power, sail only, finally with some wind in the right direction—but so *perfectly* in the right direction that we couldn't maintain the course we wanted.

The night of Tuesday 18 June, at 2100, the watch sighted the glow of light reflected off clouds at 040° magnetic. Doubtless the lights of Guam. And the next morning Chuck and Jane sighted the land mass itself. By 0800 on Wednesday we were able to pick up identifiable landmarks on shore and proceeded up the west coast of the island toward Apra Harbor. We made contact on 2182 kHz with the U.S. Coast Guard at

0915, and at 1015 talked with the Apra Harbor harbormaster's office on VHF Channel 16.

We had read in H.O. 82, *Sailing Directions for the Pacific Islands,* that the current at the entrance to Apra Harbor was fairly severe, ranging from 1½ knots to as high as 3 knots. We therefore consulted carefully with the harbormaster as to his recommendation on our entering the harbor without engine power. Quite understandably the harbormaster took the safe course and recommended that a tug be dispatched to assist us through the harbor entrance.

Just outside Apra Harbor on a gorgeous sunny spring day with the sea and sky vying as to which had the brightest sparkle, we made our rendezvous with the Dillingham tug *Mahale* under command of harbor pilot Bill Hatcher, who brought us smoothly and smartly alongside one of Dillingham's docks in Apra Harbor—well, not quite alongside the dock, but rather alongside the *Pine March No. 2,* a large Korean fishing vessel that was unloading its catch of skipjack tuna into waiting refrigerated trucks. The trucks in turn worked in round-the-clock relays to take the fish to the Guam airport, from which this delicacy was flown back to the States for consumption. This delicacy, in the midst of which we had been for over a month, without being able to catch one of the elusive buggers! We would have to talk to the Korean fishermen about *that.*

While I was far from sure that we really needed that Dillingham tug, at least we had made contact right off the bat with the right outfit to locate and cure our mechanical problems—the Dillingham tug had deposited us at the Dillingham dock, so the company couldn't very well ignore us. Also, in talking to the crew of the tug as they had towed us side-by-side after entry into the harbor, I had gathered intelligence. Our key person was Rey Johnson, head of Dillingham's marine maintenance and repair facilities on Guam.

I soon made contact with Rey, who appeared to be affable, cooperative, capable—and busy as hell. He came through loud and clear that his company's experience with servicing private yachts had not been good, that the effort expended by the company did not match the compensation received, and that Dillingham was developing a policy of not servicing private

The Dillingham tug Mihale *tows* Dagny Taggart *into Apra Harbor,*
Guam.

yachts. I believe it was only because my company had had extensive dealings with Dillingham, and that we had mutual business associates, that Rey agreed to tackle our problems.

Fortunately for us, one of Dillingham's chief trouble-shooters in the Pacific, Bob Endler, who was also a fine mechanic, was on temporary assignment on Guam and was able to help Rey in the administration of our work and with the work itself.

I wrote out in order of priority a list of work that we needed to have done in Guam and gave it to Rey Johnson. First priority was the extensive air leaks into the fuel system. I insisted that he replace the entire existing copper tubing system with aircraft neoprene hoses and fittings, install separate fuel lines for each engine, including separate water trap with pet cock for draining, and separate primary filter for each engine and fuel system; second, repair and replacement of the burned-out starter motor on the Ford diesel engine; third, check for an air leak in the Perkins diesel fuel system; fourth, repair of the damage to the battery cables and leads burned or fused as a result of overcharge from the locked-in starter motor; and fifth, repair of the autopilot.

We had various requests of lesser urgency. To our discredit, I think we in the crew sometimes lost sight of the overriding importance and urgency of just these five items and got ourselves and Dillingham bogged down with other jobs.

As soon as I had reached an agreement with Rey Johnson, I contacted Joanne by telex to let her, our families, my company, et cetera know what the hell was going on. Her immortal words by telex on 19 June 1974:

HI CHIEF—WE ARE GETTING SEASICK CHARTING YOUR COURSE ACROSS THE PACIFIC. HAVE NOTIFIED FAMILIES AND HAVE CABLED YAP AND PONAPE ADVISING OF YOUR ARRIVAL IN GUAM.

The bad news was that our prospective Ponape-to-Honolulu skipper, Bruce, had learned that it was now impossible for him to make the voyage. What bitter disappointment! Bruce reminded me that I had agreed that if he felt he couldn't make it, he would be free to secure a professional or semiprofessional skipper, and negotiate the financial arrangements.

During our stay in Guam we had numerous telexes and

telephone calls involving all the possible skippers or skipper sources we had considered over the past few months. Joanne had really beaten the bushes and her brains out for us. She not only worked with Bruce and his various leads, but also had checked again with our Wind 'n Sea buddies, with my old yacht club in Newport Beach, with the Balboa Bay Club, and again with old WW II buddy John LaMontagne.

Some of the propositions Bruce had presented, and we had turned down, were interesting insofar as they illustrated where we perhaps should have been in our thinking, but were not:

—A proposition to ship the boat from Guam to Marina del Rey for US$27,000, which seemed outrageous at the time, but perhaps, in retrospect. . . .

—An offer by Bob Sloane, whom Bruce described as the local dean of yacht deliveries, to handle the entire delivery from Guam to Marina del Rey for a flat fee of US$11,000.

—An offer by another experienced skipper who felt that under the circumstances of an owner/wife being on board, a fair arrangement would be simply to charge for the skipper's time at US$1,400 per month.

—And perhaps the most consistent and maybe the most significant position taken by the more experienced skippers: they disapproved of our route across the Central Pacific and would accept the assignment only if they could have their own crew (without those presently on board). They would head north from Guam (or wherever) far enough to catch the westerlies and head back to the States via the latitude of Vancouver/Seattle. This of course was exactly what I had considered and flirted with for lo those many months, and had rejected as being too rough, literally and figuratively, on an amateur crew and a brand new boat; certainly there was no way that we could have attracted an amateur crew for a North Pacific crossing!

And having come this far, committed to the Central Pacific route, could I afford, economically or morally, to send the crew home and turn the boat over to a professional to head north where the big boys go?

In a long letter Bruce, after reviewing various prospects, had recommended a young seaman who had come highly recommended to him by various outstanding yachtsmen/sailors in the

Southern California area. Pete had good skills, including celestial navigation, and fantastic long-distance racing experience—Transpac, Acapulco, Newport-Bermuda, Mazatlan, La Paz, as well as races in the Mediterranean—and also return voyages. Everything was a plus right down to the line with the one exception: he was only twenty-two, which was younger than any of our crew on the *Dagny Taggart*.

As I pondered the imponderables, my internal computer decreed that considering our mechanical problems and the all-important business of making all the right moves in order to avoid encountering a typhoon, the best course was for me to stick with the *Dagny Taggart* safely to Ponape, where the boat would be out of the typhoon belt, where we would have had some 900 mechanically trouble-free miles under our keel, and I would feel comfortable leaving my precious son, wife, friends, and boat in the hands of another. I authorized Joanne to hire Pete to fly to Ponape, where he would take over as skipper for the legs from Ponape to Majuro to Honolulu.

There seems to be a rule among humankind that the smaller the community the larger the hospitality, and conversely the *larger* the community the *smaller* the hospitality until you get up to places as large as New York or Los Angeles or Washington, where the hospitality almost disappears. Compared to Yap, where the hospitality had been so tremendous, Guam was a pretty big place. We were a *bit* of a novelty, but not the biggest thing that had happened in the last two years! In the overall scheme of things, however, Guam was small enough to produce some pretty good local hospitality.

The first day, Carol and Jane and I went to the Marianas Yacht Club to shower and clean up. The shower was great, except that it was simply rigged up on the branch of a tree, in the great outdoors, right next to the beach. No one else was around, and there was no modesty, false or otherwise, among Carol and Jane and myself. So no problem; well, no problem until a car drove up alongside us! Turned out to be a great guy—Chuck Griffin—who was stopping by to check his small sailboat, which he kept at the club. Chuck looked the other way while Jane and Carol grabbed some clothes. Like so many of the residents on Guam, Chuck had spent some time in the service on the island, had decided it was a great place to be, and had come back to make Guam his home.

Natural Bay, Guam, where Magellan landed. The white church marks the spot where he reportedly went ashore.

That day and later, Chuck showed us with pride all around his island with about all the hospitality that one person could give out. How many people know that the largest McDonald's *in the world* is located on Guam! Largest both in square feet and in dollar volume! Gourmet restaurants; luxury hotels; beautiful beaches for swimming, surfing, skin diving; fascinating history; ancient ruins; historical monuments; Japanese honeymooners.

Meanwhile, back at the Dillingham dock, Bob Endler, Jim King, Don Ski, and Castro were tearing out, tearing up, cutting open, cleaning out . . . what a mess! Just like being back in Anthony's Wong's yard again, only the workmen spoke English and were twice as big—which was a handicap (the size, not the language). The Dillingham people simply could not get into or even reach into some of the spots that the Chinese had been able to hop in and out of with ease. So Castro, the carpenter, simply cut bigger holes. We finally solved our leaking from the top of the starboard fuel and water tanks by cutting a giant hatch in the cabin sole, which gave us—aha, at last—easy access to the fittings leading into the tanks. Once we had access, we had it made.

Bob Endler, a big, handsome guy of German extraction, was in direct charge of the job; he was a stickler for doing things right or not doing them at all. If there was a problem with the fuel, then let's get all that old fuel out of there and put in new fuel that we are sure is water-free and dirt-free. And while we're at it, we'll clean out the tanks!

Gulp! I could see the comic strip in which dozens of little dollar signs flitted about in the sky with wings attached. But I couldn't argue with motherhood as espoused by a stubborn German about six-foot-five, who after all was doing our work solely as an accommodation to us.

As soon as Bob Endler had made his initial survey, we went over with him the list of parts that he would need. Most items on the list were available on the island, with the exception of some parts for the Ford diesel. These I wrote down. When Bob asked me why I was doing this, I told him that I would ask Joanne Davis and Bill Druitt to have the parts sent over to us by Pan Am. Bob replied that this would not be necessary; he would contact Dillingham's office in Honolulu, who would have them for us in a few days. At this time I was still counting hours, not days, to get out of Guam. I told Bob that I would go ahead and order through my channels anyway, and if we had duplication, that would be okay because we could always use the spares.

About three or four days later, Rey Johnson asked me if I could step into his office for a minute.

"Taylor, you wouldn't by any chance consider staying here on Guam, or coming back to Guam, and accepting a job as purchasing expediter for us, would you?"

He said that those parts I ordered were on the dock less than twenty-four hours after I wrote down the list! He had placed his order for the same parts at the same time over the company's computer-controlled purchasing network and hadn't yet received even an acknowledgment of the order!

On behalf of myself, Joanne Davis, Bill Druitt, and my friends with Pan Am, I declined the job. But it was a bit of a thrill. I didn't dare tell Rey that the Ford diesel injector pump that we had ordered from Guam had been located in Aberdeen, Scotland! If I *had*, I'm sure Rey would *never* have let me leave the island!

The Dillingham guys finally gave up on rewiring our burned-out starter motor or acquiring a new one on Guam, which they had originally thought possible. I ordered a new one through my private procurement network and picked it up at the airport on Wednesday 26 June. That seemed to be the signal for things to start winding up at last. Two days later I was able to make the following glorious entry in the log:

> At approximately 1830 hours, fired up both the main engine and the generator engine; in each case engine started on first turn! Ran both engines for about an hour; each sounded quieter and smoother than ever before! Hot dog!

Our one small remaining hitch was that the day before, Bob Endler had discovered that one of the injectors on the Perkins was frozen. He was able to fix the injector, but was very fearful that it might have caused permanent damage to the injector pump. He highly recommended that we acquire a spare injector pump before we left Guam.

Work one of your miracles, Taylor!

I sent Joanne a telex right away, and the next morning at 0230 hours Guam time, I called to confirm the order.

Saturday 29 June was to be our last day, *for sure*. Frequently and intermittently we had been out-prioritied when key Dillingham personnel working on our job were pulled off to more vital jobs for the U.S. Navy or commercial ships. We had been promised on stacks of holy writs that our Dillingham's electronic expert, Don Ski, would be available to us all day on our last day, Saturday, to track down and repair the problem with the autopilot.

If we could just get the autopilot to work and pick up the spare Perkins injector pump at the airport, and take on fuel, we could get the hell out of Guam. I was extremely anxious to leave right then, not only for the usual reasons of getting the boat and the crew and myself back to the States ASAP, but according to the U.S. Naval Air Station weather service, we had a marvelous weather window for the next week, which meant we could be virtually assured of no typhoon danger if we would leave *now*.

Fueling presented the usual problem. At first we tried to take fuel by hose from a Dillingham tug. The problem was the tug's pumps had only two speeds: full-off or full-blast. Hard as the crew of the tug tried, they couldn't get a flow that our small fuel inlets would accommodate. After son Bob had gotten completely soaked with diesel fuel, including eyes and ears and hair, and I had a good eyeful, we gave up with the tug and filled our tanks by siphoning from fifty-gallon barrels delivered to dockside. Just this once it was an advantage that the dock level was about twenty feet above the deck of the *Dagny Taggart*. Naturally, as we were moving the boat from place to place to take on fuel and to try to analyze and repair the autopilot problem, a series of severe line squalls came roaring across Apra Harbor!

While out in the harbor working on the autopilot, we saw frenzied waving on shore. As we powered by the Dillingham dock, the message came to us over the howling wind that I had an important call from Los Angeles. I felt that I had better get ashore and take the call, since I was about to drop out of communication with the world for a while—I hoped. So even though better judgment would have dictated waiting for a lull in the storm, I gave the wheel to son Bob and asked him to cruise by an old tug that was tied up to an old barge, so I could hop off.

Bob and I didn't get our act well enough rehearsed ahead of time; I thought for a moment that the trip was over right there in Apra Harbor. As Bob maneuvered to come by the tug close enough to let me off, he found that it was necessary to have considerable way on the boat to maintain steerage against the strong wind and waves carried by the squall. The wind caught our bow just as we approached the tug and slammed the *Dagny Taggart* hard against the side of the steel tug. I was certain that we had suffered damage, but miraculously we never found any evidence of injury from this collision.

I managed to get off the boat and take my call. It was Joanne with news re the Perkins injector pump shipment, as well as some other business and personal information, including a request from friend Tom Flattery: would I consent to accept the position of treasurer of the Los Angeles Regional Group of the American Society of Corporate Secretaries? How far away that type of thing seemed to me now!

Still at the height of the storm, the autopilot testing over, Carol brought the boat beautifully and successfully into the Dillingham dock—a considerable feat, since the visibility through the driving rain was almost zilch, and the waves in the shallow harbor were steep and mean and coming from all directions as they slammed into the solid seawall that made up the Dillingham dock. The autopilot failure had been a simple maladjustment in the limiting switches. The same problem occurred several times later on the voyage, but after watching Don Ski run the problem down, we were able to adjust and repair it easily.

We picked up the Perkins injector pump at the Guam airport later that afternoon. On the way back to the boat we stopped by Bob Endler's apartment to say goodbye, and also to check on the proper settings on the pump. All checked out okay. By the time we returned to the boat, the crew had prepared dinner. Bob Endler had driven to the dock to help us get away. So, with tropical rain beating down on the deck above us, we had a farewell dinner with Bob and Chuck Griffin and departed the Dillingham dock under power at 2140 hours on Saturday 29 June 1974, ten days after our arrival for a two-day repair job.

IN DEEP WATER AGAIN

By the time we departed from the Dillingham dock the last squall had passed, enabling us to make our exit from Apra Harbor under a clear night sky with the dignity becoming a lady such as *Dagny Taggart*—nothing like our ignominious entrance being pulled by a tug!

We passed down the west coast of Guam and were abeam of Cocos Island at 0230 hours; we lost sight of Guam about mid-morning the next day.

Studying our charts for currents, winds, navigational hazards, and the like on our course from Guam to Ponape, I realized that at about 1600 hours on the afternoon of our first day out of Guam we would be over the Marianas Trench, the deepest part of the Pacific Ocean, or of any ocean for that matter—a depth of 36,000 feet. No getting around it, we had to have a swim call *right at that point*. We checked our navigation as best we could—which was pretty good since we had so recently left Guam and still had Radio Guam on which to take RDF bearings.

With water temp in the low 80s, a beautiful sunny day, God was in his heaven, and we were in his water. All was right with the world.

After a great swim we resumed course and speed under sail and power. My log entry reads:

Underway enroute to Ponape on course 115° by compass, on main engine, fore stays'l and mizzen sail. Autopilot holding course very well within two to three degrees. Changed course to 113° compass to adjust for 2° east magnetic variation. Wind dead ahead with medium swells.

And then *zambo!* The main engine stopped right in the middle of an aspiration! Please! Let it be anything but air in the fuel!

Chuck adjusts the genoa sheet as Dagny Taggart *leaves Guam.*

We checked the main fuel filter; it had at least two cups of water in it! Not a healthy situation, but a lot better than still having an air leak. Hopefully whatever water there might be in the new fuel we picked up from Dillingham would be filtered out within a few days, since the fuel tank outlets were from the bottoms of the fuel tanks and water is heavier than diesel fuel.

As per Dal Arnold's recommendation, we had asked the Dillingham people to install two separate outlets from the fuel tanks, feeding into two separate primary filters, but in our somewhat peculiar status of Dillingham working on our boat more or less as a favor, we didn't get everything exactly as we wanted it. Bob Endler had moved the primary fuel filter higher to a more accessible spot, but had felt that two entirely separate systems were not necessary.

The leg of our voyage from Guam to Ponape was not uneventful. Our mechanical difficulties continued, and we developed a small leak in the hull. When heeling, we had a heavy and steady fuel leak from the vent in the port fuel tank, so we had to drop sails and power despite good winds. We managed a repair, but the engine continued to conk out.

The main thing we wanted to miss as we approached Ponape was a spot that a lot of our predecessors had not missed: the dreaded Minto Reef. The description in the sailing directions for the Pacific Islands tells the story:

> MINTO REEF (north end, 8° 11′ N., 154° 18′ E.), 59 miles northwestward of Oroluk Island, is an atoll reef, about 4½ miles long. A sand bank about 6 feet high stands on the north side of the reef. This reef is visible only under favorable conditions of light, and constitutes a dangerous hazard at all other times. Several wrecks lie stranded on this reef. There are several shoal passages into the lagoon.

Sounds like a nice place to live, but I'd sure hate to visit it suddenly at four o'clock in the morning! *Visible only under favorable conditions of light* . . . I know of lots of navigational hazards that are hard to see if the light is poor. This was the first one I had encountered that could be seen *only* if the light was just right.

Here we were in the goddamn doldrums, literally and

figuratively! We, mostly Bob, seemed to be able to nurse the main engine into life only occasionally. The wind gave us help only occasionally. While we felt good about our navigation, the techniques of celestial are such that if you are within a few miles of where you think you are, you're doing as well as can be expected. Besides, days would go by in which squalls, cloud cover, or haze would prevent our getting any sights. And there was that damned current! Sometimes as high as 2½ knots, and usually the wrong way.

On the same day that Bob was going through the frustration of tearing apart the Ford diesel fuel system and putting it back together again only to find no improvement; as he was being sick over the side every-hour-on-the-hour from the nauseous effect of the diesel fumes, Joanne back in the other world received a letter from Ann, a good friend of Bob's, asking for Bob's address so she could write to him. Ann stated in part of her letter to Joanne: "Maybe I should just address it: Bob Hancock, Paradise!"

OH, WHAT A BEAUTIFUL MORNING!

One exceedingly rough night in a series of exceedingly rough nights and days, as we were approaching Yap on the second leg of our voyage, I was getting up to go on watch as Carol was coming off watch, attempting to take off her outerwear and fall into the sack. The boat took a nasty lurch, tossing her against the bulkhead or into a doorknob, or something:

"Jesus, Taylor! Is this *really* your idea of a good time? We've got problems up to our eardrums. We see each other and talk less out here than we do back home when we're each working twelve hours a day. At least at home we sleep in the same bed roughly the same hours; and we have our weekends together, mostly anyhow; and I can't remember the last time we made love, it's been so damned long ago! I thought we were going to rediscover one another on this trip. Why can't we be together more often?"

Another bad lurch didn't help things much, except it gave me an excuse to get up on deck and see if everything was okay—because I really didn't have very good answers to any of Carol's questions.

Why was it that we didn't stand watches together anyway? I think I had the notion that since I had both my wife and my son on board, I wanted to do all I could to avoid the risk of either the appearance or the reality of a family-clique arrangement. I knew what could happen to the morale of the ship's crew in the face of actual or suspected favoritism by the captain.

This time I knew for *sure* that leg four, from Guam to Ponape, would be my last leg. I wanted desperately to please Carol. I still had hope that if somehow we could smooth this trip out she would fall in love with life at sea, and I did want to be with Carol. For all these reasons, and also because she was right—we didn't even get to sleep together anymore—I set the watch schedules on leg four so that Carol and I would stand our watches together—and naturally we would be off watch and in the sack at the same time.

Good arrangement!

My official log entry on the 0400-to-0800 on Sunday 1 July 1974 was:

> Underway as before in North Pacific Ocean enroute to Ponape. Making about 3 knots through the water in genoa, main and mizzen. Beautiful night and morning. Ideal sailing day, and all is well: no water in bilges; all sails drawing well; good round of morning sights.

No wonder I was so satisfied: my *real* log entry of important events would have recorded the fact that at 0615 Carol appeared topside in all her glory, naked as a jay bird! So what, she said, they've all seen my body before, and what do we have to hide? After all, we *are* man and wife and all that. I was convinced. *Sailing* wasn't the only thing it was an ideal day for!

In retrospect, I did have some qualms; I couldn't help but recall that I had dinged Randy for *reading* on watch. . . .

Son Bob, silhouetted against a build-up of clouds, wears the tattered swim trunks he lived in for five months.

ON THE WAY TO PONAPE

Except for a few delightful interludes, leg four was a nightmare.

One day we would have good wind, or would be able to keep the Ford diesel alive by nursing, or praying, or exorcising, or what have you. The next day there would be no wind, or wind in the wrong direction, or rough seas, or all three, all against us, and no way to get any power from the engine.

We had a good day on the Fourth of July—hurray hurray—but Bob somehow managed to puncture the lower palm of his hand while opening a gallon can of apples. Carol gave first aid, wrapping Bob's hand impressively.

We bled air out of the fuel, we drifted, we cursed, we sailed, we cursed, we drifted, we bled.

On 6 July, our log entry:

> Sun line at 1600 hours indicated 6 miles westerly—*westerly!* the wrong damned direction! since 0800 hours. Swimming call at 1730; delightful. Shampoos and razors and good time. Picked up Truk Radio beacon at 165° True. Lovely chicken dinner on after deck, accompanied by Hawaiian music from Radio Guam.

I know that all of our nerves were drawn taut during those trying days. Through Jane, we have a direct reading on how taut:

> Saturday 6 July: Seems like I'm bound to have a run in with someone. Bob's turn today!

We had somewhat of a turnaround on Sunday 7 July; Chuck had virtually torn apart the entire fuel filter assembly on the Ford diesel and reassembled it over a period of a couple of days. For reasons that we didn't understand then, but do now, the repairs worked and gave us a 40 or 50 percent use of the main engine when we needed it for the next few days.

And by God, with the improvement in our mechanical situation, we had a similar pickup in our human relationships.

Unfortunately it wasn't quite that simple. We still had mass failures of our fuel system, and mass efforts to cure, followed by mass failures. We still muddled through somehow. Our log entries show good meals, swimming calls, pleasant weather.

Dammit! There *had* to be a way to get our two diesel engines working properly. The answer was right there in front of us . . . someplace. We've got to start with the assumption that the brand new fuel lines installed by Dillingham in Guam are airtight. Where else could air be leaking in?

I went back to my high school physics, my college engineering courses, my Coast Guard training, my fooling around with automobile engines most of my life. I finally began to grasp a small bit of the Great Truth about what was going on in the air-in-the-fuel department. That air was being sucked in someplace. Our fuel supply system was a vacuum system, under which the electric fuel pump on each engine created a suction from the main fuel system. As I sketched this system a hundred times on paper, and a thousand times in my mind, it began to dawn on me that there could be a *thousand* places where a little or a lot of air could be sucked in and there would be no way to detect it.

Why not create a system that would be a *pressure* system, instead of a *vacuum* system? If a pressure system had a small leak, so what? So you would lose a little fuel, but no air would be allowed in. Besides, you could see where the diesel fuel was leaking and easily effect a repair.

But how does one build a pressure fuel system in the middle of the Central Pacific Ocean?

Well, I tried.

I took a five-gallon jerrycan—the kind you see strapped on the rear end of jeeps heading for the desert—cut open the top to allow access, and drilled a quarter-inch hole near the bottom. I inserted some flexible quarter-inch tubing into the lower drain hole and applied epoxy putty on both the inside and outside of the bond, in order to make a fuel-tight seal. Then I epoxied the top of the jerrycan back on.

My crew buddies didn't give me much moral support:

"How are you gonna keep that five-gallon can full of fuel all the time?"

"How are you gonna keep the diesel fuel from slopping out of the top of the can in rough weather?"

"Where are you gonna *put* the damned thing—if you ever get it made?"

"If God had wanted diesel engines to have pressure fuel systems, he would have made them that way in the first place!"

After a couple of days my Rube Goldberg device was ready for the moment of truth. We didn't want to cut off the engine just for the sport of trying out my invention, so we waited for the engine to conk out again. And do you think that damned assemblage of iron and pumps and pistons and injectors would cooperate with me?

Hell no! For the first time in two months, it just purred away, hour after hour, without even a hiccup!

Well, good! I would save my monster as a threat. If, as, and when, old Lehman Ford, you conk out again, you are gonna get what's good for you!

KEEPING IT CLEAN AT SEA

If someone made a study of dishwashing, and I suppose there are those who do such things, I bet the study would find that the ingredients most necessary to ease the task at hand are plenty of hot fresh water and a supply of good soap.

We had the soap.

We had asked our Chinese shopkeeping friend at the Bird Alley Anchor Chain Store where we could get a good supply of liquid detergent. Anna May turned the shop over to her brother and led us down and around and up the next commercial alley, which I suppose could have been called Soap Alley. We bought a couple of gallons of what turned out to be a fine detergent. We had, and have now, no idea whether it was bathtub stuff or was made by DuPont in Delaware and shipped to Hong Kong along with the California oranges, but there it was, soapy, slippery, and cheap! No fancy containers; it was in cast-off Eastman Kodak photographic chemical bottles, made of yellow plastic—but no matter about that.

We never wanted to use our precious fresh water at sea for any purpose for which seawater would suffice, and, after a fashion, seawater will do the job of washing dishes. We would heat up some seawater, and with our Hong-Kong-Soap-Alley soap the results were reasonably good. It was still a bore to pump enough seawater for a good rinse job, but having the grease well cut by the soapy hot water was 80 percent of the job.

And then once when the generator engine wasn't operating properly or at all, and we were using a two-burner kerosene/ alcohol stove, which we carried for such emergencies, we gave up the luxury of hot water for dishwashing. This meant a fair amount of the old wiping-off-the-grease-film-with-the-dish-cloth trick, but with both engines out or threatening, fuel and water leaks, an unhappy crew, and sixty-nine other panic or near-panic problems, a little grease wiped off with a dishcloth didn't seem like the end of the world.

But as the leg wore on, the greasiness at the end of the washing cycle seemed to be getting worse and worse . . . could the water be getting colder? No; our log observations showed that the seawater temp was going up as we journeyed farther south.

After about ten days, when the greasy dishes situation was nearing ridiculum, I finally asked one of my crew mates if he (or she, I've forgotten which) had noticed the same phenomenon:

"Yeah, I sure have! Miserable. I thought it was just me. What the hell could it be?"

"Hey, Jane, have you noticed any problem with the dishes having a residue of grease on them, even after you wash them?"

"Yes. I meant to say something about that last time I had cleanup duty, but by the time I finished fighting the grease, I was so tired I fell in the sack, exhausted."

There must be an answer.

The next morning on the long 0400-to-0800 watch, I held a seance with myself. Usually this works. No soap.

Soap! No soap! You don't suppose. . . .

Sure enough. I practically *tore* back to the lazarette, where the yellow plastic bottle containing the main supply of Hong-Kong-Soap-Alley soap was stored.

And there it was—the yellow plastic bottle—right next to *another* yellow plastic bottle of the same general size and configuration but containing the legend "Wesson Oil"!

No *wonder* we were all finding that the dishes were greasy even after washing—we had been washing them with Wesson Oil instead of soap! The last time I had filled the galley soap dispenser, I had poured from the yellow Wesson Oil container instead of from the yellow Soap Alley container!

I wondered how many other dumb things like that I might be doing without knowing it—things that might show up only after it was too late.

CHANNEL? WHAT CHANNEL?

We had other little unsolved mysteries. In the evening log for Tuesday 9 July, Carol wrote:

> 2005: at 40° magnetic a bright green flash with a red tail, similar to a skyrocket was sighted off our port beam, followed almost immediately by what seemed to be a normal falling star. We supposed it was a satellite re-entering the earth's atmosphere.

And we had our little indiscretions:

Mainly because I like music, and dislike the bother of changing records or cassettes, I hunted long and hard in Hong Kong for just the right sound system. I wanted a 12-volt cassette-playing stereo system that would play continuously—that is, play through to one end of a tape, reverse itself back to the beginning, and then start over. It wasn't easy, but after spending an inordinate amount of time I succeeded, even though I had to make some tough trade-offs both in cost and in features—no radio as a part of the system, for instance.

I lived to regret my decision. I had forgotten we had the Modern Generation on board and that the musical tastes of said Modern Generation were a long way from mine. And to further my agony, both Taiwan and Hong Kong are meccas for the collector of Modern Generation music; there is no concern about copyright laws or such nonsense. Pirate tapes are available at less than the cost of blank tapes in the States.

A person, this person anyhow, can tolerate almost anything one time. So it's a piece of music that I don't like, played too loudly. Big deal. But the third and fourth time it would sometimes get to me. The continuous play feature had its own little Catch-22. If I turned the thing off, I was being a killjoy. On the other hand, if I had just not lost my senses and had acquired a conventional sound system, it would have been the most natural thing in the world to slip down and put on *another* cassette when the offending one reached its ending. Hoisted on my own petard.

It was just a little after midnight on the morning of 10 July. *Jesus Christ, Superstar* was blaring out of our stereo speakers at about 120 decibels. I figured everyone else must be up, having a party, and there I was in the sack! But no, Carol was next to me conked out. Who the hell is making all that noise? The first time the tape played I more or less tolerated it, but the second time was too much!

I gathered my wits and pants and glasses about me and stumbled out to investigate. There was son Bob, at the galley in the pilothouse, singing and stomping in time to the blaring music, washing the dishes from the night before, and roaring drunk!

Earlier in the voyage I probably would have sacked him, or disowned him, or something. But he had worked so hard, so conscientiously, and literally had kept us going out there, I figured he had one coming to him!

I did suggest that perhaps the music should be turned off, or down to super soft, and that the place to stand one's watch was back at the helm, topsides, and not below in the galley doing the job that he should have done last night.

Bob's own log entry is pretty revealing:

> 0000-0400: RH on watch. Calm. Nothing goin' on 'cept that music was too loud and the party on watch was inconsiderate. Engine needs to be bled about every two hours now, at forward secondary filter; this seems to keep it truckin'.

By the afternoon of 10 July we had secured what appeared to be a very accurate navigational fix that enabled us to change course and head directly for Ponape rather than steering to the north to avoid the danger of Minto Reef. We narrowly missed a water spout—a spectacular demonstration of Mother Nature's irresistible power. We were down to bleeding the main engine every thirty minutes to keep it operating continuously.

We celebrated Carol's birthday that evening. Bob presented her with a Taiwan flag that he had saved for the occasion. Jane made a cheesecake and a way-out punch concocted of whatever she was able to pick up from the corner punch store, which turned out to be wine and vodka!

As we neared Ponape, I studied all my sources of information regarding the island and posted the highlights in which I thought the crew would be interested:

Geology:	Volcanic basalt, surrounded by barrier reef with approximately 25 islets.
Fauna:	Water buffalo.
Highest Point:	Telecome Peak at 2,595 feet; often hidden by clouds.
General:	Ponape Island is part of the Senyavin Islands which consist of Ant Atoll, Pakin Atoll, and Ponape Island. Ponape Island is the second largest land mass in the Trust Territory.
Flora:	Very fertile, coconut palms, breadfruit, various trees, cacao, pepper, cassavas.
Harbor:	Ponape Harbor. Confined, but irregular with many reefs. Main entrance 400 yards wide.
Capital:	Village of Kolonia on hilly ground about 100 feet high at SW side of inlet at head of harbor.
Lights:	Ponape Island Light, on reef on south side of Ponape Passage. White round tapered concrete tower. Fl W 6 sec. 8-11 mile range.

I also posted two work checklists, one of items on which we needed outside help and one of items that we hoped the crew could accomplish. It was pretty discouraging: neither list was

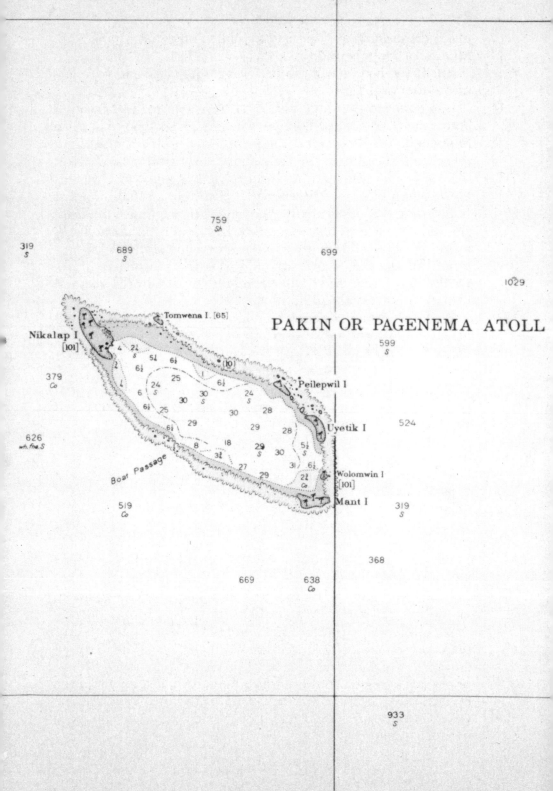

759
SA

319
S

689
S

699

1029

PAKIN OR PAGENEMA ATOLL

Tomwena I. [65]

Nikalap I
[101]

599
S

4 2½
S   5½   6¼
       6¼
       24   6½
       S   25
6   30   30
S   *S*   24
6¼ 25   *S*
       30   28
6¼   29
                29   28
       8   18   29
              29   30
       3½   5½
                         S
       27   3½ 6¼
       29   2½
                    Co
Boat Passage

Peilepwil I

524

Uyetik I

Wolomwin I
[101]

Mant I

379
Co

626
wh. fne. S

519
Co

319
S

368

669

638
Co

933
S

much different from the lists we had posted for Guam, Yap, Manila, or Hong Kong.

But at the head of all the lists was to diagnose and cure air-in-the-fuel problem!

As we moved that little pencil dot representing our position across the chart toward Ponape, what always seemed to happen happened. A good wind blew up, not only in the right direction but *exactly* in the right direction. I couldn't believe it.

Later on my watch (was *I* a jinx?) we had a new solar plexus blow. When bleeding the engine fuel system at 1630 hours, I noted that the oil pressure was only 20 psi. The crankcase showed almost zero reading, although it had been normal that morning. After I added two quarts of oil, the dipstick registered full and the oil pressure was back to its standard 40 psi. In the log, I requested all watches to check oil pressure and water temp every thirty minutes.

We kept adding abnormal amounts of oil, hoping we would get to Ponape before we used up our supply. Fortunately the winds held up fairly well and we were able to make considerable mileage under sail.

The Big Moment came right on schedule. We had secured our main engine because of the oil consumption problem, but we were making fair speed under sail:

> Sighted Ponape at 0645 hours. Started main engine at 0745 as wind dying. Oil pressure okay. Lovely morning for making landfall. DR, sun Line, and RDF all converged to indicate we are about 60 miles off Ponape. Should have no trouble making Ponape Harbor before dark.

We passed Pakin Atoll, a lovely textbook South Sea Island with no inhabitants, but looking like the perfect place to habitate and get away from it all. Very lush vegetation, beautiful clear water, protected lagoon.

We spotted Ponape Harbor Light at 1545, right on-time, and threaded our way through the reefs to make the harbor entrance. The light was a picturesque affair, only about fifteen or twenty feet high, but built as a miniature of a much larger light. Consequently, it was deceiving to the eye. Suddenly we were right upon it when I had thought that there was still some distance to go.

No problem; my study of the charts and the sailing directions had indicated that although the harbor was full of reefs, the course to the anchorage was well marked by a series of red even-numbered triangular buoys and markers on the starboard side and black odd-numbered square day markers with white reflectors on the port side.

As we turned into the Ponape Harbor channel, I called to Carol who was below checking a chart or something: "Jesus, honey, come up here! There isn't a goddamned buoy or day marker in sight. Where the hell are we?"

The broad entrance to Ponape Harbor was broad all right! But without any navigational markers or buoys. There was *no way* that I was going to try to enter that harbor without any navigational signposts along the way!

Where do we go from here?

Carol was below tearing into various drawers and bins and stowage areas. What was she doing down there? I needed her up here! Finally she came topsides with a big smile on her face and a little publication in her hands.

It was an excerpt from the published letters of the Seven Seas Cruising Association:

> Ponape Harbor with its many reefs and very shallow water is in the process of being abandoned for inter-island shipping: and Jokaj Harbor, formerly the commercial harbor only, is being developed as Ponape's principal harbor.

Yes, come to think of it, Carol *had* mentioned this situation to me previously. But the old Navy man in me had felt that the only way to fly was to stick with the charts and sailing directions, rather than to rely on some letter from an unknown sailor written to a loosely organized association of worldwide cruising folks.

But the Navy way was sure as hell wrong, and the easy-going letter-writing source was sure as hell right!

We whipped around 180° and headed out of the reef-ridden channel. By this time we had a race against time to get to the entrance to Jokaj channel before dark. That close to the equator, when the sun goes down, it goes down! No twilight.

I stationed Bob at the engine to bleed, add oil, anoint, soothe, water, check gauges; Eagle Eye Chuck in the bow

pulpit to spot reefs and rocks; Harlan and Jane standing by the
sheets and halyards in case the engine died and we needed
emergency sail power in a hurry; and Carol by the charts, the
lights, the radio, and the letters from the Seven Seas Sailing
Association.

We easily found the entrance to Jokaj channel, no thanks to
our charts, but just by the universal nautical system of markers
and buoys. The entrance was actually quite tortuous—what
would be termed hairpin turns on a mountain road—but
straightforward, as the British would say. Jokaj Harbor was
lovely, but where should we go? We came alongside and tied
up temporarily. The dock was built to accommodate small
tankers and tramp freighters. The fendering system was such
that we had to hold ourselves off the dock manually—no way
could we rig ourselves to be safe at this dock overnight.

The Micronesians on the dock were friendly. They spoke the
same language (more or less) and were cooperative, but they
didn't really know where a fifty-foot heavy-displacement sailboat should position itself for the night in Jokaj Harbor.

I decided that we couldn't stay at the dock since our hull
would take a beating against the pilings; and we'd better get
somewhere else in a hurry since we were fast losing our light.

With a lot of pointing and gesturing and drawing of pictures
in the sand, I felt I had some tenuous grasp of where the local
dock hangers-on thought we should anchor for the night.

We proceeded *very* slowly and *very* cautiously farther up the
inlet that was Jokaj Harbor.

Harlan was stationed at the starboard bow with the trusty
lead line, our only depth finder, and old Eagle Eye was in the
bow pulpit.

The Ford Lehman, God bless it, was performing beautifully.
If it had conked out as we entered that zig-zag channel, we
would have been gonners for sure!

Chuck and Harlan both saw it at the same time: "Reef ahead!
Reef ahead! Back her down! Back her down!"

I heard, and I backed. But even at the slow, cautious speed
we were making, we couldn't get that 58,000 pounds of boat to
go back the other way quickly enough.

Crunch! We were aground. But good!

PARADISE ENOW!

A few days after we arrived in Ponape, a classic schooner flying the Australian ensign cruised majestically into Jokaj Harbor and dropped its anchor not far from us. We could see the crew leisurely but professionally furling sails, running up awnings, putting on sail covers, securing from sea, and getting into an in-port mode. For *three whole days,* nobody, not anyone on that lovely vessel so much as stirred, other than to mix a gin and tonic or to plop over the side and cool off. Of course we had no way of knowing what was happening meanwhile below decks; but the point was that for three days no one left that boat! They just unwound from the voyage that took them there. We never did find out from whence they had come—we knew from simple geography that it had to have been from a long way off; Ponape is a long way from *anyplace.*

How I envied that crew! That was precisely, exactly, what I wanted to do—to cruise leisurely and comfortably from place to place with no schedule other than hitting the best weather windows, or the local Mardi Gras, Bastille Day, or whatever.

And to arrive in a port and to *just stay on board for three whole days!* Wow!

Meanwhile, back on the reef, we had discovered that we really *were* on it, even though our approach had been gentle. This particular point was perhaps the lowest of the low points of my participation in the pilgrims' progress voyage of the *Dagny Taggart.* I'm not exactly sure, but I think I more or less lost myself in despair. The grounding itself was not all that bad. I'd been aground before in conditions worse than this. But it was the culminating failure of a great series of failures.

Carol snapped me out of my momentary gloom, however: "Hey, T, let's get with it! How about kedging out an anchor and applying some simple basic seamanship principles here to get us the hell off of this reef!"

"Sure!"

Get the Avon inflated. Carry out the Danforth anchor and let it take hold. Wind the anchor line around one of our big

Barlow winches; take up the winch smartly and carefully; a little help from the main engine; there she goes! A little grinding. A lot of straining. Wheee! We lose our heel and gain equilibrium. We are afloat again! Hooray, hooray!

By this time it was practically pitch black, so we prudently gave up on any notion of retrieving our anchor that evening and devoted ourselves to securing the boat in a safe position for the night. With the Avon in the water, we had very little trouble setting another anchor and settling in under the protecting cliffs inside the harbor.

KOLONIA, NOT COLONIA

Happy to get off the reef, we nursed the Perkins diesel into service to generate a little electricity for a good hot dinner. After eating I decided that I would walk or bum my way into Kolonia, if I could find it, and do what I could to start lining up some mechanical assistance for the good ship *Dagny Taggart*.

Carol decided that she didn't want me stumbling around on the island alone in the dark, so she joined me and we stumbled around on the island together in the dark.

We found a place to tie the dinghy not far from what appeared to be a road along a causeway that seemed to run from the fuel storage area near where we were anchored toward what might be the town of Kolonia.

Our first priority was to find a place to telephone Joanne to ask for some parts and make arrangements for our new skipper to come to Ponape.

It was a long walk into town and not much when we got there. The only place we could find open by the time we arrived was the police station, so to the police station we went, traveling the last few blocks by local police car, a jeep with the word police stenciled on the side.

I suppose it's pretty much in the so-what department, but the fact that we had just come from a *Colonia* on Yap, a port that we never intended to make, to a *Kolonia* on Ponape, the *first* port we made that coincided with the port that we set out to reach, struck me as funny.

The spelling of Kolonia dated back to the pre-World War I days, when Germany had met with only mild success in attempting to build a kolonial empire in the Pacific. Somehow, through the various waves of British, Americans, and Japanese, the waves of self-determination, the old German spelling had persevered. I think one reason was simply that people on Ponape very seldom referred to Kolonia by name. It was just downtown, or the town. With no other town within a thousand miles or so there wasn't much chance for confusion.

The main street of Kolonia we have all seen a thousand times. It lives in Culver City, California. Kolonia's main street is typical of a western movie town, complete with covered sidewalks, chuckholes, mud, and a local saloon with swinging doors. Any Hollywood extra would feel right at home.

The concept of making a collect telephone call to the United States was considered pretty wild by the Ponapean police sergeant on duty. But Carol rolled her eyes a few times and pulled the old marine-emergency bit, and soon we were in the process of activating the wondrous Trust Territory Telephone Circuit.

Alexander Graham would spin in his urn. I could hear the routing: Ponape all the way *back* to Saipan, *then* to Guam, *then* to Honolulu, *then* to satellite, *then* to Los Angeles. Each time we lost a little more clarity and a little more volume. Joanne later wrote to the family that it sounded as if I was at the bottom of a barrel filled with water!

Among our various other minor requirements, we would have to try to find a better way to communicate with the States.

I suppose that once one decides to spend time cruising in the tropics, or to engage in any other activity in the tropics for that matter, one accepts, knowingly or not, the ever-present cockroach. We didn't seem to have much choice on the *Dagny Taggart* but to accept them, in at least some quantity! Some were brought from Keelung; more were taken on board at Hong Kong; others were waiting eagerly to join us in Manila.

We never kept tabs on the number of different cockroach remedies we acquired, nor the cost thereof. We had sprays, powders, liquids, poison shelf paper, even traps! Some were no good at all; others worked with varying degrees of success; but

Beautiful downtown Colonia, Yap.

none did the entire job. The cockroach population on the boat rose and fell, but never reached zero.

But of all the thousands, tens of thousands, hundreds of thousands, whatever, that we saw on the entire trip, no cockroach could compare to the Grandaddy of them all that we saw in the early morning hours at the Ponape Police Station as we waited for our gurgly call to Joanne to go through. I saw the monster come in from a crack in the side of the building, probably one that he made, and first thought it was a giant lizard. I asked the sergeant if he didn't plan to shoot it. The sergeant thought this was pretty funny, but pretty ridiculous. We have many that are bigger than that, he said, almost as if he were bragging about the size of the local pineapple.

We were able to bum a ride most of the way back to the place where we had left our dinghy tied to a rock; to our delight it was still there. We putted out to the *Dagny Taggart* and slipped into the sack.

Our first big job the next morning, Saturday, was to retrieve our stern anchor, which we had used to kedge ourselves off the reef. It was stuck. We pulled; we dived. The water in the harbor seemed to be sanitary but only medium-clear, as the harbor was essentially a river mouth with a fair amount of silt or fine sand suspended in the water as it made its way past the boat. As far as we could tell the anchor seemed to be wedged between a couple of coral heads about twenty to thirty feet deep—just beyond the skin-diving depth capacity of any of us on board.

In one last gigantic effort, using our winches, the ship's engines, and all the grunt and groan we had available, we pulled the anchor loose, but by a seamanship foul-up on my part (and seamanship was supposed to be my strong suit) we managed to drop the anchor line overboard!

We carefully made note of the location of the anchor and line, figuring that we would find someone with diving equipment to re-retrieve it for us later.

When we had finally finished with the anchor fiasco, we repositioned the boat in deeper water, riding on a single bow anchor, and I headed for shore to secure a permit from the Public Works Department to anchor in the harbor, immigration clearance from the Immigration Office, and the all-important drinking permit issued by the chief of police.

At each of our contact points on shore, we asked about the availability of a good diesel mechanic or diesel engine service. Up until about 1500 hours on Saturday, our first full day on the island, we had either negative answers (You want *what?* On Ponape? You've got to be kidding!) or blank stares.

Not too encouraging.

Our Seabee friends on Yap had told us that there was a Seabee Civil Action Team on Ponape. But here we had anchored out in the harbor and no one had come on board; we felt it would be awkward just walking into the Seabee camp and saying, "Here we are. Please help us."

But after floundering around in Kolonia for the better part of a day, with zilch results, we did just that. Carol and Jane and I approached the Seabee camp and introduced ourselves, saying that we had spent some time with the CAT group on Yap and thought we would say hello.

The Seabees were delighted. It was as if we'd never left Yap. The barracks and mess hall had the same general configuration as the camp in Yap; the Seabee team was made up of the same specialists; the missions of the two teams were the same; and the guys were every bit as cooperative and helpful to us.

"You want a good diesel mechanic? You just lucked out! Stick around for thirty minutes and the best damned diesel mechanic in the Pacific will walk right through that door!"

We had a beer—two beers—and in thirty minutes, right on, in walked Jack Adams, the best damned diesel mechanic in the Pacific.

Jack was an Australian, probably in his sixties, who had recently resigned as an employee of the Ponape Public Works Department but was still working for Public Works on an independent contract basis. Jack turned out to be a fine mechanic. He was an even better showman . . . *great* sense of the dramatic: now-I-remember-back-in-1938-when-a-typhoon-almost-washed-Ponape-off-the-map . . .

We gave Jack a general outline of our mechanical problems. He speculated on what the various possible defects might be and how they might be cured. But he was badly tied up on a big ship job and didn't know when he could get to us for personal work.

Howsomever, after the two of us, Carol especially, had done what we could to endear ourselves to Jack, all news was not bad. Jack said that he would arrange to have the *Dagny Taggart* tie up at the side of the fuel dock, so we would be accessible from the shore and not have to go back and forth by dinghy. He assured us that he would find some time to consult with us on our air-in-the-fuel problem—although we of the *Dagny*'s crew would have to do most of the actual work involved.

Fair enough!

It was certainly good news that we could get alongside a dock. For leisurely cruising it is great to be riding at anchor, away from it all, but when you are trying desperately to provision a boat, make repairs, or load on new equipment, it is a tremendous advantage to be alongside a dock, almost any dock.

As on Yap, one of the Ponape Seabees took us under his wing. Al Gerhold, Seabee electrician's mate first class (and he was!) drove us around Kolonia in a jeep and dropped us off at the South Park Hotel, where Jane and Carol and I, along with Harlan who had later joined us, had a good Japanese-style dinner.

After dinner, Al picked up the four of us to take us back to the boat, or rather back to the dinghy to get to the boat. But the road back to the dock went past the Kaselehlia Inn.

The word *Kaselehlia* in Ponapean means the same as *Aloha* in Hawaiian. Well, that led to a discussion that in turn led to our stopping at the Kaselehlia Inn for a drink before returning to the boat.

The Kaselehlia Inn, late on a Saturday night, turned out to be a booming place—tables, dancing, live band, and the *Seven Korean Virgins!*

THE SEVEN KOREAN VIRGINS

Much to our surprise, we learned that Ponape is on a kind of Central Pacific off-Broadway circuit. Various acts put together in the Far East try out for a few months in some of the little backwater spots in the Trust Territory such as Ponape, to work

Sea Bee civil action team electrician, Al Gerhold, and a Ponape trainee.

off the rough spots as well as to check audience reaction and so on.

The Seven Korean Virgins didn't have many rough spots, and the audience reaction they generated was tremendous!

They were not *billed* as virgins, but they were herded and sheltered by their Japanese impresario so carefully and assiduously that it would have been hard to have changed their sexual status while they were on Ponape. Even during the break between their appearances, they were taken, each holding the hand of one in front and the one behind, like elephants in a circus, up the stairs and into their separate rooms, with the doors locked behind them.

The specialty of the Korean girls was effecting a perfect reproduction of popular U.S. song hits. According to local legend, the girls (who spoke no English) spent eight to twelve hours per day listening to and going over and over and over the song hits that they were using or intended to use in their act. And they were good at it.

Well, we five, Carol and Jane and Al and Harlan and I, truly enjoyed the Kaselehlia Inn's hospitality, the beer, the Seven Korean Virgins, until suddenly it was one o'clock in the morning and we should be finding our dinghy and wending our way back to the *Dagny Taggart.*

We had tied our Avon at the semiofficial Marine Services dock in the Old Harbor, which we had reached by traveling through a series of ponds and inlets, and finally through a water tunnel under the causeway between the Old Harbor and Jokaj Harbor, where the *Dagny Taggart* was anchored. Sure enough, on return to the Marine Services dock, our trusty Avon with Seagull outboard was bobbingly awaiting us.

The engine started on first tug, and we headed out for deep water, to travel along the side of the causeway, to try to find the water tunnel under the causeway, and to negotiate the series of ponds and inlets back to the spot where the *Dagny Taggart* was anchored.

Soon it was clear that we not going to find the tunnel under the causeway; it was too dark. The wind was picking up. There was the feel of a rain squall in the air. Why I don't know, but we kept going.

Chances are that we would be out there to this day trying to find the tunnel if it hadn't been for one of our many Central Pacific Seabee miracles. After dropping us at the dock, our friend Al had whipped back to the Seabee base and had traded his jeep for his Yamaha. And there was Al, with his bike sideways on the causeway road, directly over the tunnel, flashing his spotlight first on us, then on the tunnel, then on the various navigational hazards that we had to avoid to get from where we were to the tunnel entrance.

His timing was so good we couldn't believe it. Just as we had reached a point abeam of the tunnel, not knowing where it was, Al had reached the tunnel by land, and had shined his light upon us!

Getting into and through the tunnel was, thanks to Al, a snap. But the picture was entirely different as we emerged on the far side of the causeway. It was as if we had been tossed into the middle of an Air Force wind tunnel testing ground!

Whamo!

The storm had struck with sudden vengeance while we were inside the tunnel. The wind must have been at least 50 knots, gusting to 60; the water was unbelievable—solid sheets coming down so hard it was difficult just to hold your head up straight.

Well, mush on. We can't just stop here and cry.

The Seagull performed perfectly through all this—with one tiny exception: whenever we got into water shallower than the depth of the Seagull's shaft, the propeller objected to hitting the rocks, coral, mud, or whatever. The tidal range was not very great on Ponape, but we had somehow managed to get ourselves in the ridiculous predicament that the tide was nearly too low to make it back to the boat—even if the weather had been good.

We found ourselves scraping the bottom so frequently with our outboard prop that we had no choice but to secure the engine and try to row or pole our way in the right direction. It worked out that we were at all times in either one of two conditions: aground trying to get off the coral or out of the mud; or floating so that the howling wind simply took over and pushed us where it wanted to push us. We were pretty much out of control.

I decided that the only thing to do was put ashore and wait for the squall to blow over. I should say I decided that the only thing to do was stop fighting the fierce wind and allow the dinghy to be blown ashore where we could wait for the storm to die.

While all this was happening, Al was cruising up and down the shore, shining his light for us, giving us encouragement. We had a flashlight on board, so we could flash back in Morse Code to let him know that we were still there, more or less.

Once I decided that the best we could do was allow ourselves to be blown ashore, it was only a few minutes until we were obliged and aground. I had feared that we might grind to a halt a considerable distance from dry ground, becoming stranded indefinitely in some shallow unknown marsh. But the wind gods were good to us. With a tremendous amount of luck and a little last-minute maneuvering we managed to get ourselves aground on a well-kept private beach adjacent to a Ponapean house. And, wonder of wonders, right there on the beach was a boat house for shelter!

Since there was a boat house it seemed only fitting to pull our boat into it, which we did, sweating and straining, soaked to the gills in the driving rainstorm. The wind was howling so loudly we had a hard time hearing each other shout even though we were just a few feet apart.

Unfortunately, the boat house was pretty dilapidated and didn't serve its purpose of keeping the rain out. The four of us sat there for five minutes or so. I tried to light a cigarette; no luck. And no letup in the storm. Worse, if anything.

We had thought that the house to which the boat house was an accouterment was empty, but a little scouting trip revealed that it was occupied by human forms rolled in blankets on the floor. We aroused them, told them of our plight, and made a pitch for them to allow us to spend the night in some spare room someplace. The floor would be great. Anyplace as long as it was dry. There was little choice, actually; for as far as we could tell there was absolutely no furniture of any kind in the house. Certainly simplifies housekeeping. But the occupants declined to allow us to enter their house. Can't blame them, really. We were pretty motley and bedraggled. If a gang of four waterlogged Ponapeans were to knock on your door during a rainstorm tonight, would *you* let them in *your* house?

And then another Seabee miracle: out of nowhere, Al showed up on his Yamaha. He should have been awarded the

U.S. Navy Annual Central Pacific Navigational Trophy for finding us in the first place in that howling gale with no landmarks and practically no roads. I was even more amazed when I went back later by daylight and observed the maze of trails, bays, inlets, and streams that he had to get over, through, or around before he could reach the spot where we were.

After a little more analysis of our situation, and general consultation with ourselves and with Al, Carol and I decided that the storm wasn't going to abate for a long time; we might as well go into town, get some sleep, and come back at daylight. This seemed logical to Carol and to me, but somehow Jane and Harlan decided that they would stay there in the leaky boat house.

Although Carol and I felt guilty about leaving them behind in the rain, we took off for Kolonia, one at a time, riding behind Al on his Yamaha.

Back to the Kaselehlia Inn! By this time it was three-ish or so in the morning or later. The Seven Korean Virgins, locked in their rooms if the stories were true, were quiet. Carol and I woke the manager to ask for a room. The manager smilingly and sleepily obliged.

We left a call for 0630 hours, which didn't give us much sleep, and in the early morning headed back for the Harlan and Jane Memorial Beachhead. The rain, believe it or not, had stopped. It was a lovely clear and even crisp morning as we trudged our way back through the mud, trying to locate the chance spot on which we had been blown last night. To our surprise, we found it.

And there was the boat house. Good. There was the Avon. *Very* good! But where were Jane and Harlan? Not good at all. Closer. The Avon was full of water, right up to the gunwales! They couldn't have just lain there and drowned! Could they?

It was unbelievable! What appeared to be some old bundles of clothing in the bottom of the dinghy turned out to be Harlan and Jane, water up to their armpits, in some state that couldn't be called sleep, but couldn't be called wakefulness either.

Hello. We are here. Get up. Are you okay?

Stiff, wet, cold, shivering, shivering, shivering. This was the tropics? I've never seen anyone appreciate a dry and lighted

The sacred ruins of Namadol, Ponape.

cigarette more than did Jane as I lit one for her and put it between her blue trembling lips.

The sun was coming up. The sky was a clear, deep blue. There was no reason not to get underway, back to the *Dagny Taggart*. We bailed out the bathtub in which Jane and Harlan had been lying, got the dinghy launched, and were off and running, back to the boat.

As soon as we reached the shelter of the *Dagny Taggart*, we nursed the Perkins into action and Carol whomped up a mess of hot oatmeal, canned sausage, and hot coffee. I doubt whether any meal before or since has tasted as good to Harlan and Jane as that hot breakfast after that miserable wet night.

After breakfast and cleanup, Carol and I, together with Bob and Chuck, gathered up our two and a half weeks of accumulated laundry and headed for the Seabee camp, where we showered, laundered, and recouped. We met the commanding officer of Seabee Civil Action Team O111, Lieutenant Junior Grade Eric Berg. We also visited Jack Adams at his shop (open on Sunday, which was a Good Sign), delivered to him a copy of our Ford diesel manual, and discussed our problem and Jack's availability to help us solve it—just like Yap!

THE GINGER HOUSE

That Sunday evening, about dinner time, friend Al Gerhold suggested that he take Carol and me to dinner. Seemed like a great idea. Al drove us in a WEP through some fantastically beautiful countryside, up a mountain road through lush forests, and finally to a lovely old wooden building known as the Ginger House. The walk up the verdant mountainside to the Ginger House was reminiscent of the climb to the Happy Talk House in the movie version of Michener's *South Pacific*. Green growth, white flowers, misty steps upward.

We were the only customers in this lovely, lovely place, which consisted largely of a wooden floor, chairs and tables, and a thatched roof. A large muu-muu-clad Ponapean woman greeted us and waited on us, and we caught occasional glimpses of a tall white-clad Ponapean chef. Between the two of them, they served good drinks and a fine fresh fish dinner.

We wound up what had been a beautiful and mildly productive Sunday with a stop at the airport bar, which was only a short distance from the *Dagny Taggart*'s dock. We had a drink with Al and met most of the other Seabees in CAT 0111, all good men tried and true.

And then came the mutiny!

Well, almost.

THE GREAT SEABEE MUTINY

We felt lucky to have found Jack Adams on Ponape; we felt that he was competent, and we liked him. But he was a one-man show, and he was unavailable. In our secret heart-of-hearts, at least in *my* secret black heart, I was hoping that the Seabee guys would be able to give us off-time help and would fathom for us once and for all the air-in-the-fuel problem.

A favor is sometimes hard to ask for; it is more to be earned and deserved by the receiver and volunteered by the giver. We tried to do all the earning and deserving that we could without going overboard. We sincerely liked and appreciated the men, and we wanted their mechanical help, but we didn't want to be in the situation of we'll-trade-you-our-goodwill-for-your-help.

We did let our buddy Al know that we sure could use some help from their diesel mechanic guys. We talked to Pete, the diesel mechanic. He said that probably Monday afternoon late he could make it down to the *Dagny Taggart* and would look things over and see if he couldn't analyze the problem and, working with Jack Adams, get us fixed up on Tuesday.

Oh joy!

But by the crooked and fickle finger of fate, the Navy admiral from Guam who was head man for all Navy groups in the Trust Territory, flew into Ponape on that same day, Monday 15 July, for an inspection and general survey of his domain.

In the late afternoon on Monday, Lieutenant Berg, commanding officer of the Ponape Seabee Team, came on board the *Dagny Taggart*; just Carol and I were there.

"Hey, hello! Come on aboard. Let us show you around to see what we've accomplished since you were here last. I'll get you a beer."

"Err . . . uh . . . no thanks; I'm here on official business."

"Business, schmizzness, that'll wait."

We showed him around, and we had that beer, but we noted that Lieutenant Berg, all 270 pounds and twenty-four years of him, was a little on the stiff and formal side.

"Umm . . . uh . . . gee, I'm sorry about this, but the admiral from Guam has put out an order that no Seabee CAT member is to spend any time, on duty or off duty, helping cruising sailboats owned by U.S. citizens. It seems that recently there was a sailboat that put into Yap with a number of mechanical problems, and the admiral feels that it is not proper for Seabee personnel to spend time assisting such vessels outside of their primary duties."

It was obvious that Berg was embarrassed and ashamed. To date *none* of his people had spent *any* time on our boat except socially. Sure, maybe we had imposed on the Seabees' hospitality by drinking their beer and watching their movies and using their laundry facilities—but only on the weekend and on off-duty hours.

We never really did know what the real problem was.

The next day a series of CAT 0111 guys came on board the *Dagny Taggart* to check in and tell us how upset they were with the special U.S. Navy order that went out all over the Pacific saying, in effect, "Don't help the *Dagny Taggart!*"

Some of the Seabee guys were particularly angry:

"Just wait 'til the next time I'm asked to work on the car of one of the local chiefs, or to build a tennis court at the mayor's house, or to build a garden wall!"

"If we can't help our friends who are in real need, I'll be damned if we're gonna take our time or the government's money to do anything here except what we have to do, strictly in accordance with regulations."

Well, it wasn't *exactly* a mutiny, but we sure had some mad Seabees on our hands, or *somebody* had them on their hands.

While we did have a fair amount of surreptitious off-time help from Al and some of the other guys, the admiral's order effectively cut off any help where we really needed it, in the diesel-fuel-line department.

That left us with good old Jack Adams.

GOOD OLD JACK ADAMS

On the plus side, thanks to the help of Jack Adams, we were tied up alongside the good ship *Kaselehlia,* not to be confused with the Kaselehlia Inn. And the great Aussie himself, Jack, was working right next door on the *Kaselehlia.*

So we enticed Jack over and down (way down) to the good ship *Dagny Taggart* for a coke or a coffee whenever we could and did our best to get him interested in our problem.

Our chief mechanics, Bob and Jane and Chuck and I, had a great Harvard-Business-School-type session with Jack on Monday afternoon.

"Okay, let's just sit here and trace the fuel system. Where does the fuel come on board? Where does it leave the boat? What happens to the fuel from entry to exit? Study that Ford Lehman Manual."

Jack enforced a silent period of ten minutes or so while each of us, on our own, traced the whole fuel system from start to finish. Not that we hadn't done this before, rocking and rolling and sweating and swearing and heaving while we were trying to get back into operation in the middle of somewhere.

Jack's discipline was good. Something we had never done before. Good lesson.

After a few more of these sessions, a lot of talk, a lot of analyzing, a lot of checking each fitting, a lot of renewing of fuel filters, renewing of fuel filter elements, testing of fuel pumps, testing of injector pumps, testing of injectors, we all reached the conclusion (actually Jack reached the conclusion, but in the Harvard-Business-School technique, Ponape style, it was a group analytical effort) that the problem had to be in the injectors. With water in the fuel, soap in the fuel, air in the fuel, fire in the fuel, stopping every eight minutes, we had just burned the hell out of the delicate injectors. Best to replace them all. But Jack felt that if the new ones didn't arrive in time for us to leave Ponape, he could work on the old ones and get them in good enough shape for us to get to Majuro.

In the voices-from-the-past department, on Tuesday 16 July, Jim, our ex-crewperson, arrived on Ponape. Jim told us that Randy had had to fly home because of blood poisoning in his feet from his encounter with the coral on Yap. And Randy, true to the end, had fouled up all of our mail by placing a change-of-address with the postal authorities in Guam. We know he didn't really mean to do it, but the change of address had included *all* mail for the *Dagny Taggart* and crew, so our mail as well as his ended up in the state of Washington, or the state of Alaska, or someplace.

We had developed a list of spares and equipment for new skipper Pete to bring over to us: 100 feet of line for our taffrail log, ten filter cartridges for our Fram oil filters, lightbulbs in various oddball sizes, sixteen feet of packing gland material, one complete (really complete) fuel filter assembly for a Ford Lehman diesel, one complete injection pump for same, four complete fuel injector assemblies, six filter elements for the Ford Lehman, six for the Perkins, 100 navigational forms for each sight.

On that same long day, which included the Seabee mutiny (or whatever it was), our session with Jack, and the realization that Old Taylor was about to leave the Great Venture, Joanne Davis came through with a great telex to cheer our spirits. She had made reservations for me to fly to Honolulu from Ponape and for Pete to fly to Honolulu from Los Angeles. We would meet, talk, and then fly off in opposite directions. Joanne had reserved rooms for both of us at International Inn so we could get some sleep while we were there.

Pete wanted to bring an extremely competent crewmember with him—a young man he had sailed with on ocean races—and who was an expert mechanic.

I spent most of the next day, Wednesday 17 July, with Jack Adams, who had become our key guy. I had grown to feel confident, with all the great recommendations Bruce had for me, that the new-skipper department was in good shape. My only remaining serious concern was the air-in-the-fuel problem, and here I felt, at last, that we had found the guy who knew the story and who was personally dedicated not only to finding out what the problem was and setting things right, but most important was dedicated to giving the crew the proper education, background, and experience to handle any future problem that might develop.

Jack's approach seemed so basically sound that it embarrassed me that we had not instituted it three years ago when we had first started flirting with the Grand Cruise concept.

Jack and I had become quite close over these short four days; he had assured me that he would not let the *Dagny Taggart* sail out of Ponape until he was satisfied that we had licked our problem.

SO LONG OLD TAYLOR

On that same day, Wednesday 17 July, we had a dramatic illustration of Jack Adams's skill at analysis and repair. In the case of the air-in-the-fuel problem, we had concluded that our problem had been a combination of many things, most of which had been cured. The present difficulty was a residual effect of the previous problems in that our poor, long-suffering injectors had gotten to the point at which they were recycling a small amount of air with each injection/explosion. This recycled air would build up on the diesel scavenging system until there was enough air to close down operations, which meant further burning and injury to the injector nozzles.

In the case of the excessive use of lubricating oil in the Ford crankcase, we had gone through another analytical exercise and concluded that the problem had to be in the heat exchanger in which the engine lubricating oil was cooled by incoming salt water. There must be a leak in the internal tubing in the heat exchanger, permitting lubricating oil to leak out into the salt water cooling system and, worse, allowing salt water to leak into the engine lubricating oil system.

Sure enough, we took the system apart and found the oil/salt water heat exchanger full of holes. We had sent for a new exchanger, and when it arrived, we put the system and the engine back together again, and she purred away like magic. No leaks in either direction! What a great feeling!

And now for those injectors! We had expected Jack to come by on Wednesday to remove the injectors and dismantle the injector pump from the engine for us—or at least to assist us in this task—or at the *very* least, to show us how to do it.

But Wednesday came and went, with only our triumph of solving the heat exchanger problem to our credit—which wasn't too shabby all by itself!

But the next day, Thursday 18 July, presented us with a mini-crisis. I was scheduled to leave on Air Micronesia at 1300 hours. I felt that I had to have one more session with Jack Adams in order to satisfy myself that our mechanical problems were really solved and I could safely leave for the States. Joanne had scheduled me to meet new skipper Pete in Honolulu that night at midnight.

In order to remove the injectors and the injector pump it was necessary to take the head off the Ford diesel engine, which is not all that big a deal for a person who has ever taken the head off a Ford diesel engine before, but for a first-time proposition, it was pretty thrilling.

How could I get the engine torn down, have a closing session with Jack Adams, and still make the 1300 flight?

Of those three demands on my time, it was obvious that I had to be the one to have the session with Jack, and that I had to be the one to be on that airplane, but in theory, someone else could tear the Ford diesel apart.

Bob was off snorkling on the reef.

"Chuck! Jane!" I asked Chuck and Jane for their undivided attention. I had spent several hours the night before with the Ford Lehman manual (much to my mate's disgust on our last night together!).

"Okay Chuck, Jane, please read pages 26 through 42, twice; then I'll check back in 30 minutes."

They did and I did. We checked whether we had all the right tools. We did.

This was at 0800 hours on 18 July. I left Chuck and Jane tackling the diesel take-apart project with verve and vig, and I went to talk with Jack. I told him that I needed his frank opinion in connection with the air-in-the fuel problem. Did he believe that if we installed new or reworked injectors we would be okay?

Jack's reply was pretty straight: Basically, yes. No gold-plated guarantees, of course, but basically, yes. He, with our help, or we with his help, had checked out every possible source of air invasion, and it had to be the overworked injectors. We had new injectors coming, and Jack had the facilities to refurbish our old injectors if the new ones did not arrive in time.

It seemed like a lousy time to leave. The engine was torn down—by amateurs yet! The new skipper, whom I had never met, hadn't arrived yet. Some people were off snorkling; others were visiting ruins.

I had a long, frank talk with Carol; she felt that things were under enough control for me to be able to leave. I figured I could stay on for days, weeks, months; but sometime, somehow, I had to get back. And now seemed to be the time to bite the bullet.

GOOD OLD AIR MICRONESIA

Somewhere in the bottom of an old sea bag stored in the lazarette, I found my summer milkman-type business suit, an old button-down shirt that wasn't too badly wrinkled, a tie, some store-bought shoes, and voila! I was a businessperson again.

The airport was reasonably close to the Mobil fuel dock where we were tied up, so Carol and I walked to the Ponape Memorial Airport around noon. We milled with the indigenous throng, a few tourists, and a few Marines.

And then suddenly, as so often at airports, the plane was there, the flight called. This was it!

Was I doing the right thing? Would my precious wife, son, friends, boat, be okay without me? Did Jack Adams have the answer to our problems? And was Pete competent enough to handle the position of master on the *Dagny Taggart*?

Deep questions. But I had, I guess, found the answers to these questions, subject to my meeting with Pete in Honolulu.

Everything was gonna be okay. Everything *was* okay.

So I said my goodbyes to my good wife, my good son, my good crewmates, my good Seabee buddies. And good old Air Micronesia, jet engines straining, coral a-flying, took off in a cloud of dust, en route for next stop: Majuro.

Dagny Taggart *leaving Ponape—bound for Kwajalein.*

I had been in Majuro before, but this time my approach and arrival took on a different and more significant meaning. This was to be the *Dagny Taggart*'s next stop. Could she find the place? Could she navigate her way through the reef into the lagoon? Would she be welcome, and would she find what she wanted when she got there? Maybe the new injectors from Scotland wouldn't make the connection at Ponape and would have to be forwarded to meet the boat at Majuro. Would all go okay there?

Well, that was it; we had Rubiconed. No turning back now. Lovely Majuro. Typical classical geological atoll. There she was ahead of us; and now she was behind. Behind me.

Long leg from Majuro to Honolulu. Long by sea, even long by jet. But finally at midnight-ish, Air Micronesia landed at Honolulu.

Immigration. Ugh!

Yes, U.S. citizen returning from Trust Territory. Yes, I was sailing a private vessel across the Pacific from west to east. No, I wasn't crazy.

Or was I?

Customs. Ugh!

No, no baggage to uncheck. Just what I have in my hand. By this time the guy was convinced; I *was* crazy.

Finally, free of the ties that bind, I walked out of the Honolulu Airport looking for Pete. And we found each other instinctively.

Long hair. But, hell, *my* hair was long. And so was that of half of the crew.

We took to each other naturally and beautifully.

In fact, we walked together introducing and talking for what amounted to several blocks, before each of us realized that neither of us knew where we were going. I thought that *Pete* was leading the way; and he thought that *I* was leading the way!

After backtracking a half mile or so, we checked in at the airport hotel that Joanne had arranged for us. We compared notes—navigationally, commandly, socially.

Everything seemed to be right-on. Pete had his own sextant, which he let me check out, and which checked out well; a good philosophy of cruising and command; a great understanding of sailing and getting along with people; many mutual friends and associates.

Pete's flight was due out at 0700, which gave us about three hours of sleep. We left a call for 0600—up, up, and at 'em.

We had a quick cup of coffee together, and it was adios, old friend. Please take good care of my precious wife, son, friends and boat.

I checked in with my Pan American buddies in Honolulu— all was just as Joanne had arranged. I not only had a valid ticket from Honolulu to LAX, but I had a return ticket from LAX back to Honolulu if I needed it.

Oh joy!

The six most beautiful harbors in the world today are reported to be Vancouver, San Francisco, Sydne, Rio de Janeiro, Hong Kong, and Waikiki.

Waikiki Beach lacks the commercial flavor the other five enjoy and possibly doesn't qualify for the same category, but what Waikiki lacks in secondary attraction, it more than makes up for in spectacular beauty. By his own admission, not even Robert Louis Stevenson could handle describing it—although he sure tried.

Well, I can't either.

But everything considered, I figured that as we jetted over Waikiki Beach, heading for the mainland and four-year-old April after three months' absence from her, it was a fairly good spot to end my segment of *Only a Damn Fool*. At the time, I was completely satisfied that all problems had been identified and solved, and the rest of the voyage would be uneventful. They weren't and it wasn't. The second half of our adventure will be Carol's story, *Only a Damn Fool, Book II*, in which she battles the U.S. Army on Kwajalein, picks up a motley crew from island to island, and survives a broach and knockdown approaching the California coast. But that will be her story . . .

The beauty that was there in that sweep from the hotels of Waikiki to hoary Diamond Head was reminiscent of all of the beauty that we had seen in our voyage across the Pacific, from lovely island to lovely island.

Would that such beauty could continue. Would that it would ever be thus.